The Places and Spaces of Fashion, 1800–2007

Routledge Research in Cultural and Media Studies

The Places and Spaces of Fashion, 1800–2007

Edited by John Potvin

Routledge
Taylor & Francis Group
New York   London

First published 2009
by Routledge
270 Madison Ave, New York, NY 10016

Simultaneously published in the UK
by Routledge
2 Park Square, Milton Park, Abingdon, Oxon OX14 4RN

Routledge is an imprint of the Taylor & Francis Group, an informa business

Library of Congress Cataloging in Publication Data

The places and spaces of fashion, 1800-2007 / edited by John Potvin.
    p. cm. — (Routledge research in cultural and media studies ; 16)
    Includes bibliographical references and index.
    1. Fashion—History. I. Potvin, John.
    GT511.P53 2008
    391.009—dc22
    2008010896

ISBN10: 0-415-96149-1 (hbk)

ISBN13: 978-0-415-96149-3 (hbk)

Contents

PART III
Window Dressing and Boutique Culture

Figures

Introduction
Inserting Fashion Into Space
John Potvin

Space is an essential framework of all modes of thought (Sack 1992: 4).

In one of the earliest scenes from the famed 1939 film *The Wizard of Oz*, the Wicked Witch of the East is tragically killed by a airborne, wayward house that was ripped from its foundation and displaced violently into the tornado, which left rural Kansas in a bit of a mess. All that we, the audience, see are her thin ankles in a pair of sparkling ruby slippers. All that remains of her material identity is her body, crushed by the (domestic) architectural weight of Dorothy's house, and her much sought after, infamously magical shoes. Taking possession of those special shoes, not unlike any coveted Manolo Blahniks or Jimmy Choos today, give Dorothy a certain spring in her step, a certain power to walk the Yellow Brick Road, perform the many tasks at hand, and face any adversity each subsequent space might conjure. And like any good and stylish pair of shoes, Dorothy's ruby slippers take her through the many spaces and places along her journey in the Land of Oz. While the movie may not be about Dorothy as a model fashion icon strutting down a yellow catwalk, the powerful visual image of those ruby slippers activated through the desire to be elsewhere serves as a vivid metaphor of fashion's ability to transport the embodied subject to another place and space.

* * * * *

Space has become fashionable again. To be "in fashion" is both and at once sartorial and spatial. Yet, discussions of space continue to be emptied of fashion; it's as if space were unchanging and sacred, beyond the vagaries of trends and fashion's cycles, beyond the purported feminine wiles of beauty and image. Likewise, spaces and places have often been overlooked in the writing of the visual and material cultures of fashion. We have been lead to believe that space involves depth and longevity often prescribed through the thickness of architecture in contrast to fashion, which privileges surface and newness. The encounters with fashion happen within a space at a given place and do not simply function as backdrops but are pivotal to the meaning and vitality that the experiences of fashion trace. More often than not, these environments mitigate, control, inform, and enhance how fashion is experienced, performed, consumed, seen, exhibited, purchased, appreciated, desired, and, of course, displayed. The design implications of these spaces and places, and even the objects contained therein, condition our responses to, and our perceptions and memories of fashion. Conversely, fashion enhances the identity, worth, pleasure, and currency of certain places and spaces, as the culture of retail environments has recently reminded us. Fashion's multiple personalities and identities are contingent on the design of an environment, enabling, altering, or enhancing the cultural significance of the fashioned subject who through these myriad spaces and fashions are given leave to perform their own multiple personalities. It must be recognized that space is itself a representational strategy that not only invests in and influences the visibility and visual and material outcome of fashion but also unveils, imposes itself upon, and narrativizes identity.

Referring to the spaces and places of consumption specific to London since the eighteenth century, Christopher Breward eloquently asserts that fashion "is a bounded thing, fixed and experienced in space—an amalgamation of seams and textiles, an interface between the body and its environment. It is a practice, a fulcrum for the display of taste and status, a site for the production of objects and beliefs, and it is an event, both spectacular and routine" (Breward 2004: 11). However, since the nineteenth century, Paris has stood as the embodiment of modernity and the transient nature of urban fashionability. The French capital achieved its iconic status, which it retained well into the twentieth century, precisely because it managed to construct spaces and enliven places for the cultures and performances of fashion. Nigel Thrift has argued for a vision of the city as a network of haptic, sensory, phenomenological experiences. But might we not think of all spaces and places in these terms, no matter how small or grand, insignificant or praiseworthy, physical or virtual? In other words, might all the spaces of fashion not become *the* places for the spectacle of everyday life, and is not the everyday itself the spectacular?

Drawing inspiration from Charles Baudelaire and his always fashionable and omnipresent *flâneur* who embodied *par excellence* the city of Paris, Walter Benjamin was the first to map out the relationship between space, fashion, and modernity (Benjamin). The *flâneur's* experiences of the city were predicated on a narrative of mobility and visibility, one "that relies on interrelation of place for its storyline rather than on a character-driven plot" (Rendell 10). Mobility implies bodies moving through, acting out, time and space. Michel de Certeau understood space as "composed of intersections of mobile elements. It is in a sense actuated by the ensemble of movements deployed within it." For him "space is a practiced place" precisely because bodies move through it and therefore enliven it (117). Space allows, therefore, the embodied subject to narrativize fashion; it translates the idea of fashion into action. And so, in these ways, space like fashion is rehearsed, that is, it is the locus of the performing subject.

For Benjamin, the arcades in particular and the city in general visually and materially accommodated the fantasies and desires of the modern urbanite. Like the everchanging fashions worn and displayed with panache by the *flâneur* whose identity was predicated on seeing and being seen, the boulevards and arcades chronicled the relentless changes and shifting meanings of modern life, despite their architectural grounding and solidity. Architectural and spatial structures are transformed by fashionable embodied agents who forever participate in the never-ending spectacle and performances of modernity as both agents and spectators. The unremitting alterations endured by a city like Paris in the late nineteenth century are revealed through myriad and shifting spaces of fashion's spectacles and displays. Arcades were at once both private and public, where the spectacle was the commodity and where thresholds were always threatened by fashion's subjects and objects. "Signifying spaces," like the Parisian arcades, at once "attract or repel a public, who convey meaning through the events and rituals performed in them" (Quinn 26).

In the case of Paris, for example, the city and couture have worked together to conjure a specific representation of both place and a fashioned identity. David Gilbert notes that, by the end of the nineteenth century, "[more] than clothes of particular designers, the fashion object that was being consumed was the city itself, and the spectacle of high fashion *in situ*" (2006: 21). This notion of the city performing as a fashion object—or subject—can surely be extended to the seemingly endless spaces and places which map out the city itself. Certain events on the calendar also call attention to certain locations within the city, heightening their involvement with fashion, such as the racetrack at Longchamp, an integral event in the bourgeois Parisian social calendar since the eighteenth century. What special events like the racetrack, the opera, theaters, nightclubs, and runway shows among others involve is movement, migration through the city, crossing through space to arrive at a desired destination.

Earlier economic literature has placed emphasis on and limited the geography of fashion to the locations of its production (Gilbert 2006: 28). However, given that fashion moves, migrates, travels particularly within an international and global culture, this volume explores the topographies of consumption, display, creation, performance, exhibition, and advertising of fashion, in other words, the final product in both its glamorized and everyday forms. Today, more than ever, fashion and mobility have come to represent global experiences encompassing certain cities and yet moving beyond them through e-commerce and other alternative modes of consumption. Virtual spaces like the Internet seem to lack space and place, that is to say, a true material sense of location, but it is equally and increasingly relevant to the experience of fashion. In addition, the current obsession with global expansion and domination makes the discussion of space and place in the histories and theories of fashion all the more pertinent and prescient. Global expansion transforms places and spaces, rendering them identical, indistinct, and uniform, leaving one city to look like every other. However, globality and virtuality are themselves experiences of space and place, representational strategies which obliquely disguise the body. Place and space also take on added significance in a global world intensified by increased travel, transience, migration, and displacement. As a result, one question worth posing is does fashion travel well? Either through commerce or immigration, fashion traverses boundaries sometimes translating well, while at other times resulting in moments of tension, confusion, and/ or alienation despite being a global marketplace.

Fashion has transformed the visual culture of cities. In Milan, for example, Giorgio Armani's ever-changing and highly recognizable Emporio Armani billboard in Via Broletto, and Donna Karan's DKNY iconic advertisement on a midtown Manhattan firewall have become key markers in cities where fashion permeates many facets of cultural and economic life. These much photographed walls, enlivened through the imposed imagery, have indelibly marked the urban fabric of cities which often operate as the commercial centers of their respective countries. Never before has fashion played such a pivotal role in the cultural, social, economic, and private lives of so many, and as a result, as Bradley Quinn claims, "it also portends a new economy of space" (Quinn 16). More recently, we have witnessed a new phase in the cultural wars of consumption and public space with the monumental expansion of evermore spectacular and grander designer boutiques, a development initiated by designers realizing their aspirations through collaborative efforts with famed architects. These designer boutiques and mega-stores have expanded and obscured the parameters of promotion and the contours of consumption to become cutting-edge environments of innovation and spectacle, as well as noteworthy cultural *milieux* and art exhibition spaces. Like the new museums and galleries which proliferated around the world in the 1980s and 1990s, these now-celebrated and much-written-about designer boutiques have become tourist destinations in their own right for art connoisseurs, architecture enthusiasts, or zealous fashionistas alike. Fashion designers have not only hired star architects to design larger than life boutiques or department stores, but they have also begun to influence other cultural and spatial spheres such as the theater, rock and roll stage, museums, and galleries, to name just a few. Architects in turn have also recognized the value of fashion in their quest for innovative ways to approach a built environment with constantly changing needs and concerns.

Not to be outdone or defeated in the trenches of the culture wars and tapping into the current scholarly and popular interest in fashion, numerous private and public art institutions also have le(n)t their spaces to explore the visual and material cultures of fashion with differing results. Fashion has transformed museums and art galleries with myriad block busters featuring past and living designers, and these hallowed institutions have adopted the cornerstone of fashionable goods marketing by creating desire and stimulating and fulfilling need. The relationship between the art gallery and fashion, to cite but one example, provocatively proves how, on the one hand, fashion can transform places and spaces, adding, deferring, or altering the identity of that environment, while, on the other hand, it can increase the cachet and cultural currency of a (living) designer. Regardless, what can surely be said of these environments, and what is often forgotten, is that desire, pleasure, and play become active accessories in the narratives of embodied subjectivity.

DEFINING THE SOCIAL RELATIONS OF SPACE

Surely one might ask whether place implies a temporal reality, a concrete moment of experience, while space remains abstract, ambiguous, and fluid. Place might simply be defined as a topographic point, a particular position, a location, while space could be understood as a continuous area or expanse which is free or unoccupied or where things are to be located. However, as Henri Lefebvre argues, "spaces [cannot] be considered empty 'mediums,' in the sense of containers distinct from their contents" (87). What Lefevbre evokes is that we might acknowledge how both place and space are constituent of the object and how in turn, as an embodied practice, both might help locate fashion on the map of political and cultural identity.

With these definitions in place, I wish to make clear that it is not the intention of this author or of this volume to conceptually reify place and space, denying the loaded history and the philosophical traditions which have attempted to deny, theorize, or deconstruct them. Both terms occupy deeply contested terrains. So rich are the histories and theories attending to the terms that my hands are tied to fully rehearse them here in the space of this brief introduction. On the other hand, I do not wish to abandon all intellectual responsibility to provide my readers with some sense of how these terms might come to bear on the case studies developed and explored by the authors in this volume. Moreover, place and space are fluid, transformed by subjects and objects, and are therefore often difficult to pin down and even more difficult to define. As Edward S. Casey ascertains:

> If it is true that there is a genuine geneaology of space—and, mutatis mutandis, of place—then we cannot maintain that place or space is simply one kind of thing, to be discovered and described once and for all. Not only is space not absolute and place not permanent, but the conception of each is subject to the most extensive historical vicissitudes (297).

In light of this, how might a volume on space and place proceed? What I suggest is to ask what might fashion reveal about how people occupy, embody, enjoy, and perform in certain places and spaces at a given moment in time? Space thickens fashion, it extends it, attenuates it, grounds it, while fashion adds texture, color, and life to space. What these two facets of the discussion reveal are the ways in which social space comes alive. As Lefebvre defines, social space "subsumes things produced, and encompasses their interrelationships in their coexistence and simultaneity" (73). However, one effective way to locate the experiences, moments, and cultures of these interrelationships is through representation itself, that is to say, the sites/sights of visuality and visibility which transform, enact, and activate the rare and mundane experiences of everyday life. These glimpses into the everyday are marked by what Lefebvre distinguishes as "a theatricality as sophisticated as it is unsought, a sort of involuntary *mise-en-scène*" of fashion (74).

In his discussion of the submersion of place into the expansiveness of space, Casey has asserted that place is not merely a site, as the latter "does not situate." He adds importantly that "[s]pace on the modernist conception ends by failing to locate things or events in any sense other than that of pinpointing positions on a planiform geometric or cartographic grid. Place, on the other hand, situates, and it does so richly and diversely. It locates things in regions whose most complete expression is neither geometric nor cartographic" (201). Casey continues: "The more we reflect on place, however, the more we recognize it to be something not merely characterizable but actually experienced in qualitative terms. These terms, for example, color, texture, and depth, are known to us only in and by the body that enters and occupies a given place" (204). If we slide fashion into the equation, an experience which also necessitates a consideration of color, texture, and depth, then we are impelled not to think of space and place as disembodied, as sites distinct from human experience and interest. Is space and place the thingness that binds people to fashion and even to each other through the interrelationships within social space? Through spatiality and emplacement, the body orients itself and its understanding of other fashioned subjects.

While there is a rich and significant body of work which has interrogated the practices of shopping and fashion as object of consumption, critical attention has viewed the places and spaces of fashion almost exclusively in terms of the capitalist system and consumer culture, obliterating the myriad nuanced layers involved in social relationships. In addition, more recently, much has been made of the connections, metaphorical or otherwise, between fashion and architecture, paying little attention to the material and visual connections as well as the objects and bodies interacting in and negotiating the spaces of fashion. In other words, attention has been paid to the surface/flesh/fabric of fashion and architecture, and little to the depth/interior/insides of fashion's environments. This volume interrogates the complexities of the display of fashion as sites and sights of spectacle, desire, pleasure, identity, and performance. In sum, what *The Places and Spaces of Fashion, 1800–2007* proposes is a sort of topography marking out various, while not all, spaces which influence the display and representation of fashion.

As the *Oxford English Dictionary* outlines, "display" as a verb is suggestive of two underlining forces. First, it means both to "place (something) prominently so that it may readily be seen," while it is also defined as a method to "give a conspicuous demonstration of (a quality, emotion, or skill)." In these terms, what is involved and investigated in the chapters of this volume is that space through visibility and visuality conspicuously give fashion meaningful shape, volume, and form. Additionally, as the second definition attests to, there is a performative and affective dimension, one that clearly implies a space to act upon and through. Exploring the display of fashion in its various spaces and places adds a neglected and compelling dimension to the synergy between material and visual cultures. As Quinn states: "The fashion system is premised on visuality; a concept essential to the consumption of fashion but often underestimated in interpretations of it. . . . Visuality is not the same as sight; it occurs when visual media and sensory perceptions intersect, where gaze meets desire" (20). This meeting requires spaces and places.

In *The Production of Space*, Lefebvre argues that space is not a mere "container without content," but rather a product of human agency and activity, not unlike fashion, I posit. As such, he attributes "spatial practice" as "all aspects, elements and moments of social practice" (8). Lefebvre looks into space through three different temporal modes, which seem readily amenable to a discussion of fashion: "the perceived, the conceived, and the lived." Spatial practice (the material expression of social relations) comprises conceptual practices, which conjure space both in imaginary, representational form and as a lived experience. Edward Soja has also argued that "spatiality is . . . a social product" (125). While the social production of space is evident in everyday and institutional practices, it ignores the imbrication of social space with mental space (Burgin 28). In the case of fashion, most people, at least initially, experience fashion through images, that is, the gaze (the optical), which is then succeeded by an experience enlivened through touch (the haptic). This relationship, then, is at once both material and visual, both social and projected mental uses of space.

Interestingly, Immanuel Kant asserted that "things *must* occupy particular places: we cannot perceive them, much less know them, except in such places" (Casey 204). He argued that the world of things in order to appear to us, as it were, must assume a form, that is representation itself. According to the philosopher, even time and space are represented; "place is part of the very world of appearances whose status is held to be representational" (Casey 203). The limitation of a Kantian approach, of course, is how the philosopher reduced the world (of objects) to a sum of representations, thereby not only reaffirming the mind/body split, but also privileging sight over the other senses, ignoring embodied space and practices in/through/because of these spaces.

BODIES IN FASHION/BODIES IN SPACE

Networks of creation, production, distribution, and consumption have long been examined, scrutinized without attending to the spatial dynamics and corporeal realities which assist in these activities. Fashion is not simply a product of labor, but a practice of being-in-the-world, a sensual activity. And so, we must not lose sight of the role the senses play in both the conceptualization and experience of both space and fashion. Lefebvre's "histories of space" is also the "histories of the body," and in this volume I wish to think through these bodies as clothed, fashionable, sartorial. For Lefebvre, the body is at the center of the social experiences of space: "The Whole of [social] space proceeds from the body" (405). In this way, space itself is not a geometric or abstract experience, but rather one marked by a haptic, visual, and complete sensory integration. Both fashion and space possess and are possessed by a body. At the hands of fashion or space, the body is not a passive agent of either, but inhabiting, wearing, altering, affecting both, an agent of transformation. Following along from Maurice Merleau-Ponty, intentions are marked by and through our physicality; our experience of the world of objects is primarily through our bodies. As a perceptive body, the subject's sensible apprehension of objects is not simply the product of consciousness but a tangible, material, and fleshy experience across the landscape of fashion.

Merleau-Ponty argued that bodily movement is "productive of space" (387). Our bodies are *the* way into the world and the object (140). Merleau-Ponty was keen to point out the significance of touch. It is the flesh that encounters the world of objects; fashion not only rubs up against our fleshy bodies, but is itself a second skin, another layered and significant sensory device of being-in-space. Fashion is a situated and embodied practice. In the twenty-first century, the body has become both virtual (mannequins, cybernetic models) and real (fleshy producing and consuming agents). Is cyberspace really and truly the last place to colonize? If cyberspace is no "real" place, then what can we make of this when the subjective experience of communication and information is disembodied? One way to measure space is through relationships between things, for as Robert David Sack has exclaimed: "space is manifested through things" (1980: 15).

Like the *flâneur* who looks, watches, gazes, desires, moves through the city, crosses the threshold of an arcade, picks up an object, puts it down, solicits the help of the sales clerk, places gold coins in the former's hand, leaves and walks the streets anew, shakes the gloved hand of a friend, caresses the elbow of his finely dressed companion, opens the door of his carriage which will take him home, to the opera, to dinner, to the racetrack, these bodily experiences (to only list a few) in the day in the life of the *flâneur* help to situate occasioning definitive coordinates that are at once real, material, and significant, if even only fleeting. de Certeau once described space as "composed of intersections of mobile elements. It is in a sense actuated by the ensemble of movements deployed within it." For him, the body's movement and mobility activate place: "space is a practiced place" (117). It is only part of the equation and is not enough. I wish to hint at a space beyond, from which to claim that the clothed body, or the embodied subject's engagement with fashion, tangibly situates economic, political, religious, cultural, and social spheres at once imagined, perceived, and concretized in space. While philosophers may discuss sensible bodies, what is crucial to our discussion here is how, through a sensual or sensory commonality, place and fashion are visually and materially linked by way of the body. Fashion is a sensuous moment of experiencing space.

How does the fashioned body, the embodied fashion subject, or just simply fashion itself produce, create, engender, elicit, represent, interpret, and transform space?

The study of fashion has more recently come to terms with the fashioned body as a signifying practice. In her seminal work on the relationship between fashion and the body, Joanne Entwistle explores the social and cultural significance associated with how the dressed body takes on various meanings in different contexts, either formal or informal, public or private. Entwistle's interest in embodied fashioned subjects is evocative of the nuanced and fleshy experience of fashion and textiles, complicated by social order, rules, protocols, and strictures.

It is the body that lends orientation to space, that locates place. More precisely, the sensual body, the tactile experience of being-in-clothes helps the subject to make *sense* of being-in-the-world as clothing and fashion visually and materially prescribe class, group or clan affiliation, ethnic and cultural locations, gender roles, and sexual identity. Fashion is one of those ways we understand our place in the world, and yet it offers us alternatives.

SOMEWHERE BETWEEN SPECTACLE AND PERFORMANCE

Recently, a much needed discussion of the performative nature of fashion has come to bear on how fashion is theorized, researched, discussed, marketed, and displayed by both scholars and professionals in the industry. However vital is a discussion of fashion's performative function, performances need locations, even if acted out within the private confines of a change room or closet. Sites can be marked out as places and spaces which define and are transformed through, by, and because of the subjects and objects of fashion. As potential sites of and for spectacle, performance, and even transformation, people often seek out locations of fashion either as participants, voyeurs, consumers, spectators, or would-be models. Fashion tailors the perception of spaces or places and the identities which occupy or traverse them.

However, the performative, according to French theorist and self-professed leader of the Situationists International Guy Debord, is suppressed in favor of the spectacle as it fulfills a greater role in the commodification of everyday life and social relations: "In societies dominated by modern conditions of production, life is presented as an immense accumulation of spectacles. Everything that was directly lived has receded into a representation" (thesis 1). Fashion is a system of continuously changing images, and both fashion and space share in common the fact that they are modes and systems of representation. What happens when they collide, merge, implicate, and imbricate at the sites/sights of display? As previously quoted, Quinn correctly states that: "[t]he fashion system is premised on visuality; a concept essential to the consumption of fashion but often underestimated in interpretations of it" (20). While this is true of fashion, it certainly rings true of space. And so, with this in mind, visuality and visibility are the conceptual glue that binds space with fashion.

In a seemingly Kantian vein, Debord maintained that "[t]he spectacle is the stage at which the commodity has succeeded in totally colonizing social life. Commodification is not only visible, we no longer see anything else; the world we see is the world of commodity" (thesis 42). Burdened by a sort of repressive hypothesis of the spectacle, Debord's Marxist methodology leaves no room for the subversive potential of images, spectacles, and performances. Reduced to "mere" spectacle, Debord viewed the social body as a monolithic entity, devoid of any bodily identity or material agency. Courted as a consumer, each individual is bombarded by images which form the spectacle of contemporary life and culture. Debord argued that society, through capitalism, divided the social body into those who produce and those who consume. However, as Regina Gagnier eloquently reminds us, we are all simultaneously workers and wanters "born of labouring bodies and desiring bodies" (Gagnier 54).

More often than not, studies end prematurely at the point of purchase, ignoring how the narratives of fashion extend beyond consumption to include the personal and public material, imagined, and visual experiences of the subject with its objects of desire. The performances of being in spaces and places within the modern metropolis provided for venues wherein and avenues through which to perform myriad identities. What is particularly prescient about the Situationists and Debord's theories in particular is the strategy of *détournement* as a sort of redirection of images or events. This French word *détournement* denotes practices which deflect, divert, distort, misuse, misappropriate, or hijack. While the term has sometimes erroneously been translated as "diversion," it would appear that this translation ironically provides for an additional signifying layer to a discussion of fashion, despite the pejorative connotations (see theses 204–09). Fashion has the power to do just this, force a *détournement* within any given culture, hijack any spatial relations, or operate as a sweet diversion.

The Places and Spaces of Fashion, 1800–2007 attempts to shift attention away from and even avoid a conversation which sees fashion and space in strict terms of theatricality for which the reasons are many. First, it presumes a separation from everyday life, that the spaces of fashion are culturally marked as special, rarefied, and hence removed and hidden from view. Fashion might provide a sort of material biography of social and cultural spaces of both the special, significant, and ephemeral as well as the everyday. Fashion's impact on spaces and places does not only make them "fashionable," but exposes and complicates social relationships within them. Second, a performance also assumes an audience distinct from the actors on the stage, detached and disinterested from the spectacle of fashion they are witnessing. Third, it also infers that fashion is scripted, and hence structurally prescribed and described, belying the interpretive potency of the spectator-viewer-consumer. The performances of fashion happen on many stages (space) and through many stages (time). In the world of embodied subjectivity, which this volume presupposes, the spectator is active, that is, as the inevitable scopophilic participant in the display of fashion, the engaged interpreter of what is seen, and finally a fashionable interloper. In this way, the intersubectivity engenders the spaces between subjects and the places which locate them. The spectacle is a visual performance made possible through the onslaught of images and, as Debord recognizes, mediates the "social relations between people" (thesis 4). More often than not within the cultures of modernity, the dialectical relationship between reality and image is collapsed; the image becomes reality and the wo/man becomes the fashion plate.

FASHIONING VOLUME

Within the space of this book, a statement like Ben Highmore's "[p]laces permit and prohibit" could not ring more true (33). The act of writing history is an act of placing importance on and placing within the frame of view; certain fashion and spatial practices have been included, while others have been excluded from this volume. While Highmore is specifically referring back to de Certeau's analysis of the production of history, that is, historiography itself, the spaces of prohibition and permission refer more broadly to the production, formation, and distribution of knowledge and subjectivities. In this case, places and spaces become sites which restrict, prescribe, limit, entertain, promote, and encourage the representation, embodiment, experience, and display of fashion through the guise and writing of intellectual history, which this volume attempts.

As a location itself or as an act of emplacement, *The Places and Spaces of Fashion, 1800–2007* does not restrict space to bricks and mortar, but looks to the auratic, secular importance attributed to and garnered in these spaces. Like the Wicked Witch of the East whose corporeal identity for the viewer was defined in strict terms of the adverse affect of (domestic) architecture, so too has the corpus on fashion and space within and beyond the academy been informed by the weighty and univocal context of architecture. A spate of books has explored the more recent trend in the current building boom of mega-stores, designer epicenters, and celebrated retail spaces. For while books like *Fashion Retail* (2004) by Eleanor Curtis, *Absolutely Fabulous* by Ruth Hanisch (2006), *Retail Design* (2000) by Otto Riewoldt and Jennifer Hudson, and finally the special issue of *Architectural Design—Fashion + Architecture* (vol. 70, 6, 2000), to name only a few, have set out to differentiate the various stylistic tendencies found in retail architecture, they limit their attention to contemporary retail stores, focus exclusively on architecture as the defining principle of place and space, ignore the visual and material cultures of these spaces, sidestep the broader cultural implications these spaces have on fashion and identities, and with the exception of the special issue of *Architectural Design,* what such books gain in breadth, they tend to lose significantly in interpretive depth. In short, they explore buildings rather than the systems, networks, and complexities of spaces and places of fashion and its display that come together in and around these outlets.

Given the infinite possibilities fashion offers and the polyvalent nature of space, this volume can only boast, at best, to be an embryonic and partial cartographic initiative. As the chapters attest to, one single map, program, or model is neither plausible nor even desirable. It does suggest, however, the multidimensionality of many types of spaces: architectural, social, virtual, conceptual, pictorial, representational, material. A volume of disparate case studies such as this one is neither bound by one theoretical model nor wedded to one methodological template and moves beyond disciplinary boundaries by negotiating terrain at the often murky backwaters of art and architectural history, visual and material studies, and fashion theory and history. It offers strategies and histories of reading fashion's many maps as the authors vacillate between the concrete and the abstract. The locations of fashion on the cultural, economic, social, and political maps have been altogether ignored or trivialized by conventional historians and scholars. What these case studies help to open up is Pandora's (jewelry) box of sorts, to worlds where space constructs narratives and where fashion is not merely an accessory but content and meaning itself.

Architecture: In Fashion, edited by Deborah Fausch, explores the myriad metaphors, analogies, relationships, connections, seams, and threads that bind fashion to architecture. While some of the case studies attend to the issue of modernity, the book, more theoretical than historical, appears less to have explored fashion as a material and visual object, privileging fashion in the service of architecture, than to have pursued discussions of the "fashionability" of various architectural practices. Whereas in *The Fashion of Architecture* Bradley Quinn skillfully explores the complex interrelationship of contemporary fashion and architecture, interrogating how fashion, particularly of avant-garde designers, informs and is informed by architectural praxis. Quinn honestly and compellingly begins to explore this complex symbiosis, but confines his analysis not only to our contemporary experience, but more precisely to radical, avant-gardist designers. Quinn's analysis, however, rarely gives way to more nuanced discussions of some specific case studies beyond the realm of high fashion to explore some of the everyday occurrences, performances, and actualities of fashion(s) and the built environment. Quinn himself concedes that "[t]he axis between fashion, architecture and identity is highly topical, but until recently, relatively unexplored" (Quinn 40). Taking off from this point, *The Places and Spaces of Fashion, 1800–2007* attempts to do exactly this. By considering different historical and geographical material, this volume moves beyond the physical and conceptual strictures of architecture as the defining principal and guiding force of fashion's spatial parameters to explore the thickness of spaces which help us to locate defining narratives of fashion's multiple identities. As a result, the goal is not to map out specific and static positions in the cartography of modernity, an impossible task to be sure, but to demonstrate the fluidity, contingency, cyclical culture, mobility, and shifting nature of space, in other words, the fashions of space.

The volume purposefully draws the reader's attention to the locations where identities blossom and fashion lives, breathes, and becomes integral to the places it occupies. Divided into three parts, the chapters explore various physical and conceptual spaces, moving from the two-dimensional with paintings, illustrations, and photographs to more traditional, concrete, and architectural physical environments. The volume also navigates some of the various sites (whether permanent or temporary) of the production, circulation, exhibition, consumption, and promotion of fashion that define meaning and knowledge about a culture or individual by providing room for a bond between embodied consumers-spectators and fashion's many objects.

Fashion and space do not occur in isolation, but in tandem with other human activities (economic, political, cultural, social). And so, in this way, separating fashion as it were, is an artificial enterprise, but I argue a necessary one. Necessary because it has rarely, if ever, figured in discussions of the study of space and place. As a result, this volume aspires to begin, or perhaps continue, to chart out fashion's myriad travels and destinations. However, I also wish to imply that the map, like all scholarship, is always being redrawn. The fashion system is always on the move, after all, never satisfied to stand still, always seeking out the new, that which is exciting and desirable. And so, the most we can hope for is a cross-section cut through layers of fashion's geography, seeing through the sediments, the layers of history built up over time. This becomes a challenging prospect when one thinks about space not only in terms of its physicality, but also its imaginary projections or idealized (spatial) abstractions. How does one chart out the imaginary onto physical maps, where the rules that govern physics, geometry, architecture, and geography do not apply?

Certain places are sought out by the fashion cognoscenti. Space within the context of the modern metropolis is itself a luxury and only serves to enhance the status of the wearer or of the fashion object. In selecting the chapters for this volume, I have attempted to include as many spatial narratives as possible from the nineteenth century to the present in both Europe and North America, whose relationship to fashion have been informed by the market economy, the vagaries of various cycles, and the modern metropolis. The chapters have been selected because they engage with questions attending to the "modern condition" by seamlessly weaving interdisciplinary discussions of the visual with material culture to explore the spatial dimension(s) of fashion. Some of the chapters explore new and exciting terrain, while others offer compelling revisionary analyses of relatively known sources. The approaches taken by the authors are purposefully diverse as they mark out the differences and diversity in the modalities of space, strategies of display, and vagaries of the performances attending to the needs of the fashionable. These discussions include the following sights/sites: department stores; museums and galleries; designer boutiques; painter's studios; streets and parks; university campuses; racetracks; shop windows; private residences; change rooms; tailor shops and haberdasheries; runway presentations; war zones; virtual and cyber sites; arcades; promenades; cities and fashion districts, among others. Some of the places and spaces have long since disappeared or no longer possess the same vitality or currency they once possessed, while others are enjoying growth or a renaissance of sorts.

This volume is set up as an arcade, department store, or website—a location to see, read, and choose fashion through locations of desire. It has amassed objects (yes, even commodities) for the readers to take pleasure in. As such, like all points of sale and display, it is incomplete; it is not a diachronic purview of the subject, but rather a promenade, a flânerie, a bricolage, a perusal of sorts. Volumes like this one invite the reader—like the consumer—to pick and choose and maybe even long for more, seduced by the histories, fantasies, mythologies, and possibilities offered by fashion and its many exciting spaces.

WORKS CITED

Architectural Design—Fashion and Architecture. Vol. 70, 6, 2000.

Benjamin, Walter. *The Arcades Project.* Cambridge and London: The Belknap Press at Harvard University Press, 1999.

Breward, Christopher. *Fashioning London: Clothing and the Modern Metropolis.* Oxford and New York: Berg, 2004.

Burgin, Victor. *In/Different Spaces.* Berkeley, Los Angeles, and London: University of California Press, 1996.

Casey, Edward S. *The Fate of Place: A Philosophical History.* Berkeley, Los Angeles, and London: University of California Press, 1997.

Curtis, Eleanor. *Fashion Retail.* West Sussex: Wiley-Academy, 2004.

Debord, Guy. *Society of the Spectacle.* London: Rebel Press, 2000.

de Certeau, Michel. *The Practice of Everyday Life.* Translated by S. Rendall. Berkeley: University of California Press, 1988.

Entwistle, Joanne. *The Fashioned Body: Fashion, Dress, and Modern Social Theory.* Cambridge, UK; Malden, MA: Polity Press, 2000.

Fausch, Deborah. *Architecture: In Fashion.* New York: Princenton Architectural Press, 1996.

Gagnier, Regenia. "Productive, Reproductive, and Consuming Bodies." In *Body Matters: Feminism Textuality Corporeality,* edited by Avril Horner and Angela Keane. Manchester and New York: Manchester University Press, 2000: 43–57.

Gilbert, David. "Introduction: From Paris to Shanghai." In *The Changing Geographies of Fashion's World Cities,* edited by Christopher Breward and David Gilbert. Oxford and New York: 2006: 3–32.

Hanisch, Ruth. *Absolutely Fabulous!: Architecture and Fashion.* Munich and London: Prestel, 2006.

Highmore, Ben. *Michel de Certeau: Analysing Cultre.* London and New York: Continuum, 2006.

Lefebvre, Henri. *The Production of Space.* Translated by Donald Nicholson-Smith. Malden, MA, Oxford: Blackwell Publishing, 1991.

Merleau-Ponty, Maurice. *The Phenomenology of Perception.* London and New York: Routledge, 1958.

Quinn, Bradley. *The Fashion of Architecture.* Oxford: Berg, 2003.

Rendell, Jane. "Between Architecture, Fashion and Identity." *Architectural Design.* Vol. 70, No. 6 (December 2000): 8–19.

Riewoldt, Otto and Jennifer Hudson. *Retail Design.* London: Te Neues, 2000.

Sack, Robert David. *Concepts of Space in Social Thought: A Geographic Perspective.* London: The Macmillan Press, 1980.

———. *Place, Modernity, and the Consumer's World: A Relational Framework for Geographical Analysis.* Baltimore and London: The Johns Hopkins University Press, 1992.

Soja, Edward W. *Postmodern Geographies: The Reassertion of Space Into Social Critical Theory.* London and New York: Verso, 1989.

Thrift, Nigel. *Spatial Formations.* London: Sage, 1996.

Part I

Picturing Fashion/ Fashionable Pictures

1 Tracking Fashions
Risking It All at the Hippodrome de Longchamp

Heidi Brevik-Zender

Late-nineteenth-century Paris was the setting for myriad sites of fashionable display. Along its tree-lined boulevards, stylishly dressed bourgeois citizens paraded past trendsetting courtesans during afternoon promenades. At the Palais Garnier, the capital's gilded opera house, audience members' opulent garments often enjoyed more scrutiny than did the performances on stage. Sale days at *Le Bon Marché,* one of the city's lavish department stores, were occasions to exhibit the latest styles on one's body while purchasing them. Even visits to view cadavers at the city morgue—a popular if morbid tourist attraction of the period—were instances where smartly dressed dandies and "well-dressed women nonchalantly trailing silk dresses" (Zola 1970: 132)[1] demonstrated their sartorial skills to crowds of onlookers drawn to a space where both corpses and clothes were on display.[2] Yet, of the many events that drew a fashion-conscious crowd to particular venues of metropolitan Paris, few could rival in spectacle and importance the horse races of Longchamp.

At least once a year, the Hippodrome de Longchamp became Paris's most significant nexus of stylish display. Refurbished in 1857 under Baron Haussmann (1809–91) and lying just west of the city limits in the Bois de Boulogne park, the race track at Longchamp was, by the late nineteenth century, the most popular racecourse in France and an incomparable site of fashionable pageantry. The Grand Prix de Paris, held every spring starting in 1863, was a daylong affair that attracted thousands of spectators, as much for the chance to observe the well-dressed attendees and to witness the new clothing styles that inevitably made their debut as for the high-stakes horse race.

Festivities commenced in the morning, when fashionable Parisians in carriages and on horseback processed down the Champs-Elysées toward the racetrack to the delight of observers seated on benches placed there by the city for the occasion (Herbert 152). Upon arrival at the sporting grounds, viewers arranged themselves according to a hierarchical schema that located the aristocracy, government officials, prominent social figures, and members of the exclusive Jockey Club in covered stands, while the bourgeoisie and lower classes sat in open carriages and on the grass around the track. Following the race, high society convened at gala balls where evening fashions were put on parade.

This chapter analyzes the ways in which the Longchamp racetrack served as a vital—if incidental—location of fashionable display in late-nineteenth-century Paris. Drawing on paintings of the races by Edgar Degas (1834–1917) and Édouard Manet (1832–83), as well as on the serial novel *Nana* by naturalist writer Émile Zola (1840–1902), I examine artistic portrayals of the pageantry, physical arrangement, and metaphorical function of sartorial exhibition at Longchamp. How, according to these writers and artists, did fashionable display play a role in both reinforcing and weakening the hierarchies of a socially stratified society? How did differences of class inform the sartorial topography of the racecourse, and how was it represented? In addressing these questions, I focus in particular on the notions of danger and risk that were important elements of late-nineteenth-century fashion, horse racing, and modernity alike.

Risk-taking informed many of the leisure practices of the nineteenth century, an era that witnessed an increase in the popularity and incidence of gambling. For a rising bourgeois population with a growing expendable income, gambling represented a publicly sanctioned way in which thrills could be purchased for an ostensibly affordable price. "Gambling and its transformation of every social gathering and chance encounter into an arena of desire," observes historian Thomas M. Kavanagh, "held the power to infuse the humdrum reality of everyday life with real excitement" (2000: 507).[3] The sport of horse racing, which rapidly gained in popularity following its late-eighteenth-century debut in France, developed in tandem with betting. The *pari,* or wager, which could be placed with any of the racecourses' ubiquitous bookmakers, was one of the most compelling elements of this growing spectator sport. The connection between gambling and horse racing was cemented in 1863 with the advent of the Grand Prix de Paris, whose total purse of 100,000 francs made it the highest endowed race in the world. Often drawing crowds of over 100,000 people (Gaillard 88), the Grand Prix quickly became both a mecca for public gambling and a premiere event on the chic Parisian social scene (Jones 214).

Yet for all its thrilling popularity, gambling at the races could be extremely dangerous, for the financial risks incurred by patrons could have grave consequences. In Zola's novel *Nana,* the horse owner Vandeuvres loses his entire fortune at the Grand Prix, a loss that compels him to end his life in spectacular fashion by setting fire to his own stables and burning inside them. At once a celebration of the glamour and excitement of Longchamp and a cautionary tale about the vices it promotes, this episode of *Nana* serves as an extreme reminder of the very real risks incurred at the track.

Risk was also an important factor in nineteenth-century sartorial fashion. In public, much depended upon appearance, for what one wore could dictate who one was *perceived* to be, which was perhaps more important than who one actually was. Members of the lower and middle bourgeoisie who had aspirations of social ascendancy, like those already at the height of public standing, needed to obey the ever-changing edicts of fashion by donning the very latest in dresses, hats, jackets, jewels, and accessories. "Fashion has exercised in Paris, for several centuries, an absolute power," wrote Madame Emmeline Raymond, editor of the long-running periodical *La mode illustrée,* in 1867 (923). Violations of this seemingly omnipotent, uncompromising Parisian fashion system were a danger to one's social standing and thus were to be avoided at all costs.

In bourgeois and high society alike, fashionable garments were necessary in order to manifest a wearer's fiscal worth. It was risky from a social standpoint to appear at important functions without the appropriately fine garments. Specific spaces, from the private salon to the public park and theater, each required its own specific brand of sartorial chic. In turn, the stylish outfits donned by smart Parisians helped to identify these milieus as particularly fashionable. Elegant attire in these settings, it was assumed, bore witness to a person's elevated social class and, in some cases, could serve as an entryway to an even higher public rank. Notes Thérèse Dolan, "costume was of great importance for those who wish[ed] to appear to have what they d[id] not possess, because that [wa]s the best way of getting it later on" (380). Clothes were thus indispensable tools for the aspirations of bourgeois social climbers. Some risked a great deal for fashion, a trend of which, not surprisingly, some nineteenth-century writers were highly critical. For example, in *Pot Bouille,* his cynical portrait of Third Empire bourgeois mores, Émile Zola portrayed the destruction of the Josserand family, whose ruinous obsession to clothe daughters of marriageable age in the latest fashions results in a father's premature death and the adulterous, unhappy union of its younger daughter.

Fashion was thus an area of risk for economic reasons as well as social: one needed to invest in articles of clothing in order to gain access to privileged spaces and attain or sometimes hold on to a preferred social standing, despite the fact that these desired results were far from guaranteed. Moreover, risk could also be incurred on a symbolic level, for the meaning of any given garment was constantly subject to dangerous slippage. In *The Fashion System,* Roland Barthes argues that clothing, like most cultural objects, is imbued with significations that transcend its functionality: a garment easily disassociates from an earlier function to assume numerous new significations (265). The problem with this ever-expanding set of meanings, note the authors of "Toward Formalizing

Fashion Theory," is that it destabilizes the ways in which articles of clothing are read and understood, which in turn creates a higher level of risk for wearers as they attempt to conform to fashion's fluctuating meanings. "Changing adopted styles involves risk to the individual," they argue, "because a substantial resource investment must be made . . . and the future meaning, and therefore symbolic utility [of a garment] is uncertain" (Miller et al. 147). This underlying uncertainty is a characteristic of a dynamic and risky fashion process by which individuals determine which new styles to adopt.

Risks in fashion were accentuated during the Longchamp Grand Prix because the event was a well-known showcase for unveiling the newest styles in fashionable garments. Offers historian Marc Gaillard, "[e]very Grand Prix was the occasion for a veritable fashion show at which the greatest Parisian couturiers presented their new designs and society women rivaled each others' elegance" (73). Professional clothing designers began treating the Longchamp races as an opportunity to unveil their newest gowns to a public keen on viewing, and eventually purchasing, the most up-to-date styles. Charles Frederick Worth, the nineteenth-century father of haute couture, famously enlisted the help of his wife, who donned his latest creations to debut them at the Longchamp races (Steele 170). Moreover, because the majority of illustrated publications from the second half of the nineteenth century featured numerous images of spectators at important races, designers could capitalize on the free publicity provided them by the mass-circulating press (Gaillard 101). The Grand Prix racetrack thus provided a milieu that was mutually beneficial for fashionable Parisians and couturiers, although the sartorial pageantry of the event was not without risk. At Longchamp, one could introduce a new fashion to great public acclaim, yet a wearer also risked ridicule should a gown be poorly received, while a designer chanced a devastating blow to his newest design and potential financial disaster in the case of a fashion flop.

I submit that it was this exhilarating combination of social, financial, and sartorial risk that caused Longchamp to become one of the most electrifying sites of fashionable display in nineteenth-century Paris. As it happened, the element of risk at the races was underscored by the very real threat of physical peril present at the track. In 1890, writer Louis Baron juxtaposed the glamour of horse racing with its hazards, describing the event as both "attractive and dangerous" (in Gaillard 129). The existence of corporeal danger was spectacularly captured by several artists of the period. For example, Edgar Degas' 1866 *The Fallen Jockey* depicts a thrown rider lying unconscious—or perhaps dead—on the track while horses leap over his inert body (Bogg 50). In his 1864 watercolor, *Races at Longchamp,* Édouard Manet similarly evoked the inherent dangers of a horse race, painting a group of steeds bearing down at the finish line and aiming toward a group of well-dressed

Figure 1.1 Edouard Manet. *Races at Longchamp; Verso: Section of Grandstand Area,* 1864. Watercolor and gouache over graphite on white wove paper on two sheets, joined; verso: graphite; actual: 22.1 x 56.4 cm (8 11/16" x 22 3/16"). Harvard University Art Museums, Fogg Art Museum, Bequest of Grenville L. Winthrop, 1943.387. Photo: Katya Kallsen © President and Fellows of Harvard College.

spectators (Figure 1.1). As we shall presently see, interplay between risk and fashion informs the depictions of the track painted by these two artists of Parisian modernity.

FASHION IN HARM'S WAY: ÉDOUARD MANET AND EDGAR DEGAS

In the images of Longchamp seen through the eyes of Manet and Degas, fashion plays a capital role. In Manet's *Races at Longchamp,* fashion is located literally at the center of the composition. A group of spectators gathered at the track's edge dominates the middle portion of the work, which features several women dressed in the fashionable bell-shaped crinoline skirts of the Second Empire and a number of coach drivers and gentlemen sporting shiny top hats and crisp blue and black coats. Splashes of pink, red, and blue in the stands denote garments and parasols in the crowd and echo the bright colors of the racers' jerseys. The eye is especially drawn to the sumptuous wash of gray and cream-colored fabric of the expansive dresses worn by two of the women in the foreground.

The dynamic action of the scene is displaced to the right side of the painting, where rapid forward motion of the charging horses is suggested both by gray clouds of dust at the animals' feet and their diagonally set front legs. As the horses race toward the onlookers, their sideways momentum sends them careening in the direction of the immobile female spectators in the foreground, who appear to be placed in a somewhat risky position: a line drawn from the hooves of the horse on the front left of the pack and extending into the crowd suggests that the animal is aimed directly at the women, whose pouf skirts appear to be extending out past the very limits of the safety railing that separates spectator from sportsman. Although it is unlikely that the onlookers will actually be trampled by the stampeding steeds, it seems inevitable that, at the very least, the horses will draw close enough to muddy their expensive garments.[4] Manet here juxtaposes the wild instability of the horses with the cool stylishness of the chic bystanders. The potential for sartorial harm adds to the excitement of the event, even as the viewer is cautioned against the true physical, not to mention fiscal, dangers at the races. In this moment caught on canvas, Manet turns Longchamp into a symbol for the glamorous Second Empire society that, by decade's end, would meet its demise; the opulence of Parisian life is put on display while impending danger speeds toward it down the final stretch.

Most of the onlookers have their eyes trained on the race; that we can only see the backs of their heads indicates a heightened sense of apprehension over the many wagers most likely at stake. However, pieces that survive of an oil version of the painting from 1865 confirm what is suggested in the 1864 watercolor with respect to the direction of the central female character's gaze: she is not focused on the approaching racehorses but rather on someone or something—an eye-catching new dress style or the latest in shawls perhaps?—on the opposite side of the track. Distracted by a sight so compelling as to turn her attention from the din of the horses' pounding hooves, the elegant female spectator is in turn watched by the well-dressed gentleman behind her who is mounted on horseback on the far left of the painting. Robert L. Herbert observes that "one went to the races, as to the theater, partly to look over the women and their apparel" (159). It is likely that Manet is suggesting in this layered series of gazes that for many, fashionable ladies, more than horses, were the ultimate spectacle at Longchamp.

The thrilling speed of the racers, the slightly precarious position of the main female bystanders, the nervous energy of a crowd fixated on high financial stakes and the prominent role of fashion at the races are all captured in this painting, which is informed by multiple levels of risk. Many of these elements are also present in works by Degas, whose lifelong fascination for the racecourse was eclipsed only by his interest in dance. In *The False Start* (1869–72), the composition is backgrounded with an extended view of the stands, where bright patches of blue, pink, white, and red signify the dresses, wraps, parasols, and accessories of the many spectators on display at the races (Figure 1.2). Against this elegant pastel backdrop, on the left side of the work, a horse leaps forward while its jockey attempts to control it by pulling sharply on the reins. As the large horse in the foreground springs forth, another horse closer to the stands rears its head; the dynamic energy of both animals is emphasized by their flying tails and manes and gaping mouths. The dark blocks of

Figure 1.2 Edgar Degas, *The False Start,* c. 1869–72. Oil on wood panel. 32.1 x 40.3 cm (12 5/8" x 15 78"). Yale University Art Gallery. John Hay Whitney, B.A. 1926, Hon. 1956, Collection.

color of the two horses' deep chocolate coats stand out in stark contrast to the hazy pale hues that represent the leisured class behind them. In contrast to Manet's paintings, here the spectators are in no physical danger, for they are located at some distance from the horses, protected in their covered stand. Rather, it is the jockeys, embodying man's struggle to gain mastery over animal, who risk life and limb.

Sartorially speaking, it is not the crowds that draw our attention, for the dabs of color that Degas used to represent them do not allow us to distinguish details of dress or tailoring. Instead, jockey fashions take center stage. In the middle distance, the bold canary yellow outfit worn by the racer on the right jumps out against the more neutral backdrop of trees and pastel ladies behind him, matching in brightness and intensity the red flag of the starter to his left. The sheen on the black silk jersey of the jockey in the foreground, the sensuous volume of his ballooning shirt, and the tight folds on his jodhpurs are highlighted with quick gray, tan, and black brushstrokes. Degas' typical attention to tailoring in garments is here concentrated on the jockeys, who become the vehicles for his exploration of fit, cut, and style.

This interest in the texture and color of jockey uniforms runs as a leitmotif through Degas' paintings of the track. In *Racehorses at Longchamp* (1871), he emphasized the pinks, blues, yellows, oranges, and reds of jockeys' jerseys and caps, creating a swath of pretty colors across the center of an otherwise dark and heavy composition (Figure 1.3). Interestingly, Degas uses soft, feminized shades for his jockey uniforms, picking up on colors that are more reminiscent of elegant ball gowns than of masculine sporting events. Indeed, this same palate of pastel hues reappears in the bows and ribbons on dancer costumes in his paintings of the ballet, as well as in the shades of fabrics used to make fashionable ladies' hats in his milliners series.[5] With this particular choice of colors for his racers' attire, Degas connects the chic venue of the theater and the hats of stylish Parisian women to the races at the Bois de Boulogne. In *Racehorses at Longchamp*, the well-dressed spectators in the stands are replaced with horses and riders, but they are not forgotten: the modern, curved rooftops visible above the tree line on the left suggest the imminent presence of a sophisticated nineteenth-century capital city, while the sartorial spectacle of Paris is echoed in the eye-catching silks worn by the jockeys.

Figure 1.3 Edgar Degas, *Racehorses at Longchamp,* 1871, possibly reworked in 1874. Oil on canvas. 34.0 x 41.9 cm (13 3/8" x 16 ½"). Museum of Fine Arts, Boston. S. A. Denio Collection—Sylvanus Adams Denio Fund and General Income, 03.1034.

In focusing so frequently on the colorful uniforms of jockeys at the track, Degas underscored the unique fashion role played by these sportsmen at the races. In keeping with a tradition passed down from England, the decorative silks that professional jockeys wore often corresponded to colors chosen by the owners of the horses they rode. Certainly, then, silks were useful to distinguish one rider from another during a race and to denote each jockey's employer. But these bright silks that Degas so clearly enjoyed painting also highlighted riders' status as fashionable objects. An American journalist reporting on racetrack fashions in 1869 noted that, among the "remarkable toilettes" worn to the races, "the favorite colors seem to be pale blue, pale green, lavender, pink, pearly gray, and maize color" (Herbert 168). It can be no coincidence that Degas, painting during this same period, used such similar hues in his depictions of riders at the Longchamp races. In Degas' works, jockeys are themselves fashionable accessories, to be flaunted and admired by the wealthy men who hired them just as their wives admired each others' new silk purses and scarves. Beautiful objects in motion, Degas' jockeys represent a fashionable modernity of high speed, rapid change, phantasmagorical entertainment—and underlying danger.

THE HUSTLE AND THE BUSTLE: ÉMILE ZOLA'S *NANA*

Jockey fashion and its ties to haute couture garments are also highlighted in the Longchamp scene of Zola's 1880 novel, *Nana*. The story of a beautiful, seductive courtesan who lays waste to the fortunes and lives of wealthy and powerful men of Second Empire Paris, *Nana* features one of the most vivid nineteenth-century accounts of the Grand Prix de Paris. In it, the title character debuts a remarkable blue and white outfit that mirrors the colors worn by the jockeys employed by Vandeuvres, one of her many suitors. Nana accessorizes her look by donning "a little blue cap with a white feather" that she wears "to look even more like a jockey" (1397). By wearing the colors of the Vandeuvres stables and her sporty cap, Nana not only playfully appropriates the role of the jockey, but also turns the professional uniform of the racers into a fashion statement, further insuring that all attention turns from the race to the spectacle of her attire.

Indeed, Zola understood that the Grand Prix was an event analogous to a fashion parade, where all eyes were drawn not just to the horses but also to the spectators and their outfits. His famous preparatory notebooks, in which he observed with minute detail the milieus that he chronicled in his novels, include passages on the pageantry of Longchamp: what was worn at the 1879 races, the colors, the movement of forms, and the physical arrangements of the crowd. In *Nana*, fashion is a major preoccupation, and Zola makes his title character the very definition of what is in vogue. Capturing envy and fascination, Nana embodies all that is chic. Innumerable male lovers desire her, while high-society women, including her wealthy alter ego, the Comtesse Sabine, emulate her fashion style and wardrobe. To be in Nana's presence is fashionable: the glamorous Parisian set congregates at her parties, assembles at her country house, and draws around her at the races. Nana, the very incarnation of chic style, creates fashionable spaces wherever she goes.

In keeping with her reputation as a Parisian trendsetter, Nana chooses to unveil a remarkable cutting-edge look during the Grand Prix races. In addition to the jockey cap, her outfit features what Zola describes as "a blue silk tunic that clung to the body and lifted in the rear in an enormous poof, which conformed to the backside in a bold manner for this era of ballooning skirts" (1376). In this passage, Zola seems to be evoking a bustle, a style of skirt that features a flat front and a large pad or cage that protrudes from the back. And yet, during the Second Empire, the period in which Nana's story is set, it was not the bustle but rather the bell-shaped crinoline skirt that dominated ladies' fashions. Indeed, the crinoline has become something of an emblem of the period, due in part to Baudelaire's homage to artist Constantin Guys, who immortalized the wide silhouette of the crinoline in his famous illustrations of Parisian women. For its part, the bustle did not actually gain in popularity until the early years of the Third Republic, several fashion seasons after Nana's story takes place.

Nana's skirt is thus "bold" because it represents an innovation in fashion design that follows decades of the crinoline's reign.[6] She unabashedly unveils this risky new dress design, one that clings to her lower body and calls erotic attention to her *derrière,* during a period in which the overall roundness of the crinoline cage and its "ballooning skirts" served to hide the contours of the lower body rather than to expose them. Moreover, the bustle's exaggerated posterior curve recalls the haunches of the identically named racehorse Nana, a long-shot filly who speeds to Grand Prix victory as the crowd excitedly screams her name. As the voluptuous shape of her protruding skirt mimics the back legs of the horse named for her, the garment is itself infused with Nana's animal sexuality. Sensual and daring, this risky new fashion makes its debut at the Longchamp races because its clever and capricious wearer knows how to take advantage of a milieu where flair in fashion reigns supreme.

Part of what contributes to Nana's success as a Second Empire trendsetter is her status as a courtesan. Perhaps because of their need to attract wealthy clients by putting their bodies on constant display, high-end prostitutes were frequently looked to as arbiters of the very latest in clothing styles. Valerie Steele suggests the privileged position these women held with regard to fashion, quoting Arsène Houssaye who noted that "demi-mondaines seemed a little more chic" than respectable Parisian ladies, though ironically both frequented the same dressmakers (170). The erotic lure of the courtesan, who often overshadowed the reputable woman of Paris, can be perceived especially in the realm of nineteenth-century artistic representation: caricaturists such as Honoré Daumier echoed Constantin

Guy's fascination of the crinolined courtesan, while Manet scandalized the Salons with his brazen prostitutes in *Olympia* (1863) and *Le déjeuner sur l'herbe* (1863), and Charles Baudelaire, Alexandre Dumas, Pierre Louÿs, and Alphonse Daudet, among others, joined Zola in memorializing the coquettes, actresses, performers, and demi-mondaines of nineteenth-century Paris.

In the Longchamp chapter of *Nana,* Zola's focus is entirely on the courtesan class at the expense of the aristocracy. From her vantage point across the track, Nana observes as countesses and duchesses rub elbows in the imperial stands with the Empress Eugénie, a faithful client of Charles Frederick Worth who was noted for her smart fashion sense and her ability to make wildly popular whatever garment she chose to wear. Yet, in Zola's depiction of the exclusive stands at Longchamp, the fine garments of the French royalty, like those of the spectators in Degas' *The False Start,* seem to blend together in a colorful, but vague pastiche, "a profound mass of toilettes, mixing their lively colors in the gaiety of the open air" (1393). In contrast, the details of the outfits worn by the title character and her prostitute friends remain in focus under the novelist's fixed gaze. Dolan observes that "Zola thus adorns the demi-monde with the glitter of imperial regalia and devotes to this underclass the type of reportage usually reserved for the Empress and her entourage" (381). By focusing on the lower classes, Zola suggests a collapse of the formerly rigid hierarchies between high society and the courtesan class. Not only is the Empress Eugénie, a noted fashion icon, underreported at Longchamp, but her presence is eclipsed by the courtesan's emboldened sartorial display.

By insuring that all spectators at the races linger on Nana's eroticized bustle rather than on the Empress Eugenie's evidently forgettable Grand Prix gown, Zola uses the metaphor of fashion to allude to larger nineteenth-century fears over the blurring of social demarcations, easing of class restrictions, and intersecting of formerly disparate social groups. Referencing largely upper-class anxieties that the century was succumbing to a systemic dissolution of formerly stable class divisions, Zola crafts a scene in which his courtesan heroine quite literally crosses the threshold of a space into which she, and other demimondaines, are not to be allowed. During a lull before the start of the races, Nana defiantly enters the jockey-weighing area of the arena, a space that she knows to be "absolutely forbidden to prostitutes" (1387), and crosses directly in front of the luxury tribunes where she stares down the Comtesse Sabine and makes loud, disparaging remarks about her lover and Sabine's husband, the Comte Muffat. As Nana's confident gaze passes over the grandstands, the pale fabrics worn by the aristocracy and the wealthy appear to fade into the building, "melting into the fine shadows of its framework" (1393). As the silver lace ornamenting Nana's white satin gown sparkles in the sun, in the grandstands, "the dresses seem to lose their color" (1386). Sartorially and socially, the tribunes appear to fade in the presence of Zola's brightly attired courtesan, who steps proudly onto this "forbidden soil" (1393) and effortlessly subverts accepted rules of both costume and comportment.

Nana's violation of the "no prostitute" rule at the weighing zone symbolizes more than simply a threat to traditional structures of power and public accessibility; it also suggests a dangerous contagion of the upper classes by the lower. Rita Felski notes that "public space is associated in *Nana* with a fear of contamination and disorder arising from a leveling of class distinctions" (75). Indeed, Nana's commanding presence at the races is an impertinent reminder to the aristocracy of her lascivious role in facilitating, on a truly seminal level, the intermingling of social classes; sleeping with nobles, businessmen, actors, journalists, and workers alike, Nana turns her body into a living receptacle in which the seed of royalty literally mixes with that of the street poor. Longchamp, like other fashionable venues of entertainment in the capital city, emerges in Zola's novel as a site where upper-class fears of subversion by the lower classes and social commingling fester behind its elegant facade.

Nana's encroachment upon the imperial stands suggests a failure of the physical layout of the racecourse to reinforce separation of the nobility, the bourgeoisie, and the general populace, in spite of the fact that Longchamp's architectural design aimed for just such a separation. The arena's stands, constructed by the wealthy association of aristocrats and powerful businessmen known as "Le Jockey Club," were divided into clearly demarcated sections that emphasized class divisions. In the center of the stands was the Imperial tribune, which one journalist described as "entirely isolated . . . and decorated with remarkable luxury" (*L'Illustration: journal universel,* 2 mai 1857: 279). On either side of the royal tribune were covered grandstands that housed members of the Jockey Club and various ministers, while ticket holders filled in the uncovered portions of these platforms. A large majority of the population watched the races from secondary pavilions built on both sides of the grandstands, on uncovered terraces above them, and from the grassy area directly in front of them.[7]

Although these seating areas at Longchamp certainly provided well-dressed viewers ample opportunity to see and be seen, perhaps the greatest focal point for sartorial pageantry was the *pelouse,* or the oval of grass located in the center of the racecourse and across the track from the grandstands. On race days, spectators in the oval could enjoy an entire afternoon in full view of the tribunes, and could further enhance the visibility of their garments by perching above the crowd on ornamented carriages. Critical writings on the topography of class at the races present a slight discrepancy regarding the spectators in the inner oval. Herbert notes, for example, that those in the grassy area, like Manet's viewers in *Races at Longchamp,* were "an élite among the élite" because they were required to pay an extra supplement for the privilege of entering this coveted space (158). Jones, meanwhile, echoes Zola in suggesting that the *pelouse* was home to "the more mondaine crowd," while the stands were reserved for the arena's "respectable" patrons (215).

As regards fashion, there is truth to both of these assessments. For, as many contemporaries agreed, it was the *mondaine* crowd that comprised the sartorial elite, since it was to them, and not to ladies of reputable classes, that one looked for the latest styles. In Zola's novel, it is over the center oval that the courtesan class, the fashion elite, reign. When Nana arrives at the racecourse in a flashy carriage and works her way over to the grassy area in the center of the track, the crowd scrambles to see her, "as with the passing of a queen" (1376). It is no accident that it is at this point in the narrative that Zola inserts a meticulous description of Nana's blue and white outfit; the relationship between space (the center oval) and cutting-edge fashion (the courtesan's audacious bustle) is thus cemented. Deposing the true Empress with the power of her chic, Nana insures that the oval, rather than the imperial tribune, is the most fashionable spot in the arena.

The late-nineteenth-century journalist Émile de la Bédolière wrote of Longchamp: "The splendid exhibitions of outfits and carriages at the Grand Prix . . . this is what fills, animates and imprints the Bois de Boulogne with its particular charms. Devoid of these . . . the Bois would be like a ruined theater, abandoned by its actors and its public, silent and mournful" (in Gaillard 122–24). What I hope to have shown here is the ways in which, as Bédolière contends, fashion and its display were an integral part of the popularity and success of the Hippodrome de Longchamp. A culture of danger and risk informed sartorial display at the Grand Prix races and profoundly marked representations of the track by Manet, Degas, and Zola, three chief chroniclers of post-Haussmannization Paris. Examining the discourse of fashion in their works suggests the ways in which nineteenth-century artists used stylish garments to posit upended social hierarchies, evoke the profound transformations of modernity, and perhaps even predict the very fall of the Second Empire.

NOTES

1. All translations are my own. This description of elegant feminine onlookers derives from Zola's novelistic portrait of spectators at the Paris morgue in *Thérèse Raquin*.
2. For more on visitors to the nineteenth-century public morgue see Vanessa R. Schwartz, *Spectacular Realities: Early Mass Culture in Fin-de-siècle Paris*.
3. Paris' infamous Palais Royal, "the most important center of gambling in early nineteenth-century Europe," (Kavanagh *Dice* 132) had over 100 card and dice tables that were open to all walks of public life. It was at this time that legalized gambling first became available not only to the aristocracy, but also to the lower and middle classes. Gambling also flourished in Parisian casinos and exclusive private game rooms where the elite met over high-stakes card matches (187).

4. Manet reworked *The Races at Longchamp* in an 1866 oil version in which the racers are placed in the center foreground of the work and the crowds extend across the left section of the canvas. Although these modifications in the second painting clearly transfer the focus of the work from the onlookers to the horses on the track, fashion remains a priority. In particular, Manet takes the opportunity in this second version to highlight the airy groupings of dresses and parasols in the stands with larger patches of pastel yellows, creams, and blues.

5. See in particular *The Dancing Class* (1873–75) and *The Milliners* (c. 1882).

6. I am indebted to Sima Godfrey for bringing to my attention the writings of Cora Pearl, a wealthy and audacious nineteenth-century courtesan on whom Zola based, in part, his literary portrait of Nana. In an 1890 memoir attributed to her name, the notorious courtesan suggests that it was she—and not the Empress Eugénie as had often been reported—who first brought the crinoline fashion to its demise (Godfrey 83).

7. For a full description of the Longchamp arena in the nineteenth century, see "Inauguration du champ de courses du bois de Boulogne" in *L'Illustration: journal universel,* 2 mai 1857.

WORKS CITED

Barthes, Roland. *The Fashion System*. Translated by Matthew Ward and Richard Howard. Berkeley and Los Angeles: University of California Press, 1990.

Bogg, Jean Sutherland. *Degas at the Races*. New Haven: Yale University Press, 1998.

Cooper, Barbara T. and Mary Donaldson-Evans. *Modernity and Revolution in Late Nineteenth-Century France*. London & Toronto: Associate University Press, 1992.

Dolan, Thérèse. "Guise and Dolls: Dis/covering Power, Re/covering Nana." *Nineteenth-Century French Studies* 26 (1998): 368–86.

Felski, Rita. *The Gender of Modernity*. Cambridge: Harvard University Press, 1995.

Gaillard, Marc. *Les Hippodromes*. Paris: Bibliothèques des Arts, 1984.

Godfrey, Sima. "Baudelaire, Gautier, and 'une toilette savamment composée'." In *Modernity and Revolution in Late Nineteenth-Century France,* edited by Barbara T. Cooper and Mary Donaldson-Evans. London & Toronto: Associate University Press, 1992: 74–87.

Herbert, Robert L. *Art, Leisure, and Parisian Society*. New Haven: Yale University Press, 1988.

"Inauguration du champ de courses du bois de Boulogne." *L'Illustration: journal universel* (2 mai 1857): 279–81.

Jones, Kimberly. "A Day at the Races: A Brief History of Horse Racing in France." In *Degas at the Races,* edited by Jean Sutherland. New Haven: Yale University Press, 1998: 208–23.

Kavanagh, Thomas M. "The Libertine's Bluff: Cards and Culture in Eighteenth-Century France."

Eighteenth-Century Studies 33.4 (2000): 505–21.

———. *Dice, Cards, Wheels: A Different History of French Culture,Critical Authors and Issues*. Philadelphia: University of Pennsylvania Press, 2005.

Miller, Christopher M., Shelby H. McIntyre, and Murali K. Mantrala. "Toward Formalizing Fashion Theory." *Journal of Marketing Research* 30.2 (1993): 142–57.

Raymond, Emmeline. "La Mode et la Parisienne." In *Paris Guide: La Vie par les principaux écrivains et artistes de la France*. Bruxelles: A. Lacroix, 1867.

Schwartz, Vanessa R. *Spectacular Realities: Early Mass Culture in Fin-de-siècle Paris*. Berkeley: University of California Press, 1998.

Steele, Valerie. *Paris Fashion: A Cultural History*. New York: Berg, 1998.

Zola, Émile. *Nana* (Vol. 2). In *Les Rougon-Macquart* (5 vols.), edited by Henri Mitterand. Paris: Bibliothèque de la Pléiade, Gallimard, 1960–67.

———. *Thérèse Raquin*. Paris: Flammarion, 1970.

2 Framing the Victorians
Photography, Fashion, and Identity

Margaret Denny

> Fashion comprises the outward criterion for judging whether or not one "belongs to polite society." Whoever does not repudiate it altogether must go along, even where he ... firmly refuses some new development.
>
> —Rudolph von Jhering in Benjamin (1999: 75)

In the public spaces of nineteenth-century Victorian society, men and women seized center stage in ritualistic performances as fashionable and respectable citizens. Opportunities for public display flourished in the urban environment: the parks, boulevards, transportation systems, shopping emporiums, and entertainment venues of the world's industrialized cities. Equally, the subtle nuances and transformations of fashion adornment materialized in the many illustrated manifestations of the day: posters, prints, and an array of fashion journals. Before the inauguration of halftone screen printing in the 1890s, the basis for modern advertising and illustration, photography provided Victorian society edifying material on the art of dress, decorum, and self-construction. Moreover, in a highly complex industrialized society, knowing how to present oneself in polite society through the knowledge attained by looking at photographs gave one comfort and confidence.

In this chapter, I discuss photography's role in creating spaces for identity formation and reinforcing societal norms of deportment and decorum through fashion. I argue that within the spaces of photographic studios, expositions, salons, and domestic parlors, the medium offered Victorians new opportunities for performance and rituals of fashion presentation and self construction. The literature to date has overlooked photography's propensity to create spaces of and for fashion's articulation, places to express one's personae to wear the latest fashionable attire, or to experience vicariously the character of others when donning "dress-up" clothes. As I show, each space elicits a certain type of performance opportunity to elevate, maintain, and/or promote a subject's status. In the spaces of photography, people could see how they looked photographed, how they constructed themselves through fashion, hairstyles, and pose, in relationship to other people in photographic images, in particular famous individuals—royalty, political figures, and celebrities.

RESPECTABILITY AND SOCIAL EXPECTATION

The early days of photography coincided with a more conservative dress mode for women advocated by the "cult of true womanhood," the criteria to which middle-class women were supposed to adhere: purity, piety, domesticity, and submissiveness (Welter 152). When a woman's primary responsibility was to motherhood and maintenance of the hearth, propriety marked the period in fashion as well. An early calotype from c. 1847 by the photographers David Octavius Hill (1802–70) and Robert Adamson (1821–48) illustrates the demure dress style worn by respectable women of the day. Posed outdoors in front of a doorway and framed by domestic accoutrements, Mary Hamilton, Lady Ruthven (1789–1885), is reminiscent of a Victorian fashion plate. A painter and patron of the arts, Lady Ruthven and her husband James Hamilton, Lord Ruthven, were the lairds of Winton House, their ancestral estate located in the East Lothian countryside near Edinburgh. *Lady Ruthven,* her back to the camera, is shown wearing a striped silk day dress, black lace mantle, poke bonnet with *bavolet* (a curtain covering the back of the neck), and veil (Figure 2.1).

As in the majority of Hill and Adamson photographs, this image was taken at Rock House, Edinburgh, at the "daylight" studio, a protected "set" on the south-west wall of the house which they furnished with drapery, chairs, and various props to give an interior appearance (Bruce 22). Writing on the structure of fashion in relationship to photography, Roland Barthes has argued that "[t]he world is usually photographed as a décor, a background or a scene, in short, as a theater" (1983: 301). Surrounded by elaborately carved furniture, patterned drapery, and latticework props, the decorous Lady Ruthven occupies the shallow stage-like setting, in space corresponding to Barthes' description of "theater." While theater, display, and performance comprise the photographic process, for Lady Ruthven, her staged presentation is a reflection of her public world. Apparently at ease in this constructed space of performance, demonstrating her role as lady of the house and estate, we get a sense of her subtle beauty and grace of her presence, and an idea of her distinct individualism. Further, as Barthes has suggested, the photograph brings out fashion's plasticity—the spatial relationship between shape, lines, and surface. The image expresses the correspondence between the physical attributes of the space and objects within the space. Contrasting areas of light and shade reveal the forms and patterns of Lady Ruthven's attire. The latticework and carved furniture props echo the diagonal lines of her elegant shawl and its intricate woven pattern, while the stage on which she stands insures an extended area for the gathers of her day dress.

Figure 2.1 David Octavius Hill, Scottish, 1802–70, Robert Adamson, Scottish, 1821–48, *Lady Ruthven*, ca. 1845, Salted paper print from paper negative, 19.9 x 15 cm (7 13/16" x 5 7/8"). The Metropolitan Museum of Art, The Rubel Collection, Purchase, Manfred Heiting and Lila Acheson Wallace Gifts, 1997 (1997.382.18) Image © The Metropolitan Museum of Art.

Since direct eye contact with a woman wearing a poke bonnet could only be made from a frontal view, by choosing to show Lady Ruthven's reserved back view, the photographer draws attention to the exquisite lace mantle and makes the subject even more mysterious. Honoré de Balzac had observed that a woman's outfit is "a permanent revelation of her most secret thoughts, a language and a symbol" (Gernsheim 31). The conservative dress and bonnet styles that marked the early nineteenth century allowed little outward expression. In the Hill and Adamson photograph, the subject—covered, protected, and demure—epitomizes the period's true woman whose body was shielded from both the sun and the gaze of male viewers other than her husband's.

PHOTOGRAPHY DISPLAYS AT FAIRS AND EXHIBITIONS

The nineteenth century predilection for showcasing new and innovative consumer products at international expositions, industrial fairs, and exhibitions offered new outlets for photographs to be seen by a mass audience. The rapidity with which the latest fashion styles moved across the western world is preserved in the photographs from this period. Beginning in London in 1851 with the century's first important exposition, the Exhibition of the Works of Industry of all Nations later known as the Great Exhibition, and continuing throughout the century at regional, national, and international fairs and expositions, the display of fashion and fashionable accessories in photographs became yet another way mass audiences recognized and assimilated fashion changes. As author Julie K. Brown argues: "[i]ndustrial fairs placed photographs within a specific marketplace of business and commerce, international expositions created a space for photographs that were demonstrations of national identity and progress, and institutional exhibitions provided sites where the cultural content of the photographs could be expressed" (174).

The Great Exhibition stimulated a public interest in photography and simultaneously exposed fair viewers to the rich cultures, architecture, and costumes of colonial native peoples. The iron and glass structure of the Crystal Palace itself formed a wondrous space to view fabric and costume displays and other elegantly dressed fairgoers. Bathed by natural light coming through the transparent structure, and filled with enormous plants, colorful flowers, and a crystal fountain centerpiece, the Palace became a stage on which attendees could elucidate fashion and fashionable knowledge.

The technically improved stereoscopic viewer enhanced by Sir David Brewster and its accompanying stereographs debuted at the Great Exhibition. Queen Victoria (1819–1901) and Prince Albert (1819–61) were among the visitors enthralled by the stereo viewer demonstrated by Jules Duboscq, who had been commissioned by Brewster to produce his stereoscopes. Duboscq later arranged to have Brewster present the Royal Couple with a viewer and set of stereograph cards. The introduction of the stereoscope into the Royal household captivated a middle-class audience of consumers. Experiencing a landscape, architectural monument, or genre picture through a stereoscope, one is magically transported to a simulacrum of three-dimensional space. The viewer, whose sight is isolated from his surroundings and directed towards the image, absorbs the visual information embedded within the stereograph. The magical quality of illusion of the stereoscope created a demand for more images. Photographers began making views at the Crystal Palace site, group portraits, architectural views, or group scenes. The experienced spaces of fashion display constructed for the photographer were reproduced an infinite number of times in the stereo photographs. Hand coloring was prevalent, introduced for even more verisimilitude. What ensued was a mania for the new visual home entertainment. Collecting stereograph cards and sharing them in one's own parlor with friends and family became essential domestic activities which entailed surveying fashion in photographs; the London Stereoscopic Company envisioned "[a] stereoscope for every home" (Darrah 1977: 2–4). Exceptionally popular were images of foreign lands. Although many stereographs were of landscape views, the images introduced remote places and the people who occupied them, their customs, architecture, and costume. As William C. Darrah has pointed out, "[t]he well-known travel sets include thousands of excellent views showing costumes of every description" (155). Costume and accessories envisioned in the spaces of the stereo viewer whetted Victorian consumer appetites for new and innovative fashions. The activity of viewing these photographic images from within private domestic spaces carries with it a deeper meaning—an opportunity to consider one's own identity in relationship to others, and an interest in the innovative costuming, fabrics, and customs of those previously unknown peoples. The fashionable display experienced in photographs could then be enacted within domestic spaces.

During the industrial age, as groups of people and their lifestyles were rapidly changing, a nostalgic point of view that these folk traditions and costumes might vanish created a renewed interest in the recording of material culture. In England, William Henry Fox-Talbot photographed the workmen on his country estate at Lacock Abbey. His followers, Hill and Adamson, assiduously recorded the customs and activities of local people in the Scottish fishing village of Newhaven.

Picturing peasants in their natural environment to celebrate preindustrial cultures was quite incongruent to the parlor activities of the upperset, dressing up to create *tableaux vivants*, exploring ideas of identity and experiencing the fantasies that occupied these spaces of performance. The photographs by Lady Clementina Hawarden (1822–65) suggest she and her daughters shared equally an interest in the narrative possibilities of costume, foreign dress, and the art of portrayal. Her eldest daughters, Clementina and Isabella Grace Maude, pose for their mother in a complex composition—one standing on an outside balcony with her body pressed against the glass window as she peers inside and the another facing the viewer from within the room (Figure 2.2). Wearing a "peasant" outfit, Isabella performs in front of the French doors leading to the terrace of their family home seemingly indifferent to her sister; Clementina, on the exterior terrace, leans against the French windows gazing longingly at her sister. The sister in the interior

Figure 2.2 Lady Clementina Hawarden, *Clementina and Isabella Grace,* c. 1864, Albumen print. ©V & A Images/Victoria and Albert Museum, London.

space wears a peasant costume—with a *bongrace coif* headpiece, ribbon-decorated apron, laced-corset bodice, white chemisette, and gathered dark skirt. Doubled around her neck is a long strand of beads. The girl on the exterior space wears what appears to be a luxurious morning gown.

Between 1859 and 1864, Hawarden photographed her children in the studio space created on the second floor of their South Kensington home at 5 Princes Garden. The rooms facing north opened on to the terrace and communal garden, and the rooms with a southern exposure led to a balcony.

These spaces operated as the stage for performance and costume *tableaux* for Hawarden's photographs. The grand windows filled the photographic space with magnificent natural light allowing Hawarden full expression to accentuate the dresses, costumes, and accessories worn by her daughters. Contemporary viewers may be struck by an association of ideas related to fashion and window shopping. Clementina appears to play the window shopper and Isabella, the costumed mannequin. As the window shopper, seeing one's reflection in a store window, one momentarily connects to the desired object located within the space of the display window. Hawarden's fluid use of space between the interior domestic world and the exterior public world of the garden and adjacent terraces offers endless possibilities of fictional narrative, performance, and make-believe.

While the narrative created by the Hawarden sisters may be a reminder of the many *carte-de-visite* portraits of real peasants made during the 1850s and 1860s by photographers anxious to capture the last remnants of these cultures, in fact, their representation is quite the opposite. Their full-figured costumed poses perpetuate a peasant "type." As members of the titled aristocracy in the domestic space of their town home, the Hawarden sisters were only performing a constructed fantasy and transformation through dress in collaboration with their photographer mother. For most Victorians, obtaining their picture meant a visit to the photographer's studio.

PUBLIC DISPLAY AT THE PHOTOGRAPHER'S STUDIO

In the early days of the medium, having one's portrait taken developed into an occasion. The urban photographer's studio, as Alan Trachtenberg has argued, was "[n]ot a museum of natural history, however, but a theater of desire, the gallery had become a new kind of city place devoted to performance: the making of oneself over into a social image" (1989: 40). The elaborately furnished waiting rooms found in upscale studios, renowned as meeting places where people of all classes mingled freely, embodied the comfort and elegance of the residential parlor. The photographer's studio and accompanying reception room or parlor served to discriminate, guide, and affirm genteel behavior in its furnishings and accessibility. As Shirley T. Wajda has shown, "[t]he best clues to how photographic parlors worked are found in the constant attention to social performance within the space" (222). At Mathew Brady's studio in New York, customers found a reception room, with rosewood furniture, needle-worked lace drapes, satin and gold-papered walls, and a frescoed ceiling highlighted by chandeliers. The highly decorated room was enhanced by ceiling to floor mirrors thus offering an opportunity for clients to see themselves dressed in their finest, look at other fashionably dressed people, and be looked at in turn (Wajda 219). Equally in the space of photography galleries, customers observed stylistic transitions and modes of dress in the images on photographed-lined walls and in display windows. As was the case in most fashionable photographic galleries, images of illustrious public figures and celebrities photographed by the studio, or acquired for promotional purposes, decorated the reception rooms. That the spaces of upscale photographer's studio provided wealthy and fashionable ladies a satisfying experience can be read in Mary Chesnut's repeated visits to Quinby's studio in Charleston, South Carolina, chronicled in her diary of 1861. After one visit, she recorded, she "[b]ought 2 dozen cartes de visite of all the celebrities" (Wajda 225). Part of the allure of the photographer's studio was the association with one's own social circle in a refined space and the confirmation of one's social standing and identity, being with people of compatible hierarchy. One studio in Augusta, Georgia, catered to female customers with its tastefully appointed parlor and elegant piano where friends or newly acquainted women could entertain themselves comfortably prior to a sitting (Wajda 219). Further, within the spaces of the studio, an arena of performance and display, photographers passed along to their clients tips on what to wear and how to pose for the camera: what color outfits photographed best, what fabrics to avoid, and how to sit or stand so the light enhanced the sitter's features.

POSING AND IDENTITY CONSTRUCTION

The prototype for how to construct one's social being had it roots in the oldest art forms—sculpture and painting—models that were known to many photographers and their customers alike. Photography, like fashion, necessitates and facilitates self-construction. For Victorians, self-construction required knowledge of appropriate attire, proper behavior, and deportment, and other subtleties which advanced respectability and upward mobility. Having one's portrait taken meant dressing up in one's best outfit wearing very contemporary and stylish clothing. Fashion produces conflicting responses in the beholder: the need for individuality and the need for conformity and acceptance—the revelation of the public persona created in the privacy of the boudoir, recreated, and recorded in the photographer's studio. In the pose, the dress, and the attitude, one constructs the impression, identity, and persona one wishes to project. As Roland Barthes has observed: "Now, once I feel myself observed by the lens, everything changes: I constitute myself in the process of 'posing,' I instantaneously make another body for myself, I transform myself in advance into an image" (Barthes 22).

In 1895, when Catharine Barnes Ward (1851–1913) published "Hints to Sitters," the photographer placed responsibility for "how to dress for the portrait session" with the sitter but equally she advised the photographer to provide more direction in the matter. Ward found many people's attire to be lacking: "want of good judgment, not to say taste displayed by the majority of sitters" (Palmquist 70). Drawing on her experience in the reception rooms of leading photographers' studios and her own, Ward suggested that "[h]aving had some experience in painters' studios as well as in dramatic performances, added to my experience with photographic sitters, I feel that I can be of assistance to the latter" (Palmquist 69). She proposed that the professional photographer longed to offer suggestions to the sitter but hesitated to dictate—perhaps afraid to offend some customers. Ward admonished photographers: "It is a delicate matter to advise sitters unless one is strongly enough entrenched in popular favor to be independent, and refuse to pose sitters who do injustice to themselves by inappropriate or unbecoming costumes" (Palmquist 70).

With thirty years of experience in Quincy, Illinois, commercial studio photographer Candace Reed (1818–1900) managed to solve the problem by suggesting what a sitter should wear. Her advertisement in 1862 announcing the opening of a branch studio in Palmyra, Missouri, advised that "[p]ersons wishing pictures should remember to wear dark clothes, as much better pictures can thus be taken than in light clothing" ("Classified"). A contemporary historian might wonder if the apparent preponderance of dark attire found in nineteenth-century portraiture was a reflection of what people actually wore or their adherence to photographers' dictates. Studios, especially the more upscale ones, offered the service of makeup and complementary assistance with accessories as needed. Women frequently wore jewelry for their portrait sitting, earrings, a pin or brooch, and bracelets—the wearing of jewelry, long a symbol of wealth and prestige, especially among women. In the 1870s, when crosses were a popular jewelry accessory, photographers frequently supplemented their sitters' attire with crosses from their studio props (Darrah 1981: 137).

On a number of occasions, the French photographer Antoine Samuel Adam-Salomon (1811–81), a contemporary of Nadar, whose portraits were known for their rich tonal qualities, supplemented his sitters' attire. In 1868, a British journalist for *The Photographic News* observed Salomon's working habits—to accentuate a light colored silk dress worn by one female sitter he supplied a black lace shawl. For another, a gentleman whose portrait was taken, he added port-wine-colored velvet over one shoulder to aim for a more dignified appearance ("Visits to Noteworthy Studios" 31 January 1868). Salomon apparently had the confidence, following, and artistic conviction to which Ward alluded. The *British Journal of Photography* found in one instance, a female sitter was persuaded to change her attire altogether.

> My friend was dressed in a black repp dress, with black velvet jacket, M. Salomon having previously desired her to come arrayed in black. "You are a difficult subject," he said, "and therefore I should like to try and take a portrait of you. I will have as much contrast as possible with your light complexion, eyes, and eyelashes and the black dress" ("Correspondence. Foreign" 28 June 1867: 307).

When the dress didn't suit the artist because there was no play of light and shadow upon the material, he ran off to his house and produced a deep, purple cotton-velvet skirt which he suggested she put on over the dress. With this small addition, the photographer could capture the desired light and shadow in the folds of the fabric (307–08).

PRIVATE DISPLAY

Just as the display spaces of the photographer's galleries and institutional expositions showcased photographs of stylishly attired individuals, Victorians learned about fashionable dress, hair styles, and makeup in the privacy of their domestic parlors from the images in their photographic albums and individual photographs. People saw each other in an accessible and permanent medium possibly for the first time. By the 1860s, the *carte-de-visite* photographs that had gained in popularity were traded, collected, and arranged in albums. As Walter Benjamin observed: "In the coldest places in the house, on consoles or gueridons in the drawing room, they [photograph albums] were most likely to be found: leather covered with metal latches and gilt-edged pages as thick as a finger on which the foolishly draped or embellished figures were distributed" (Benjamin 1980: 206). Celebrity *carte-de-visite* photographs circulated widely. A rare studio sample sheet used by photographers and traveling salesmen to sell images of the Royal Family, political figures, stage and music hall performers, and celebrities of the day illustrates how ordinary people might acquire images of nineteenth-century cultural icons and be influenced by their fashionable appearance. Displayed for mail-order purchase were images of the actress Lillie Langtry, Queen Victoria, and Alexandra the Princess of Wales (Mann and Collins 197–200). A *carte* portrait of Alexandra, the Princess Diana of her day, is reported to have sold 300,000 copies. Author Kathy Peiss has argued that stage actresses were among the first renowned nineteenth-century women to use make-up in public, opening up a dialogue for more widespread application among genteel society. Beginning with Nadar's unequivocally beautiful images of actress Sarah Bernhardt, women had visual representations from which to model their appearance, gestures, and attire. That these images of retouched and idealized actresses and royalty were collected and assembled in albums alongside pictures of family and friends had its influence on men's and women's fashion decisions (Peiss 320–21).

ROYAL AND CELEBRITY INFLUENCES

Until more recently, fashion was derived from royalty, upper class, and celebrities. Writer Mary Philadelphia Merrifield pointed out "[f]ashion is extremely aristocratic in its tendencies, every change emanates from the highest circles, who reject it when it has descended to the vulgar" (Gernsheim 40). Georg Simmel affirmed "fashions differ for different classes—

the fashions of the upper stratum of society are never identical with those of the lower; in fact, they are abandoned by the former as soon as the latter prepares to appropriate them" (Benjamin 1999: 77). When Victoria was crowned Queen of England in 1837, her name gave distinction to the period of her reign and launched a mode and manner that was followed by her admirers. Although the Queen "shunned elaborate, opulent clothes," choosing instead simpler styles with an "accent on plainness and modesty," she nevertheless established a model of female decorum. The American editor of *Godey's Lady's Magazine,* Sarah J. Hale enlisted the help of correspondent Lydia H. Sigourney to follow the royal activities. Whether a vanguard of fashion or not, author Edith Saunders credited her with the introduction of tartan plaids (Saunders 40). Although the official court was Windsor, the Royals made Osbourne House on the Isle of Wight and Balmoral Castle in Scotland their homes away from formal duties. When descendants of Queen Victoria visited Balmoral during her lifetime, they were expected to adopt the Scottish national costume. Photographs taken at the Queen's residence at Balmoral show that within the confines of this space, and in deference to her Scottish subjects, it was customary for members of the Royal family and guests to wear plaid kilts. Even German princes on holiday at Balmoral were expected to acquiesce.

Queen Victoria and Prince Albert were passionate leaders in the relatively new medium of photography. In 1860, John J. E. Mayall (1810–1901), an American photographer living in England, was honored with a commission to visit Buckingham Palace to take photographs of the British royal family. In August, he published his "Royal Album," a collection of *cartes de visite* of Queen Victoria, Prince Albert, and their children photographed earlier that year. Each print bore an inscription with Mayall's name and the date. Published in an edition of 60,000, the albums were sold in England, America, and the colonies. Great numbers of original prints and pirated copies (with Mayall's name removed) were sold in the United States and England (Darrah 1981: 6). Mayall, who became a favorite of the British court, issued a second series of Royal Family portraits in 1861 and additional titles in 1862. The sale of these small pictures of the Royals, at a moderate rate, "gave the British people the pleasure of possessing the life-like representations of their universally loved Queen and her interesting family" (Root 381). Moreover, they gave the public a visual representation from which to emulate her style.

The crinoline had been in vogue before Victoria came to the throne in 1837, but her interest in this silhouette stimulated its popularity. A photograph taken 1 March 1861 by Mayall, possibly from one of his published albums, shows the fashionably attired Queen and Prince Albert (Figure 2.3). Posed in profile Queen Victoria wears a dark silk-taffeta dress accented by checked flounces cascading over the crinolines. The Prince Consort complements her attire with his boldly striped waistcoat. The Royal Couple was photographed at Mayhall's studio in a spatial setting reminiscent of a formal interior room, walls with wainscoting offset by a fluted column on a square base. A soft drape cuts across the top of the column helping to soften the otherwise austere background. Victoria maximizes the performative function of the studio and fashion. Her silk-taffeta dress occupies most of the bottom width of the photograph, balancing the vertical height of the Prince who leans comfortably on the column base. The Queen and her Prince Consort standing in this formalized studio space, her hands entwined in his arm, project the power of the monarchy and establish a model of decorum for her subjects.

The Queen's appearance may have been imitated by Isabella II of Spain who was a great admirer of Queen Victoria. From the Rocamora costume collection [now located in the Museum of Textiles in Barcelona], a plaid-silk ball gown designed for the Spanish queen by Charles Frederick Worth (1826–95) emulates Queen Victoria's taste. The extent to which Isabella II was a devotee of Queen Victoria is established by the fact that she hired the photographer Charles Clifford, an Englishman living in Madrid, to take a portrait of the Queen. The image taken 14 November 1861, was among Victoria's favorite photographs (Darrah 1981: 44). Although the House of Worth never succeeded in making Queen Victoria a direct client due to her loyalties to English manufacturers, the Queen "bought" designs by Worth ostensibly through her English dressmakers (Worth 116–17).

* * *

Political events and the powerful figures associated with them influenced the creation and absorption of new trends and styles into mainstream dress. Photography advanced these new modes of fashion through the display of images, the distribution of inexpensive prints made from original photographs or published texts, and its accompanying illustrations, usually woodblock relief printing from a photograph. The *Zouave,* a bolero-style jacket, short with rounded fronts, with or without sleeves, gained popularity in the early 1860s, derived from the French army infantry group composed initially of Algerians and distinguished for their picturesque uniform. Frequently, the Zouave jacket was paired with a "Garibaldi chemisette" a full-sleeved shirtwaist blouse made in red, black, or more often white cotton, with the full front gathered or pleated into the neckline. Worn as casual day dress by women and children, the design was introduced in a wave of admiration for the great Italian patriot and freedom fighter Giuseppe Garibaldi (1807–82), whose troops wore red shirts of this shape, following his successful invasion of Sicily in 1860. A photograph taken in June 1860 in Palermo by Gustave Le Gray shows the bareheaded, bearded Garibaldi wearing a loosely gathered red shirt and baggy pants that would become the signature style (Figure 2.4). Taken outdoors at the Palazzo Reale where Garibaldi and the French contingent Alexander Dumas and Le Gray were staying, in the apartments of the viceroy, the photograph shows Garibaldi in front of a cream-colored stone wall. Posing contrapposto style with his

Figure 2.3 John J. E. Mayall, *Queen Victoria and Prince Albert*, 1861, *Carte-de-visite*. ©V & A Images/Victoria and Albert Museum, London.

sword, Garibaldi projects a casual, confident, and proud demeanor. In the space of the palace, quite separate from the city's rubble-filled streets also documented by Le Gray, the photographer maximized the symbolic possibilities of posing a man of strong leadership character before the enduring stone structure. Lithographic prints and engraved representations of this original photograph were widely disseminated, showing a similar background but with the artist's addition of foliage. On 21 July 1860, an engraving of Le Gray's photograph appeared in *Le Monde Illustré*. At the same sitting and location, Le Gray photographed General Istvàn Türr, the young Hungarian patriot who had joined Garibaldi's forces in 1860. Türr

Figure 2.4 Gustave Le Gray, French, 1820–84, *Portrait of Giuseppe Garibaldi,* June 1860, Albumen silver, Image (oval) 25.7 x 19.7 cm (10 1/8" x 7 ¾"). The J. Paul Getty Museum, Los Angeles.

wears a Garibaldi-inspired cap and shirt promoting further the stylistic ensemble (Aubenas 168–71).

During the 1860s, a number of variations of the Garibaldi style were developed for women's casual dress and children's wear—particularly boy's attire. Garibaldi's mode of dress launched a series of separates: loose-fitting pants worn primarily by boys and a pillbox hat embellished with ornate braiding for women. Worn tipped forward, the *casquette,* a woman's hat resembling an old-fashioned telegraph boy's or hotel page boy's cap, evolved from the Garibaldi cap. One follower of the Garibaldi style was Empress Eugénie (1826–1920) of France.

* * *

Following Louis Napoleon's rise to power in 1852 and subsequent marriage in 1855 to Eugénie de Montijo, the Countess de Téba of Spain, the fashion industry and economy in general received a welcome boost supported by the Emperor's predilection for opulence and ceremony. The lavishness of the Second Empire was so great that only the wealthiest individuals could accept an invitation to the country Chateau Compiègne in the Oise region without trepidation. It was known the Emperor and Empress did not like to see their guests appear in the same dress twice. A week's visit required twenty-eight separate outfits—four changes a day (Gernsheim 51).

A favorite subject of photographers, painters, and sculptors during her reign, Empress Eugénie projected the image of a reserved and modest yet very well dressed lady suggestive of the virtues her position demanded. The Empress's popularity as a cult figure from her marriage to Napoleon III to her departure from France in 1870 was confirmed by the number of her portraits displayed in shop windows lining the picturesque arcades threaded throughout the principal cities of Europe: Vienna, Cologne, and Madrid (Saunders 46). The arcades offered promenades past rows of glittering shop windows extending nearly the full height of the storefronts. Photographic specimens in the spaces of street-level display windows gave photography studios, most often located on the top floor of buildings, much needed promotional opportunities, and images of beautiful women, especially those of celebrity status dressed in the latest fashions, attracted clientele. Hundreds of *cartes* of Eugénie in a variety of poses, costumes, and locations were sold by Disdéri, Legroupy, Levitsky, Mayer, and Pierson, Thiebault, and Spingler, among others (McCauley 68). Women viewed the Empress with fascination and wonderment, considering her success could be achieved by imitation. Her golden-reddish hair color was copied, and a wide-temple hairstyle worn drawn off the face—*à la Impératrice,* pictured in *carte* portraits by Disdéri—became the vogue to which women aspired (Gernsheim 41; Severa 277). Seeing her ride through the Tuileries or along the Champs Élysées in an open carriage escorted by troops, which she did in almost all weather, smiling and bedecked in satin, silk, and ribbons, the feminine viewer saw in her beauty and charm, the ultimate expression of success; women attempted to replicate her style.

Considered conservative by her *couturier* Charles Worth, who suggested the Empress waited to see how a style was received rather than take the lead, Eugénie nonetheless promoted an era of elegance and grace. One report found that "[t]he Empress Eugénie appeared at a ball in 1859, wearing a white satin dress trimmed with no fewer than 103 tulle flounces" (in Gernsheim 43). Despite protests from her husband, Eugénie promoted the crinoline "cage" invented in England but introduced by the House of Worth—its fantastic and absurd form suited the high spirits of the prosperous Second Empire. Ridiculed by the press in the summer months of 1856, nevertheless the style prevailed, eventually adopted by all. A decade later, when Worth launched the flat-fronted dress, the Empress appeared in the new style, still the world's leader of fashion (Saunders 50–52).

THE START OF A NEW ERA

As argued in this chapter, photography provided new spaces of fashion display and performance, identity exploration, and the advancement of individual personae through fashion and fashionable knowledge. Since the sitters usually wore their best and most contemporary attire, the process of being photographed and seeing photographs of other fashionably dressed individuals, particularly those of political, royal, and/or celebrity status, provided Victorian society edifying material from which to observe and participate in the continually changing world of fashion. Photographs displayed at expositions and salons and used as the basis for media illustration disseminated ideas of dress, decorum, and style. In the more private spaces of Victorian parlors, photographic albums, stereograph cards, and individual portraits informed viewers how fashionable attire and "posing" before the camera supported self-exploration and identity building, providing further opportunities for performative expression.

In the early days, photographs were as much a novelty as were new fashion accessories. People sought out the latest visual information, poured over the details found in photographs, and were influenced by what they saw. During the nineteenth century, the fashions of contemporary cultural icons, emanating from the heights of society and shared among its ranks disseminated through the proliferation of photographs, gave rise to popular fashions. Although the advent of modern "fashion photography" as we know it today developed at the end of the nineteenth century with the perfection of halftone printing, facilitating photography reproduction in its full tonal range in books, magazines, and newspaper advertisements, early photography fulfilled a major role in advancing fashion, style, and taste. From mid-century on, in the spaces of photography's production, absorption, and exchange, Victorians experienced the possibilities of fashionable display and self-construction.

WORKS CITED

Aubenas, Sylvie. *Gustave Le Gray: 1820–84*. Los Angeles: The J. Paul Getty Museum, 2002.

Barthes, Roland. "Extracts from *Camera Lucida*." In *The Photographer Reader*, edited by Liz Wells. London and New York: Routledge Taylor & Francis Group, 2003: 19–30.

———. *The Fashion System*. Translated by Matthew Ward and Richard Howard. New York: Hill and Wang, 1983.

Benjamin, Walter. "A Short History of Photography." In *Classical Essays on Photography*, edited by Alan Trachtenberg. New Haven, CT: Leete's Island Books, 1980: 199–216.

———. *The Arcades Project*. Translated by Howard Eiland and Kevin McLaughlin. Cambridge, MA: The Belknap Press of Harvard University Press, 1999.

Brown, Julie K. *Making Culture Visible: The Public Display of Photography at Fairs, Expositions and Exhibitions in the United States, 1847–1900*. Amsterdam: Harwood Academic Publishers, 2001.

Bruce, David. *Sun Pictures, the Hill-Adamson Calotypes*. Greenwich, CT: New York Graphic Society, 1973.

"Classified." *Palmyra Courier* (5 February 1862).

"Correspondence. Foreign." *The British Journal of Photography* (28 June 1867): 307–08.

Darrah, William Culp. *The World of Stereographs*. Gettysburg, PA: W. C. Darrah, 1977.

———. *Cartes de Visite in Nineteenth Century Photography*. Gettysburg, PA: W. C. Darrah, 1981.

Gernsheim, Alison. *Victorian and Edwardian Fashion: A Photographic Survey* (2nd ed.). New York: Dover Publications, 1981.

Mann, Charles and Kathleen Collins. "Studio Sample Sheet." *History of Photography* 8.3 (1984): 197–200.

McCauley, Elizabeth Anne. *A. A. E. Disdéri and the Carte de Visite Portrait Photograph*. New Haven and London: Yale University Press, 1985.

Palmquist, Peter E. *Catharine Weed Barnes Ward: Pioneer Advocate for Women in Photography*. Arcata, CA: Peter E. Palmquist, 1992.

Peiss, Kathy. "Making Up, Making Over: Cosmetics, Consumer Culture and Women's Identity." In *The Sex of Things*, edited by Victoria De Grazia and Ellen Tenlough. Berkeley: University of California Press, 1996: 331–36.

Root, Marcus Aurelius. *The Camera and the Pencil*. Philadelphia: Lippincott, 1864.

Saunders, Edith. *The Age of Worth: Couturier to the Empress Eugénie*. Bloomington: Indiana University Press, 1955.

Severa, Joan L. *Dressed for the Photographer: Ordinary Americans and Fashion, 1840–1900*. Kent, OH, and London: The Kent State University Press, 1995.

Trachtenberg, Alan. *Reading American Photographs: Images as History Mathew Brady to Walker Evans*. New York: Hill and Wang/The Noonday Press, 1989.

"Visits to Noteworthy Studios." *The Photographic News* (31 January 1868): 49–51.

Wajda, Shirley Teresa. "The Commercial Photographic Parlor, 1839–1889." *Perspectives in Vernacular Architecture* 6 (1997): 216–30.

Welter, Barbara. "The Cult of True Womanhood, 1820–1860." *American Quarterly* 18.2 (1966): 151–74.

Worth, Jean Philippe. *A Century of Fashion*. Boston: Little, Brown, 1928.

3 On *The Golden Stairs*
The Spectacle of the Victorian Woman in White

Anne Anderson

The effect was to make her appear like an inhabitant of picture-land. . . .

—Hilda the Dove,
Nathaniel Hawthorne,
The Marble Fawn (1860)

The opening of the Grosvenor Gallery in 1877, as a rival to the Royal Academy exhibitions, provided a new space for the reception of art, albeit still exclusive, providing an arena for the Aesthetes, those declared lovers of beauty and those who exploited art as a vehicle for rising through society: "The glamour of fashion was over it, and the great help that Lady Lindsay was able to give by holding Sunday receptions there made it one of the most fashionable resorts of the London season" (Gere 19). Lady Blanche Lindsay, whose mother was a Rothschild, offered an array of Red Carpet events, from the Grosvenor's famous opening banquet to not-so-private Private Views (Gillet 40–49).[1] With the Lindsay's connections, the Grosvenor enjoyed the cache of showing work by socially distinguished practitioners: Princess Louise, the Marchioness of Lorne and Duchess of Argyll; the Marchioness of Waterford; Lady Wentworth; Archie Stuart Wortley; George Howard, 9th Earl of Carlisle, and Roddam Spencer Stanhope. According to the *Illustrated London News*, "the cant of elegant litterateurs and professional dilettante" ruled the Grosvenor Gallery (Anon c. 1880). Many of the exhibiting artists, including the owner-director, Sir Coutts Lindsay, practiced art for pleasure rather than profit. Painters, sculptors, writers, and musicians forged an artistic elite that mixed freely with the cream of London Society, a Bohemian world in which conventional class distinctions were of little account. Whistler declared that "[A]rt Is upon the Town!" as looking at pictures and high society coalesced, while George du Maurier, from the pages of *Punch,* opined that gallery-goers viewed the audience with greater interest than the art (Staley 63). Aesthetes looked extraordinary, acceptance into the Bohemian milieu signified by unconventional dress and aloofness. To be an artist one had to dress artistically, a notion of difference infecting the audiences at the Grosvenor. To outsiders, so-called artistic costumes appeared "more or less singular and ridiculous" (Gere 15). With art commodified, those seeking cultural capital needed to be seen in the right place with the right people in the right clothes: "It was in 1880 that Private Views became necessary functions of fashion. I should like to have been at a Private View of the old Grosvenor Gallery. . . . What interesting folk! What a wonderful scene" (Beerbohm 275). At the Private Views, "The Clothes of the Period" were paraded: "For the pictures . . . they can be attended to at any time; but the Private View costumes are in that of the 'limited quantity of pickled salmon,' and cannot" (Anon 1881: 601) (Figure 3.1).

HOW TO SEE AND BE SEEN AT A PRIVATE VIEW.

TAKE YOUR STAND EXACTLY OPPOSITE ONE OF THE PICTURES OF THE YEAR, WITH YOUR BACK TO THE PICTURE.

Figure 3.1 "How to See and Be Seen at a Private View," *Punch or The London Charivari*, 7 May 1881, 207.

May, when the Private Views began, was a time for assuming the "'Terry' countenance," this affectation effected by "assuming a fixed stare, keeping the mouth open, and 'tip-tilting' the nose" (Anon 1881: 601). Ellen Terry, the famous Shakespearian actress, was an It Girl, a type also known as a Stunner or Professional Beauty (PB), "more strictly, a Philistine production" (Beerbohm 280), those who set the benchmark in dress and appearance, whose personal and individual taste marked them out as fashion leaders rather than merely followers. The Tragedi-ennes Terry and Helena Modjeska headed the list, while the Pre-Rapha-elite Stunners (both model and muse), so romantically "discovered on the streets," numbered Lizzie Siddal, who became Dante Gabriel Rossetti's wife and Jane Morris, allegedly his lover. Rossetti forged new types of beauty with his long-necked and full-lipped *femme fatales,* yet the stun-ners assumed their own personas, acquiring celebrity status. Vernon Lee (pseudonym for the author Violet Paget) observed that girls were transformed into a "sort of live picture" (Lee 150), as they attempted to emulate the Pre-Raphaelite, classical, and even modern beauties seen on canvases or in the windows of photographic galleries.[2] The Burne-Jones ideal came to life in the guise of the *High Art Maiden:* pale-faced, emaci-ated, draped in white, and floppy. Oscar Wilde, writing in *The Decay of Lying,* observed that life was now imitating art, for the aesthetic type had indeed escaped from the canvas:

> We have all seen in our own day in England how a certain curious and fascinating type of beauty, invented and emphasized by two imagina-tive painters, has so influenced Life that whenever one goes to a private view or to an artistic salon one sees, here the mystic eyes of Rossetti's dream, the long ivory throat, the strange square-cut jaw, the loosened shadowy hair that he so ardently loved, there the sweet maidenhood of "The Golden Stair," the blossom-like mouth and weary loveliness of the "Laus Amoris," the passion-pale face of Andromeda, the thin hands and lithe beauty of the Vivian in "Merlin's Dream." And it has always been so. A great artist invents a type and Life tries to copy it, to reproduce it in a popular form, like an enterprising publisher (Wilde 30–31).

Suddenly the streets were filled with girls who looked as if they belonged in picture-land. As E. F. Benson reminisced, "Burne-Jones's wan women (in swiftly increasing numbers) were often seen about the London streets" and "it became fashionable in cultured circles to be pensive and willowy" (Benson 258–59). This new fashion was likely to become as conventional as the old style it had swept away: "Certainly all trace of Victorian conven-tion was banished . . . but it might be questioned if with this extinguish-ing of the smoky wick of banal Victorian convention, there has not been kindled another flame which might become as conventional as the other" (Benson 258):

ladies drooped and were wilted, and clad themselves in Liberty fabrics
. . . and let fall over their eyes a tangle of hair, through which they
miserably peered. *Punch,* week by week, was full of them, but they
were not the invention of the comic newspapers, and scarcely an exag-
geration: they actually existed in considerable numbers, until in the
manner of fashionable stunts, the glow of the aesthetic movement as a
free translation of Pre-Raphaelitism into life, began to grow as wan as
its practitioners. It was better to look at Burne-Jones's pictures than to
look like them, for women found that it did not really suit them to be
haggard and sad (Benson 259).

For Harry Quilter, art critic of the *Spectator,* the spread of aesthetic values
from art to life was cancerous: "As might be expected the evil is spreading from
pictures and poems into private life" (Quilter 392). This evil had "attacked"
women's clothes and although an "actual creed [or] rule of conduct" had not
yet been established, it "has become in some sort effective as a standard of
manners" (Quilter 392). Quilter declared: "There may now be seen at many
a social gathering young men and women whose lack-lustre eyes, dishevelled
hair, eccentricity of attire and general appearance of weary passion, proclaim
them to be members of the new school" (Quilter 392–93).

The new school became synonymous with Burne-Jones's nymphs, who
were brought to life in Gilbert and Sullivan's *Patience* (1881) swathed in
Liberty fabrics. In honor of *The Golden Stairs* (1880, Tate Britian), "a
choir of virgins clad in tints of silver and pearl" (Stephens 1880b: 605),
Punch invented the Scraggington girls:

Who go in for wasp waists and Rossetti—though he's a bit 'fleshly' . . .
(which is very much more than she is, for her flesh scarcely covers her
bones,)
    And gush till their eyes grow like saucers concerning that fellow
Burne-Jones . . .
    I give you my word I'm so sick of her sausage-skin dress and her
bangles,her voice which is always a gasp, and her hair which is always
in tangles,
    I'd like, yes, by Jingo, to dose her with one of Medea's worst messes,
    Or choke the last 'oh' from her thorax with one of her own snaky
tresses . . .
    But the deuce of it is they aren't pretty, these painter's she-creatures.
    A hag with a face like a sea-sick consumptive, a neck that's a regular
scrag, for a beauty is rather *too* rich . . .
    The worst is that girls dress up now to the daubs of each dashed
High Art Pump (Anon 1880a: 253).

The Golden Stairs signaled the culmination of the Aesthetic trope that had
been evolving since the 1850s through the works of Rossetti, Burne-Jones,

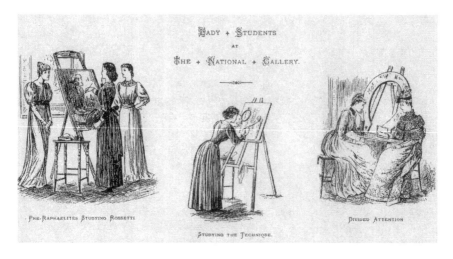

Figure 3.2 (a, b) "Lady Students at the National Gallery" from *The Queen*, February 1881.

Whistler, Watts, Leighton, and Moore. Burne-Jones's eighteen beauties, who inspired the chorus of lovesick maidens in *Patience*, was a very tangible tribute to "Life imitating Art," as the public believed the artist had included portraits of leading social beauties in the work. The Great British Matron began to fret about the effects of art on morality, as well as physical appearance, as the painted Stunners were all too often adulteresses, mistresses, and vamps, hardly the sort of material that young girls should be emulating. The models themselves were often little better in terms of their social or moral standing; being a professional model was a dubious occupation. Yet clearly, being beautiful could be turned to one's advantage regardless of class—Jane Burden became Mrs William Morris, Eleanor

(Nellie) Bromley, famed for her role in *Trial By Jury,* married Archie Stuart Wortley and Ellen Terry was rescued from the stage by G. F. Watts, "England's Michelangelo," albeit briefly.

In the search for Beauty, models were sought from both end of the spectrum, with the Pattles of Little Holland House and Spartalis (Christina and Maria) from London's wealthy Greek colony from the upper end, and Jane Morris, Jo Hiffernan, and Fanny Cornforth from the lower. On *The Golden Stairs,* the public identified with Margaret, the artist's own daughter, May Morris, Mary Gladstone, Frances Graham, later Lady Horner, the infamous Tennant girls, Laura Lyttelton, Margot Asquith, and Mary Stuart Wortley, later Lady Lovelace: "These likenesses helped to give the painting contemporary relevance and make it a key image for popular, fashionable Aestheticism" (Christian 236). The life of the model then as now appeared glamorous, offering an escape from conventional society into chic artistic circles. New gallery spaces in Bond Street and Regent Street and select parties in the new purpose built studios of Holland Park, Kensington, and Chelsea offered women new ways in which to mediate between art and society. Frank Miles, aided by Oscar Wilde, held "beauty parties" at his studio house on Tite Street, created by that aesthete of aesthetes, E. W. Godwin, which attracted Princess Louise and Lillie Langtry. Miles was the first artist to publicize the Jersey Lily, so named by her Jersey-born compatriot Millais, who painted her with the flower. Reality and fiction elided as the Stunners and PBs moved through English society, using their personas as part of a personal strategy of advancement, although, as Psomiades notes, there was an enormous gap between the artist's ideological projection and social praxis (Psomiades 177).

The aesthetic ideal appealed to those striving to make a personal statement, a commitment to a set of values, or who simply wanted to stand out in the crowd: "Why should writing people, painting people, singing people, persons presumably intelligent, since they all do something that pleases the public and is paid for in money, array themselves in garments . . . which render them distressingly conspicuous?" (Anon 1881: 601) Women were evidently "infected with eccentricity and affectation . . . the décor of the play-acting in which their life is passed." This "perversion of the purpose of dress" was an "inartistic playing at art" as the wearers of such clothes only did so to gain notoriety, now regarded as "the salt of life." Max Nordau condemned the aesthete for failing to express his real idiosyncrasies, for "trying to present something that they are not . . . The fixed idea is to produce an effect at any price" (Nordau 9). This masquerade demanded a stage, the equivalent of today's Red Carpet: "It is the passion for being remarked that makes the young women and the girls of the present day dress so absurdly and so hideously. . . . Fancy having a 'lane' made for one on account of one's clothes, and taking that for fame!" (Anon 1881: 601). Quilter, rounded on the sham-aesthetes who:

have for the last three or four years run about the picture galleries, and other spots where men do most congregate, in garments expressly invented . . . to make the men stare. Sometimes it would be a hoydenish short-frock and tippet, and perky, would-be coal-scuttle bonnet; at others, the young lady had become demure, and shrouded herself entirely in a long, loose, "wobbling" cloak, of a dull brick-dust or sage green, with a close fitting bonnet to match, which turned a naturally good complexion into the faint, grey hue of boiled sago. The sham aesthete never chooses pretty colours and forgets that dress is intended to heighten beauty, and not destroy it altogether (Quilter 859).

Quilter made a clear distinction between the genuine aesthetes, the true reformers and leaders who dressed in a certain style because they believed in it, and the copycats, for "whom mere singularity passes for beauty and who conceive that the more people there are who mutter 'How frightful!' when they see them, the more artistically beautiful their attire must be" (Quilter 1881: 859). The sham-aesthete copied his betters, especially the artists themselves, the "painter turned performer" who became the living embodiment of his art; Wilde debuted at the private view of the Grosvenor in a custom-made coat based on a cello (Gillet 53). While creating a sensation, adding to his fame and the notoriety of the Grosvenor, such a display also reduced Wilde to an object of derision. Gilbert, who quickly spotted an easy target, created outlandish eighteenth-century style costumes for his two rival poets, by mixing the personas of Whistler, Wilde, and Walter Crane.

Being conspicuous became a necessity at the Grosvenor:

> There were quaint, beautiful, extraordinary costumes walking about—ultra-aesthetics, artistic aesthetics, aesthetics that made up their mind to be daring, and suddenly gave way in some important point—put a frivolous bonnet on the top of a grave and glowing garment that Albert Durer might have designed for a mantle (Beerbohm 279).

Standing out in the crowd meant the "possession of unique gowns and incredible mantles," which the Aesthetes claimed as an expression of individuality: "It awakened people to the idea that it was possible to wear a style of dress which was unique to their personality, you did not have to be a slave to fashion to be stylish" (Wilson 36). Aesthetic dress codes required imagination rather than money, and appealed to those who wished to be novel on a limited budget. According to *The Journal of the Healthy and Artistic Dress Union:* "a little ingenuity and a keen perception of what is really beautiful in form and colour are all that is required to enable women's clothes to become what they seldom are, things of beauty and joys forever" (Wilson 32). Aesthetes claimed that they had turned dress into an art form. George Fleming (Constance Fletcher) asked her readers to imagine themselves as figures in a painting and dress themselves according to the rules of composition (Schaffer 103). Ostensibly, a person could create their own look but rather than springing from the wearer's imagination ideas were taken from historical models and contemporary books, particularly those by Walter Crane and Kate Greenaway, as well as paintings and stage productions. *Fancy Dresses Described or What to Wear at Fancy Dress Balls* by Ardern Holt (1882) illustrated an outfit for an aesthetic maiden based on the lovesick chorus in *Patience.*

Fashion experts often proposed recreating the effects seen in paintings. In *The Art of Dress* (1879), Mrs Haweis recommended her readers to draw their sleeves and caps from Renaissance paintings. She based her approach on a thorough understanding of historical costume, displaying the type of knowledge associated with connoisseurship. Mrs. Haweis did not favor any specific period or style; as long as the outfit proved its wearer had studied old paintings, it did not matter which particular paintings inspired the outfit (Haweis 52). The Old Masters offered a wide range of options, as illustrated in "Lady Students at the National Gallery" (1881), a series of sketches in *The Queen,* in which female artists have adopted the style of dress seen in the paintings they are copying. In homage to their favorite practitioners, each look was named after the artist or period that inspired it, Watteau, Pre-Raphaelite, or Classic school (Figure 3.2a,b).

Artistic dress required unstructured, loose-fitting garments with a natural or high waistline that were inspired by Greece and Rome, but also drew on medieval and even early nineteenth-century Empire fashions. White was the quintessential color, popularized by a whole series of images, from Whistler's Little White Girls, the first appearing 1862, to Albert Moore's

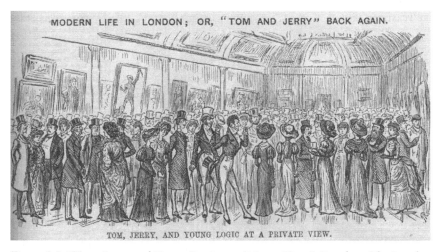

Figure 3.3 "Tom, Jerry, and Young Logic at a Private View," *Punch or The London Charivari,* 13 May 1882, 225.

creamy *Dreamers* (1882) and the silvery tints of the girls on *The Golden Stairs*. Rossetti maintained that his *Ecce Ancilla Domini* or *Annunciation* (1850) was in effect the first of the Women in White, the archetypal "stainless maiden" or "angel-watered lily." Although darker shades were worn, particularly dark brown, sage green, and gold, the "greenery, yallery" of the Grosvenor Gallery, white signaled purity, being "purged of the meretricious trappings of cheap modishness" (Gere 22). White, associated with mourning in the ancient world, also suggested allegiance to a religious or enclosed order, the withdrawal from active life advocated by many aesthetes, who sought a life of introspective contemplation and dreamlike reverie. Simplicity and other-worldliness heightened the penitential effect of aesthetic dress. The aesthetic woman was not of this world; she existed on a higher plain, being all soul. Mediated by Burne-Jones, white became increasingly associated with a flawed innocence that was equated with the world-weariness of the aesthete: "The soul has begun to awake, to some sense of what a world we live in. And so we have the 19th century weariness [which] we see just shadowed on those lovely faces of Burne-Jones's'" (Forsyth 59–60). Grief spread through her body like a systemic infection, eroding and numbing, ultimately destroying her physical and mental well-being. In Wilkie Collin's *The Woman in White* (1862), the central motif is "a figure of death in the realm of the living [a] decaying body [or] the impossible women on the edge of death" (Bronfen 298). Despair and weariness become her defining aspects, physical manifestations of her knowledge of sin. Hawthorne's Hilda the Dove, in *The Marble Fawn,* is another "poor sufferer for another's sin!" (Hawthorne 694) a "poor, lonely girl, whom God has set here in an evil world, and given her only a white robe, and bid her wear it back to Him, as white as when she put it on" (Hawthorne 612).[3] Hilda's glimpse of evil, a murder initiated by her best friend, "allowed a throng of torturing recollections to escape from their dungeons into the pure air and white radiance of her soul, [while] straying farther into the intricate passages of our nature, she stumbled, ever and again, over this deadly idea of mortal guilt" (Hawthorne 612). Hilda is overcome with "torpor," a "chill and heavy misery, which only the innocent can experience," a "heart sickness [or] that dismal certainty of the existence of evil in the world" (Hawthorne 693). An all-pervading sense of sadness haunts the Woman in White: "Of sorrow, slender as she seems, Hilda might bear a great burden; of sin, not a feather's weight" (Hawthorne 559).

Pale and "Intense," the Woman in White appears to be a mourner at her own funeral, the look immortalized by G. F. Watts in his portrayal of *Lady Sophia Dalrymple* (c. 1854, Watts Gallery), one of the seven famous Pattle girls.[4] In this work Watts visualized the personification of High Culture, the loose-fitting diaphanous shift-dress, caught at the waist by a cord, the absence of ostentatious jewelery, the simply dressed hair and the penetrating dark soulful eyes, for which the sitter was justly famous. She was once described as the "Elgin marbles with dark eyes" (Blunt 79). Although a portrait, Sophia Dalrymple still functions as the artist's muse, a combination of fact and fiction.⁵ She and her sisters forged distinctive identities thorough their artistic and idiosyncratic clothing. The Pattles dressed in an unconventional manner; crinolines were replaced with long cloaks, fine Indian shawls, hairnets, and tinkling Indian bangles. All the Pattle girls were born and raised in India. They naturally favored Indian muslin and fine cottons, materials that would drape and fall softly. According to one observer, their appearance was always "somewhat shapeless and sloppy," due she naturally supposed to long residence in a hot climate (Squire 1996a 43):

> to see one of this sisterhood float into a room with sweeping robes and falling folds was almost an event in itself, and not to be forgotten. They did not in the least trouble themselves about public opinion (their own family was large enough to contain all the elements of interest and criticism). They had unconventional rules for life which excellently suited themselves, and which also interested and stimulated other people. They were unconscious artists, diving beauty and living with it (Anne Thackery Ritchie qtd. in Gere 17).

Stunners invariably dressed with striking originality, deemed freakish by conventional society. Virginia Pattle, later Lady Somers and chatelaine of Eastnor Castle, wore her garb like a queen, creating an aura of superiority. Constance Lascelles, Lady Wenlock, was equally eccentric: "an elfin grace and originality—a far away look in her face as if she belonged to another world" (Abdy and Gere 169). She wore delicate muslins draped with Indian shawls in grey and pink. Her appearance was so unconventional that when in public her fashionable nieces felt a desire to dissociate themselves. The garb of Lady Wenlock's great friend, Mary Stuart Wortley, later Lady Lovelace, another favorite of Burne-Jones, also caused consternation. Her taste in clothes was considered to be "odd and deplorable": she never wore corsets. Such women eschewed the latest Parisian fashions, refusing to be designated simply coat-hangers; their ethereal look implied that much lay below the surface.

The aesthetic persona suggested spiritual and emotional depth. Whistler fashioned his Woman in White with the aid of Joanna Hiffernan, *La Belle Irelandais*. *The White Girl* (1862) portrayed "Jo," Whistler's model and mistress for five years, as a young woman dressed in a simple white dress, holding a white lily and standing on a bear-skin. Jules Antoine Castaganary, unable to accept a subject-less work felt impelled to concoct his own narrative:

> Let me instead see in your work something more elevated, the morning after the wedding night, the disquieting minute in the course of which the young woman questions herself, is astonished not to recognise any longer her recent virginity (Dorra 65).

Courbet declared it to be an apparition but for him the image was compromised by its "air of mystery and spiritual intensity" (Dorment and Macdonald 77). It did not help that Wilkie Collins's *The Woman in White* was serialized from 1859 to 1860, *The White Girl* being erroneously exhibited under that title at Matthew Morgan's gallery in 1862. As far as the public were concerned, it was all too easy to the see *The White Girl* as a woman driven to madness by love or yet another Mary Magdalene, a redeemed sinner, suggested by the unbound red hair and look of ecstatic transport. She might even be a suspected adulteress, like Mrs. Strong in Dickens's *David Copperfield* (1850), described by David as having:

> such a face as I never saw. It was so beautiful in its form, it was so ashy pale, it was so fixed in its abstraction, it was so full of a wild, sleepwalking, dreamy horror of I don't know what. The eyes were wide open, and her brown hair fell in two rich clusters on her shoulders, and on her white dress (Dickens 304).

Whistler's *Symphony in White No. 2: The Little White Girl* (1864) was equally mysterious. Joanna is portrayed in a beautiful, uncorseted, white gown, worn with great style, contemplating her reflection in a mirror and surrounded by artistic objects: a fan, an "Old Blue" Chinese vase, lacquer ware, and an azalea. Whistler, perhaps as a concession to the English taste for narrative, exhibited the work with the poem *Before the Mirror,* written by Swinburne in homage to the beauty of the painting, which indirectly implied the idea of love and loss: "and the notion of sad and glad mystery in the face languidly contemplative of its own phantom and all other things seen by their phantoms" (Swinburne letter to Whistler, 2 April 1865, in Spencer 76). Joanna, like Lizzie Siddal and Jane Morris, greatly contributed to the concept of the artistic woman. Courbet, for whom she also modeled, noted her "feeling and talent for art" (Squire 40). Joanna adopted clothing with a distinctive and highly personal character. Whistler told du Maurier that she took fashion-conscious Parisians by surprise. The dress she wore for *The White Girl,* begun in Paris in 1861, "has a stylishness of detail and general quality of chic setting it apart from alternative dress in England at that time" (Squire 41–42). What part Whistler played in designing the costume is open to conjecture. The artist was always persnickety and dictatorial about what his sitters wore. He is known to have designed the flowing white gown worn by Mrs. Frances Leyland for her portrait (1871–74). However, in Squire's opinion, "Jo's feelings and talent for art is surely evident in the clothes she wore and the way she wore them" (Squire 42). There is every reason to suppose that the model designed and made her clothes, as was the custom of the day.

Lizzie Siddal and Jane Morris also did much to foster their own images; in 1857 Siddal worked for four months at the Sheffield School of Art, where a fellow student thought her dress "uncommon but pleasing," although admitting the other girls "considered it unbecoming and absurd." They made jokes and caricatures about it—a penalty exacted even by peers from those courageously showing their convictions (Squire 1996a 37–39). Drawn into the Pre-Raphaelite circle as models, for works of a mythological, medieval, or religious nature, Lizzie and Jane posed in princess-line gowns and surcoats. At the same time, perhaps under the prompting of Rossetti and Morris, they adapted the uncorseted, flowing garments for everyday wear. After Lizzie's death in 1862, Jane assumed the role of Rossetti's muse, creating a legend in her lifetime until her death in 1914. The clothes she wore were carefully handcrafted, often with elaborate embroidery, and the wearer would have been "intimately aware of the hands which made them" (Weathers 101). Practicalities and ethics, as well as looks, may have steered her in the direction of loose comfortable clothes but such unbound dress suggested to a general public, who expected women to be physically constrained by their garments, a loose or immoral nature: "A woman without a corset or expansive skirt in "poetic" paintings and within the bohemian confines of the Pre-Raphaelite circle was an exotic inspiration, but alone in the streets, she was a doomed harlot" (Weathers 103).

In *The Golden Stairs*, Burne-Jones favored the Empire silhouette, resulting in a smooth bodyline, the clinging "nightgown" effect satirized by Gilbert's "love-sick" maidens. Fine fabrics were used that clung and yet were diaphanous and floating, as seen in the paintings of Lord Leighton, Albert Moore, and Alma Tadema. Fine pleats fascinated Burne-Jones, the fabric gathered or bunched up, derived in part from the works of Piero della Francesca, Mantegna, and Botticelli. Vernon Lee has Anne Brown transformed by Burne-Jones style pleating, although the diaphanous clinging folds are also suggestive of immodesty and impropriety:

> Miss Brown was by this time tolerably accustomed to the eccentric garb of aesthetic circles, and she firmly believed that it was the only one which a self-respecting woman might wear; but when she saw the dress which Hamlin had designed for her, she could not help shrinking in dismay. It was of that Cretan silk, not much thicker than muslin, which is woven in minute wrinkles of palest yellowy; it was made, it seemed to her, more like a nightgown than anything else, shapeless and yet clinging with large folds, and creases like those of damp sculptor's drapery, or the garments of Mantegna's women (Lee 148).

In Pygmalion fashion, the artist transforms life into art, in this instance creating a veritable Grecian sculpture in silk. Whistler's white dresses similarly transformed his mistress Joanna, while Rossetti elevated Jane, clad in "dead purple stuff," onto her pedestal. But when the artist leaves the room, his creation questions the "ravishing tableau": "That colossal woman, with wrinkled drapery, clinging to her in half-antique, half-medieval guise—that great solemn, theatrical creature, could that be herself? . . . Did he care for her only as a sort of live picture? she thought bitterly"

(Lee 150). More prosaically, *Vanity Fair* likened Burne-Jones's Mantegna folds to tin-foil: "They are robed in tin-foil night-gowns, like the necks of champagne bottles and they are, I am informed, 'attuned to a secret sad unison'" (Anon 1880b: 182).

Nevertheless, pleating became a craze, with Mary Anderson's striking Grecian draped mode making its mark at the Grosvenor. The American actress enjoyed an enthusiastic welcome in London, partly because she seemed less an actress than "a woman of surpassing loveliness with some taste for acting" (Gillet 52). She had an "innocence of manner that set off her personal beauty." During her time as the Prince of Wales's mistress, c.1879–80, Lillie Langtry also adopted innocent white. The Jersey Lily elicited a frenzied level of interest even amongst the highest echelons of Society; ladies would even stand on chairs to see her entrance. Many were awed by Lillie's beauty, who turned up at a late Monday evening party at the Grosvenor "in white, no flowers or jewels, and really very handsome" (Adams in Gillet 53). Ellen Terry shared with Langtry a dubious reputation, including her failed marriage to Watts and her affair with E. W. Godwin, which resulted in two children. Terry's dressmaker, Mrs. Alice Carr, wife of Joseph Comyns Carr, the manager of the Grosvenor Gallery, helped to construct her persona. Her costumes for Faust in 1885 utilized accordion pleats: "it was not long before the full kilted skirts were so much in demand amongst women of fashion that machines were set up to make what became known as accordion pleating" (Wilson 32). The draped and pleated effect was typical garb of The Souls. Lady Pembroke, Lady Lothian, and Lady Brownlow were famous for their unusual sense of color and diaphanous concoctions: Lady Brownlow "was seated between Lady Lothian and Lady Pembroke, the former in trailing black and the latter in trailing white draperies. Lady Brownlow was in sober grey of the same make and they looked like the Three Fates" (Abdy and Gere 164). Lord Leighton's stunning portrait of *Lady Brownlow,* which now hangs at Belton House, depicts the famous hostess in a white silk dress of vaguely medieval inspiration that could be characterized as the haute couture version of aesthetic dress (Squire 1996a: 47).

Through the auspices of the Grosvenor Gallery, what had begun as alternative dress in the 1850s, seen by the majority as outlandish, became an artistic trope that signified one's acceptance into the Bohemian set. The Grosvenor, the "Haunt of Beauty," was the home of the *beau monde* where one went to see the people as much as the pictures, "the notabilities, the dandies, and the ladies of the highest fashion":

> "Who . . . are these extraordinary beings with strange hats and dresses of blue, yellow and sickly green, who look limp and forlorn?" . . ."Those are aesthetic young ladies, who sigh for sunflowers, languish over lilies, and peruse improper poems. . . ."I marvel how long this strange fashion will last . . . and we shall not readily forget the rich scenes at the Private View of the Grosvenor Gallery (Anon 13 May 1882: 225) (Figure 3.3).

Although dress was alleged to be an individual statement akin to a declaration of independence, signifying difference, the aesthetic coterie laid down rules. Like the current obsession for size zero, aestheticism demanded molding one's body into a proscribed type, with the attendant physical sacrifices. Deprivations resulted in the required skeletal frame, proving that aesthetic woman was all soul, a negation of the body. *Punch* summarized the salient attributes:

> Behold the Hideous Thing! Attired in wreathed robe of ruddy flame, Through the mysterious shadows slowly came, Fulvous she was, with frizzed, flamboyant hair. . . . Her cheeks were cavernous, her form was spare. . . . One might see its osseous framework, fashioned curiously, And study its scarce-veiled anatomy, She stood as one from whom each garment slips, Limp. . . . And to the earth in hopeless languor turned, As they for restful death and darkness yearned (Anon 1879: 120).

The fulvous hair came from Jane Morris, while the robe of ruddy flame alludes to Burne-Jones's *Laus Veneris* (1873–78), shown at the Grosvenor in 1878 and considered his most decadent work, Venus being "stricken with

HOW TO EFFECT A GOOD RIDDANCE.

Scene—*Royal Academy Private View.*

Boreham Jones, Esq., M.P. "AH, HOW D'YE DO, MRS. TOMKYNS! SO GLAD TO MEET YOU—A—I——"
Mrs. Ponsonby de Tomkyns (who thinks Mr. Boreham Jones all very well, but doesn't want him just as she's talking to the Duke of Wimbledon), "OH, DEAR MR. JONES! HAVE YOU SEEN MR. SOPELY'S PICTURE? IT'S IN ROOM NO. 10. DO LOOK AT IT, AND TELL ME WHAT YOU THINK OF IT!"
[*Exit Boreham Jones, much flattered, to perform Mrs. Tomkyns's commission. Exeunt also Mrs. Tomkyns and his Grace, in the opposite direction.*

Figure 3.4 "How to Effect a Good Riddance," *Punch or The London Charivari*, 20 May 1882, 234. Scene: Royal Academy Private View.

disease of the soul . . . eaten up and gnawed away with disappointment and desire. . . . The very body is unpleasant and uncomely, and the soul behind it . . . ghastly" (Frederick Wedmore in Parris 229–30). Such condemnation did not deter those who dreamt of bringing such paintings to life, enacting the Pre-Raphaelite tragic heroine, but to the uninformed the type was downright ugly and morally dubious.

Yet aestheticism was destined to pass out of fashion; in *The Colonel* and *Patience* the girls were transformed back into healthy, well-padded, corseted conventional beauties. Condemned as ugly, the aesthetic look required too much bodily denial and certainly was not good for the couturier or jeweler. It was a sign of the times, life-style aestheticism momentarily attaining the mainstream, offering new objects of desire, shawls, bangles, and viper-like tresses. The Woman in White, originally conceived as an alternative, may have vanished like a ghost but she would continue to set the "standard for artistic resistance to the tyranny of fashionable dress" (Squire 1996a: 44). The New Woman, who combined intellectualism with women's rights, would resurrect the trope in the 1890s, embodying the Mind rather than the Soul.

NOTES

1. Lady Lindsay's direct involvement with the gallery ended in 1882, when she separated from her husband and withdrew her capital from the venture.
2. The social enactment, "a sort of live picture," is further discussed in Anne Anderson, "Life into Art and Art into Life: The Aesthetic Woman or *High Art Maiden* of the Victorian Renaissance," *Women's History Review,* Autumn, 2001.
3. Coincidentally, one of Rossetti's nicknames for Lizzie Siddal was the Dove.
4. G. F. Watts also painted Mrs. Julia Margaret Cameron, her sister, four years after her return from India in 1852, in a white dress with an unusually full, loose bodice.
5. It was the misfortune of Watts to be always moving in circles "above his station," falling in love with ladies beyond his reach. His feelings may have been reflected in the portraits that he painted of the sisters, suggesting not only his own hopeless love but also the loveless marriages which society forced on women in their position.

WORKS CITED

Abdy, Jane, and Charlotte Gere. *The Souls: An Elite in English Society 1885–1930.* London: Sidgwick & Jackson: 1894.

Anon. "The Two Ideals." *Punch or The London Charivari* (13 September 1879): 20.

———. "Fred on Pretty Girls and Pictures." *Punch or The London Charivari* (5 June 1880a): 253.

———. "The Grosvenor Gallery." *Vanity Fair,* 15 May, from *The Artist* (June 1880b): 182.

———. *Illustrated London News* (8 May 1880c).

———. "The Clothes of the Period." *The Spectator* (7 May 1881): 601.

————. "Tom, Jerry and Young Logic at a Private View." *Punch or The London Charivari* (13 May 1882): 225.

Beerbohm, Max. "1880." *The Yellow Book* (Vol. IV). London: Bodley Head, 1895: 275–83.

Benson, E. F. *As We Were*. London, New York, Toronto: Longmans, Green and Co., 1930.

Blunt, Wilfred. *England's Michelangelo: A Biography of George Frederick Watts*. London: Columbus Books, 1989.

Bronfen, Elisabeth. *Over Her Dead Body: Death, Femininity and the Aesthetic*. Manchester: Manchester University Press, 1992.

Christian, John. In *The Pre-Raphaelites,* edited by Leslie Parris [exhibition catalogue]. London: Tate Gallery, 1984.

Dickens, Charles. *The Personal History of David Copperfield*. London: Dent, Everyman, 1850, reprinted 1979.

Dorment, Richard, and Margaret Macdonald. *Whistler* [exhibition catalogue]. London: Tate Gallery Publications, 1995.

Dorra, Henry. *Symbolist Art Theories: A Critical Anthology*. Berkeley: University of California, 1994.

Forsyth, P.T. *Religion in Recent Art*. London: Hodder and Stoughton, 1901.

Gere, Charlotte. "The Art of Dress, Victorian Artists and the Aesthetic Style." In *Simply Stunning: The Pre-Raphaelite Art of Dressing,* edited by Geoffrey Squire. Cheltenham: Cheltenham Art Gallery and Museums, 1996: 13–24.

Gillet, Paula. "Art Audiences at the Grosvenor Gallery." In *The Grosvenor Gallery: A Palace of Art in Victorian England,* edited by Susan P. Casteras and Colleen Denney. New Haven and London: Yale University Press, 1996: 39–58.

Haweis, Mrs. Mary Eliza. *The Art of Dress*. New York: Garland, 1879.

Hawthorne, Nathaniel. *The Marble Faun, The Complete Novels and Selected Tales of Nathaniel Hawthorne* (Vol II). New York: The Modern Library, 1860, reprinted 1993.

Holt, Ardern. *Fancy Dresses Described or What to Wear at Fancy Dress Balls,* London: Debenham and Freebody, 1882.

Lee, Vernon. *Miss Brown*. reprinted Doylestown, Pennsylvania: Wildside Press, 1884.

Nordau, Max. *Degeneration*. London: William Heineman, 1895.

Parris, Leslie (ed.) *The Pre-Raphaelites,* exhibition catalogue, London: Tate Gallery/Penguin, 1984.

Psomiades, Kathy. *Beauty's Body: Femininity and Representation in British Aestheticism*. Stanford: Stanford University, 1997.

————. "'Still Burning From this Strangling Embrace': Vernon Lee on Desire and Aesthetics." In *Victorian Sexual Dissidence,* edited by Richard Dellamora. Chicago and London: Chicago University Press, 1999: 21–42.

Quilter, Harry. "The New Renaissance or the Gospel of Intensity." *Macmillan's Magazine* (1880): 391–400.

————. "An Aesthetic Forecast." *The Spectator* (2 July 1881): 859.

Schaffer, Talia. *The Forgotten Female Aesthetes: Literary Culture in Late Victorian Britain*. Charlottesville and London: University of Virginia Press, 2000.

Spencer, Robin (ed.). *Whistler: A Retrospective*. New York: Hugh Lauter Levin Associates, 1989.

Squire, Geoffrey (ed.) "Clothed in Our Right Minds: Some Wearers of Aesthetic Dress." In *Simply Stunning: The Pre-Raphaelite Art of Dressing,* edited by Geoffrey Squire. Cheltenham: Cheltenham Art Gallery and Museums, 1996a: 37–48.

————. *Simply Stunning: The Pre-Raphaelite Art of Dressing*. Cheltenham: Cheltenham Art Gallery and Museums, 1996b.

Staley, Allen. "Art Is upon the Town! The Grosvenor Gallery Winter Exhibitions." In *The Grosvenor Gallery: A Palace of Art in Victorian England*, edited by Susan P. Casteras and Colleen Denney. New Haven and London: Yale University Press, 1996: 59–74.

Stephens, F. G. *The Athenaeum* (3 April 1880a): 447–48.

————. "The Grosvenor Gallery." *The Athenaeum* (8 May 1880b): 605.

Weathers, Rachael. "The Pre-Raphaelite Movement and Nineteenth Century Ladies' Dress: A Study in Victorian Views of the Female Body." In *Collecting the Pre-Raphaelites: The Anglo-American Enchantment*, edited by Margaretta Frederick Watson. Aldershot: Ashgate, 1997: 95–108.

Wilde, Oscar. "The Decay of Lying." *Intentions*. London: Methuen, 1891, twelfth edition 1919.

Wilson, Sophie. "Away with the Corsets, on with the Shifts." In *Simply Stunning: The Pre-Raphaelite Art of Dressing*, edited by Geoffrey Squire. Cheltenham: Cheltenham Art Gallery and Museums, 1996: 25–36.

4 Maurice de Rothschild's "Remembrances of Things Past"

Costume Obsession and Decadence, the Collection of a *Belle Époque* Dandy

Christopher Bedford

Male masquerades were seen as problematic, but male disguises emerged as a cornerstone of both nineteenth-century fashion and moral behavior. The man was not allowed to put on a show, but he could put one over on anyone he liked. Double identity, double entendres, even double lives were acceptable to any who could master their challenges. His duplicity depended, in fact, on his ability to bring the masquerades of others into his service (Matlock 57).

In her study of "abnormal" sexual psychology in France at the turn-of-the-century, historian Jann Matlock observes that clothing obsession and costume obsession were two kinds of behavioral abnormalities that "focused concerns over homosexuality, masturbation, criminality, and degeneracy." For a male to be invested in the aesthetic appeal of costume, rather than the carnal attraction of the flesh was, according to contemporary French psychiatric theory, an expression of abnormal sexuality and one that threatened the normative, procreative status of the Parisian male. While conventions of male taste and behavior during this period were customarily somber, certain men found ways to negotiate these constraints by fashioning private spaces in which they brought "the masquerades of others into their service" (Matlock 57).

One such Parisian male was baron Maurice de Rothschild (1881–1957). Unlike most members of his highly conservative, Jewish banking family whose famous art collections consisted predominantly of Dutch seventh-century, French eighteenth-century and Old Master works, Maurice gravitated toward contemporary painting that signified his affiliation with the tastes and lifestyle of the Decadent Movement, emblematized most notably by "their leader," Robert de Montesquiou (1855–1921). Chief among Maurice's passions were the paintings of the French *Belle Époque* society painter Giovanni Boldini (1842–1931) (Proust 1963: 386) (Figure 4.1). Maurice befriended Boldini and bought numerous works directly from him, probably beginning around 1907, for a period of approximately twenty-five years. A large number, but by no means all of the Boldini paintings purchased by Maurice are full-length depictions of well-known society women, draped in conspicuous garments that shimmer with the artist's energetic brushstrokes. Boldini's interest in and emphasis on contemporary fashion is well-documented in the scholarly literature on the artist. However, the significance of this emphasis on female clothing and costume and its relationship to turn-of-the-century Parisian masculinity and sexual politics has not been thoroughly explored. Similarly unexplored are the implications inherent in a young, prominent Parisian male's decision to collect such conspicuous works in such quantity and to display those objects in his various homes.

This chapter suggests that, for Maurice de Rothschild, the act of collecting and displaying Boldini's pictures of women was an expression of his fascination with female fashion of the *Belle Époque,* a well-known preoccupation of so-called dandies like Montesquiou. Maurice displayed Boldini's imposing full-length portraits of women in shimmering, graceful garments throughout his various homes in France and Switzerland, creating at once a show room for contemporary fashion and a covert space for identity formation. Just as designers used Boldini's renowned paintings as showcases for their latest designs, similarly Boldini exploited those designs as inspiration for his lively brushwork. In turn, collectors, like Maurice, purchased the paintings, transforming their extravagant homes into complex interior spaces at odds with the prevailing social codes that governed male taste. Though Maurice conformed in many ways to the traditional collecting patterns established by his family and was a brilliant banker, both his flamboyant lifestyle and his taste for Boldini can be understood as symptoms of what Matlock calls a "double life," and of the "unhealthy" male fascination with clothing and costume that for contemporary French psychiatrists signified a debased masculinity particular to this historical period. My contention that Maurice conducted a "double life" is born out equally well by the dual—one might even suggest schizophrenic—nature of this art collection and by the details of his biography. Therefore, based on an analysis of Maurice's life and patronage, I argue that Boldini's paintings of women must be recognized not solely as expressions of *fin-de-siècle* female glamour, as scholarship to this point has suggested, but also as complex indices of contemporary male identity, created to appeal to a segment of the moneyed bourgeoisie whose tastes have come to denote the archetypal late-nineteenth and early-twentieth century Parisian dandy.

BARON MAURICE DE ROTHSCHILD

In his article "Mapping the Origins of Glamour: Giovanni Boldini, Paris and the *Belle Époque*," Stephen Gundle notes that turn-of-the-century Paris was a city marked by a far-reaching shift in the Victorian social

Figure 4.1 Giovanni Boldini, *Portrait of the Countess Zichy,* 1905, oil on canvas, (86 ½" x 47").

order. A heterogeneous bourgeoisie composed of artists, writers, dancers, courtesans, and businessmen alike, he holds, had replaced the aristocracy as the most visible social class. Money and consumerism had usurped family lineage and breeding as social currency; similar leisure activities were experienced by many different segments of the populace; an obsession with the feminine became a central cultural codifier (Gundle 277). The fragmentary accounts that together compose Maurice de Rothschild's biography tell us that it was this milieu that most fascinated the young baron. Historian Herbert H. Lottman, who provides the most biographical information on Maurice, remarks that he was "the elegant young man about town, taking summers at Marienbad, winters in Saint-Moritz, raising horses, hunting in India, passing the rest of the time with the prettiest women of Paris (the women as expensive as the horses and hunting parties)" (163). Lottman concludes that Maurice was the only Rothschild to have truly experienced the "[c]razy years" in Paris (173).

The sensationalism, generalizations, and clichés that dominate Maurice's biography as recorded in Rothschild family histories are revealing when considered in conjunction with other significant, though sporadic, references to his life found particularly in the novels and correspondence of his Parisian contemporary, Marcel Proust. As we shall see, Proust on a number of occasions characterizes Maurice very pointedly as a dandy and describes the baron's dealings with socially prominent affiliates of the Decadent Movement, most notably Robert de Montesquiou, a personality whose historical character has come to epitomize the decadence of the *Belle Époque*. While the skeletal coverage of Maurice's life given by modern historians and biographers glosses over and thus suppresses the details of his "man about town" lifestyle, reference to Proust's treatment of Maurice begins to fill in some of those gaps.

From the moment Mayer Amschel Rothschild (1743–1812) laid the foundations for an enduring family fortune by supplying William of Hesse-Kassel (later William IX, Landgrave of Hesse-Kassel) with rare coins, the art of business and the business of art were irrevocably intertwined. Works of art were as much capital investments as adornments for their homes around Europe. Art and collecting played a very different role in the life of Maurice. Born at Boulogne-sur-Seine on 19 May 1881, Maurice Edmond Charles de Rothschild was the second son of Edmond James de Rothschild (1845–1934). In 1907, Maurice de Rothschild inherited a major art collection and two magnificent houses, one in Paris and one in Switzerland—he was twenty-five years old. Beyond these basic documentary facts, the specifics of Maurice's life are often eschewed in favor of a glossy, general narrative that dismisses him as a capricious, irresponsible playboy. The dominant archetype of the Parisian playboy of the *fin-de-siècle*, however, contains far more complexity and interest than is made clear by Maurice's biographers, and it is to those issues that we now turn.

AN ALTERNATIVE LIFE: PROUST, MONTESQUIOU, AND THE CULTURE OF DECADENCE

Marcel Proust's *A la recherché du temps perdu* is the most vivid and informative chronicle of Paris from the 1880s to the 1920s, as the following quote aptly illustrates:

> If in a period of twenty years, like this that had elapsed since my first entry, the conglomerations of social groups had disintegrated and reformed under the magnetic influence of new stars destined themselves to fade away and then to reappear. . . . But all this combined had produced effects that were dazzling, while the causes were already remote and not merely unknown to many people but also forgotten by those who had once known them and whose minds now dwelt much more upon their apparent brilliance than upon the ignominy of her past, since people always accept a name at its current valuation (Proust 1993: 239).

One prominent image in Proust's kaleidoscope of personalities is that of the Parisian dandy, a type he made famous in his character baron Charlus Guermantes. In *A la recherché du temps perdu*, Proust cites Charlus' decadence, fetishism, and homosexuality as the major factors in the decay of the Guermentes family. The principal model for Proust's Charlus was his friend the comte Robert de Montesquiou. However, according to historian Heather McPhearson, "the comte's existence was more artistic and less sordid" than that of Charlus. Visionary artist or self-indulgent hedonist, de Montesquiou was nonetheless the most conspicuous and influential "dandy, esthete, poet, and eccentric" of his time (McPherson 37). In his novel, Proust uses de Montesquiou's well-known emphasis on dress, ornament, and elegance as a way to introduce Charlus' decadence. The fact that identity was commonly denoted by self-image in the *fin-de-siècle,* and that such a manner of self-presentation was common in Paris and familiar to the broader public is further emphasized by a remark Proust makes in a essay on de Montesquiou: "there has ensued a generation of young men who with scarcely an exception persist in resembling each other, and whom we would like to distinguish from M. de Montesquiou, instead of making them out to be their leader, as he is their God" (Proust 1963: 386). For Proust, de Montesquiou is the unwilling figurehead of the Decadents, in fact, the "Prince of the Decadents, ruling as whimsical despot over every corruption of the mind and every refinement of the imagination" (Proust 1963: 384).

That Maurice was one of a slightly later generation of young men who cast themselves in the mold of Robert de Montesquiou is evident in an undated photograph of Maurice, probably from around 1900 (Figure 4.2). Here, his manicured appearance, elegant posture, and carefully chosen attire are reminiscent of de Montesquiou's obsessive attention to his clothing and appearance, captured in Boldini's portrait of 1897 in which the turquoise of de Montesquiou's cane carefully matches his cufflinks (Figure 4.3). Evidence of Maurice's imitation of de Montesquiou, or at the very least, his shared sensibility, can be observed quite literally in a series of visits he made to Fabergé London in 1913. On 21 July 1913, while visiting the shop in the company of his cousin Albert von Goldsmidt-Rothschild, Maurice purchased a yellow enamel and gold cigarette holder. Then, in September of the same year he brought a cane handle for repair by Fabergé, enameled with the blue and gold of the Rothschild family. In much the same way that he was able to merge conventional Rothschild taste in art collecting with his own penchant for Boldini, so his blue and yellow accoutrements may be understood as signifiers of his dual status as avowed dandy and proud member of the Rothschild family.

Figure 4.2 Undated photograph of Maurice de Rothschild.

Figure 4.3 Giovanni Boldini, *Count Robert de Montesquiou*, 1897, oil on canvas, Paris, Musée d'Orsay.

Proust's written descriptions of Maurice's physical appearance similarly allude to the baron's publicly legible dandyism. From Proust's biographer, George D. Painter, we learn that on 21 May 1911 Proust attended the dress rehearsal of D'Annunazio's play *Le Martyre de Saint-Sebastien*.

According to Painter, Proust and de Montesquiou sat next to one another and marveled at Ida Rubenstein's portrayal of St. Sebastian, her appearance as the martyred saint apparently reminiscent of Perugino's "lovely boy" in the Louvre (129). While de Montesquiou's fascination with Rubenstein's famously androgynous appearance is well documented, on this occasion it was Proust who was apparently most impressed by the actress, describing her appearance as "a cross between Clomesnil and Maurice de Rothschild" (Painter 171).

This characterization of Maurice as effeminate or androgynous takes visual form in a caricature circulated in 1924 when he ran for French office. This drawing shows a chubby, naked Maurice with wings of a putti, floating carelessly in a field of money, a contented grin on his face. As historian Robert A. Nye notes, "it was believed that the diminished sexual economies of inverts was expressed in their bodies as a regression to the hermaphroditic center of the sexual spectrum, whereby males took on feminine aspects" (229). As is apparent from his extensive discussion of the concept of inversion in *A la recherché du temps perdu,* Proust was well aware of the implications of drawing attention to a man's androgynous appearance, and clearly his account of Rubenstein serves equally well as a description of Maurice. Similarly, the political caricature of Maurice circulated to discredit his candidacy for office obviously drew on the notion of visible effeminacy as a marker of inversion to portray the baron as an irresponsible, moneyed dandy.

Proust provides yet more evidence of the way Maurice's character and coded self-presentation were understood in the context of the *Belle Époque*. According to Painter, "one of Proust's favorite stories was of de Montesquiou's request to Maurice de Rothschild for the loan of some diamonds to wear to a fancy dress ball" (Painter 171). According to Proust, de Montesquiou was outraged to receive only a very small broach from a man renowned for his jewelry collection. Indeed, de Montesquiou frequently displayed his taste for flamboyant gems unabashedly at large social gatherings. Lottman, for example, describes "the great costume ball of the summer" of 1942 where guests were required to wear costumes inspired by Racine. Maurice attended, "garbed as the Ottoman Bajazet, displaying his mother's famous diamonds on his turban, and on his sash the rare Renaissance jewels which are part of his family's Cellini collection" (Lottman 212). In an age when the "outer husk of [conventional] masculinity was a dignified sober affair," Maurice's social identity quite obviously departed from this model, a fact that may in part explain his exclusion from the family banking business, and the glossy, vague treatment he has been afforded in his biographies (Garb 81). Just as the fictional character baron Charlus brought about the decline of his once-great family with his perversity and effeminacy, so, it seems, the Rothschilds averted what they assumed might be a similar deterioration by barring Maurice from the family business.

As Nye notes, "the biomedical discourse of sexuality that emerged in the course of the nineteenth century placed a positive and 'normative' value on marital, heterosexual relations, the virtues of family life and a healthy abundant progeny, and specified a set of pathological conditions and practices to be abominated and marked for elimination or 'cure'" (Nye 228). In contradistinction to the preferred practices laid out by this list of positive values, Maurice had only one child and spent most of his years divorced and single, led a life of frivolity and excess and displayed many of the "pathological conditions," including effeminacy and, as we shall see shortly, fetishism, that would classify him as a "perverse adult," dandy, Decadent, or invert, condemned by the nineteenth-century French medical establishment.

None of the biographical fragments already cited, however, are intended, nor are they adequate, to map Maurice's character onto that of Robert de Montesquiou or indeed any other Parisian man whose tastes, behaviors, ideas, and sexuality ran counter to normative ideals. Rather, de Montesquiou is presented here as a paradigm of the *Belle Époque* dandy that enables us to understand more concretely the tastes and values of the Decadent Movement, and how Maurice's interests and manner of self-presentation intersected with these countercultural trends. To pursue this line of reasoning further leads us naturally to the significance of Maurice's art patronage.

FETISHISM AND "INVERSION" AT THE TURN OF THE CENTURY

One particularly objectionable attribute of the male sexual deviant according to turn-of-the-century French medical discourse was an attraction to and fetishization of women's attire. Much of this concern was catalyzed by the very public displays of nontraditional masculinity seen in the tastes and appearance of the dandy. De Montesquiou made his fascination for certain extravagant women of the new bourgeois social order and their elaborate manner of self-presentation public knowledge. As Heather McPhearson has remarked, "Montesquiou developed a veritable cult" for the Comtesse de La Castiglione who had been the mistress of Napoleon III, collecting over 400 portraits of her, mostly photographs, and sketching out her personality in *La Divine Comtesse* (1913) (38). In the essay, de Montequiou celebrates her aesthetic eccentricities and elaborate attire. Among his other preoccupations were Eleanora Duse, Isadora Duncan, and Ida Rubenstein. De Montesquiou's interest in these women was strictly nonprocreative and therefore typical of the diminished virility understood as characteristic of the invert. This is made quite evident in a story recounted by Painter in which de Montesquiou went to bed, for the first and only time, with the legendary French actress

Sarah Bernhardt, only to suffer thereafter a week of uncontrollable vomiting (129).

As is clear in the preceding anecdote, de Montesquiou's interest in women like the comtesse Castiglione was far more aesthetic than it was sexual, and it was just such an obsession with fashion and costume, Matlock claims, that was defined as symptomatic of homosexuality, criminality, and degeneration in France from 1880 to 1935. She argues that the practices of clothing fetishists played a decisive role in the commonly understood differences between "normal" procreative heterosexuality, and debased, fetishistic perversion. "The clothes obsessions of male fetishists" she holds, "emerged as intimately related to the masquerades psychiatrists attributed to women" (35). According to this formulation, the elaborate nature of women's attire was the literal cause of fetishistic behavior in men: "the way women dressed was lending perverse manners to men" (35). Ultimately, the concern for the French medical and psychiatric communities was that the degenerate fascinations of clothing obsession led the male subject further away from the flesh and the natural desire to procreate and towards a perverse aesthetic fetishism and a desire to share vicariously in "commodified femininity" (57). Much of this theorizing was of course aimed at men who either cross-dressed or collected women's clothing, though undoubtedly Montesquiou's avowedly nonsexual fascination with collecting images of particular women would have been categorized under the same pathological rubric of costume obsession. The same kind of clothing fetishism seen in Boldini's paintings, however, allowed the collector to pursue his interests in fashion and costume under the guise of traditional art patronage.

MASQUERADE, COSTUME OBSESSION, AND THE DOUBLE LIFE OF THE COLLECTOR

The difficulties in precisely reconstructing Maurice de Rothschild's collection are many. The works of art at his Swiss chateau Prégny, either inherited or bought by Maurice, have never been published, but those that were in his four French properties—two houses in Paris, the château de Boulogne, and a little villa la Clairère at Gap in the Hautes-Alpes—were confiscated by the Germans during World War II and restituted in 1946. This list is the clearest evidence for Maurice's personal, as opposed to inherited, taste. This document includes items that were returned to him after the war. It mentions over 200 paintings, watercolors, and drawings, being the bulk of his share of his father's collection, some works from Adolphe and Julie, but also a large number of modern and contemporary works that had been purchased by Maurice, presumably from 1907, when he first became financially independent, until the outbreak of World War II.

A document known as the *Repetoire des Biens Spoliés* lists 116 objects confiscated by the Nazis and returned to Maurice after World War II. Maurice de Rothschild's collection in this list gives the name of the artist—though often only the last name—a title, sometimes dimensions, and frequently a note of a signature. This list includes a large number of works by Boldini, in a variety of media. Of these, only eleven works are in oil, and all of these are portraits or figure studies. Of these eleven, only two can tentatively be identified amongst the fifteen works sold from Maurice de Rothschild's collection in 1995; these are *Portrait of Madame Lideck* [*sic*] and *A lady seated on a canapé*. There were forty-eight other works by Boldini in watercolor, thirty-three of which were studies for ladies heads, wearing hats or feathers, in revealing dresses, or at the theater. His entire collection of works by Boldini, including those works not seized by the Germans and therefore presumably in Switzerland, must have numbered over seventy in total, a tally that far exceeds any other artist represented in his collection. As Boldini died in 1931 and seems to have abandoned painting on any serious scale by the early 1920s, and since Maurice was in no financial position to spend comparatively large sums of money on art before 1907, it can safely be assumed that he acquired the bulk of the collection between those dates.

The *Belle Époque* and Boldini's career reached a simultaneous apogee in the middle years of the 1890s and flourished until 1914. Boldini was, at this point, so established as a portraitist that his sitters would often arrive at his studio in dresses specifically designed by *couturiers* such as Worth, Drécoll, and Doucet to provide appropriate stimulus for the artist's brush. Montesquiou's desire to find women he could "admire, refine, and display as living works of art" assumed literal resonance in the context of Boldini's portraits where his subject's appearance was specifically designed to be easily translatable into a work of art (Munhall 41). Boldini's technique, with its primary emphasis on surface, effectively mimics the reduction of female character to a function of public image, a process described by Tamar Garb in *Bodies of Modernity: Figure and Flesh in Fin-de-Siècle France*. Boldini's canvases were, therefore, both works of art and spaces for the display of contemporary fashion. It is this reductive commodity fetishism that made Boldini's images so appealing to the dandy, invert, or Decadent who desired only the aesthetic effects of the female costume and the generic subjectivity afforded these glamorous women. Though, according to Stephen Gundle, it was Boldini's "lecherous, heterosexual lasciviousness" that caused him to paint women the way he did, the content of his portraits also appealed to the "barely concealed misogyny" of the Decadent fetishist, who was content to view the Parisienne not as a sexual commodity but as the embodiment of an anonymous type: an aesthetic commodity (282).

Maurice purchased at least eleven major full-length portraits of women by Boldini, all executed during the artist's prime, and all of which display the emphasis on glamour and costume that fascinated Decadents like Montesquiou but inflamed the French psychiatric commentators of the late nineteenth and early twentieth centuries. Though it is impossible to recreate their installation precisely, one can easily imagine that these brassy, vibrant, almost life-size portraits rendered in Boldini's frenetic style would be a commanding, flamboyant presence in any space. We do know, however, that Prégny was at least one setting for Maurice's collection of Boldini's from a significant contemporary source, significant in that it was the diary of a bisexual multimillionaire socialite and politician named Sir Henry "Chips" Channon. American in origin, married to a Guinness heiress, and an M.P. in the Conservative interest, "Chips" famously recreated the silver and porcelain rococo salon at the Amalienburg Palace in Munich as his dining room in his house in Belgrave Square, London, and kept a spasmodic diary from 1928 until his death in 1958 with inordinate attention given to the jewels and dresses of his royal, noble, and wealthy plebeian circle of friends. In 1938, at the invitation of Prime Minister Neville Chamberlain, "Chips" led a British delegation to a League of Nations meeting in Geneva. On 15 September 1938, the diary records: "This evening I dined with Maurice de Rothschild, a dinner of 17, in his Rich house, full of amazing Boldinis and medium Tiepolos. Dinner was indifferent but the wines staggering." This appears to be the only evidence of the location of the Boldini collection during Maurice's lifetime. The nature of this environment is of obvious and vast importance in the context of this chapter. Pregny was Maurice's space, far from the watchful eye of his critical, conservative family. If, as this chapter suggests, Maurice's fascination with Boldini's portraits of women reflects his investment in Decadent culture, then we must conclude that installed at Maurice's Swiss chateau, the dazzlingly objecthood of these paintings helped activate a space in which he was able to realize and perform his identity as a part of that group.

While Montesquiou was famously invested in particular figures and pursued multiple images of the same woman, Maurice, conversely, was evidently more interested in collecting notable society women, draped in the most elaborate of costumes and reduced to a consumable image by an artist whose use of paint, treatment of surface, and relative lack of attention to facial specificity was itself a metonym for woman-as-decoration. Maurice's homes, in turn, became exhibition spaces for these painted ladies. Two particular examples from Maurice's collection will illustrate this point. *Rita de Acosta Lydig,* 1911 (Figure 4.4). was purchased by the sitter in 1911, bought by Wildenstein and Co., and then sold to Maurice de Rothschild in 1931. Known as "the fabulous Mrs. Lydig," Boldini depicts her seated in a serpentine, mannerist pose, her skin the color of gray porcelain and her face like a painted mask (Christie's 27). Lydig was celebrated for her material extravagances, particularly her clothes and shoes. She personally financed Callot Seours, Paris *couturiers* who specialized in dresses made from antique fabric and lace. Lydig frequently commissioned extravagant garments from these designers, such as a dressing gown made of one seamless piece of eleventh-century lace. Similarly, she had her shoes designed exclusively by Ny Yanturni, a curator at the musée Cluny who made footwear for only a few select clients. Lydig, who owned in excess of 300, typically had her day shoes fashioned from eleventh- and twelfth-century velvet and her night-ware made from gold tissue or brocade and lace. Boldini's portrait of her is less a depiction of the woman than it is an opportunity for the artist's paint to play with and mimic the legendary finery of her lacy garments. The dual commodities of Boldini's paint and Lydig's costume work symbiotically in this image to produce the perfect picture of material fetishism, in which the subjectivity of the person vanishes and is replaced by a seamless vision of commodifed, public persona. It is additionally significant to note that Lydig floats against a shadowy, nebulous space that works against an understanding of her as purposeful subject, with personal agency, set in a particular context. Rather, the "no-space" of the painting allows the viewer, or more saliently, the collector, to incorporate Lydig into the context in which the picture is beheld. In other words, Boldini's inattention to the space of the picture plane allows the space of installation to function as Lydig's most immediate context—her space, then, belongs to the viewer.

Perhaps the crowning glory of Maurice de Rothschild's collection of painted ladies is *Marchesa Louisa Casati, with a greyhound,* 1908 (Figure 4.5). This painting was sold directly by the artist to Maurice, probably at the time of execution, though no evidence exists to suggest that Maurice commissioned the work. No other figure, with the possible exception of Sarah Bernhardt, so typifies the richly embroidered manner of female self-presentation prevalent in *Belle Époque*. Like Lydig, who was renowned for her clothing and shoes, Casati was revered for a multitude of material eccentricities. Revealingly, she was amongst the select ranks of women that Montesquiou singled out for particular reverence. Upon seeing Boldini's portrait of Casati the comte was moved to compose the following verse:

> *Madame Casati devant elle a sa grace*
> *Son mystère, ses chiens, son énorme chapeau*
> *Et son bouquet de fleurs qu'un seul coup d'oeil embrasse*
> *Lorsque le tempps est clair et que le jour est beau*[1] (Christie's 36).

Casati's trademark accoutrements included the pieces of black velvet she used to line her eye and a seven-meter pearl necklace she wore constantly. Taking her lead from the "divine Sarah" Bernhardt, Casati went to great lengths to cultivate and promote her extravagant appearance and amassed outlandish collections to match, including a menagerie of exotic animals that roamed freely around her home in Venice. However, she was most renowned for her eccentric costumes, the extent of which were described by the Polish sculptor Catherine Barjansky in 1913:

Figure 4.4 Giovanni Boldini, *Portrait of Rita de Acosta Lydig*, 1911, oil on canvas, (71" x 43 ¼").

That evening she wore the long Persian trousers of heavy gold brocade, fastened tightly around her slim ankles and held by diamond bangles of fine workmanship. Her feet were encased in gold sandals with high diamond heals . . . An immensely large black pearl on one hand, an equally large one on the other. . . . She smoked cigarettes out of a black mouthpiece studded with diamonds (Christie's 39).

Women like Casati and Lydig were assuredly fetishists themselves and Boldini, cognizant of the public fascination with this notion (particularly among the Decadents), developed a uniquely synthetic treatment of these women and their accoutrements that all but erased the particularity of the person, in favor of a method that reproduced the public fantasy of the eccentric, bourgeois woman as carrier of aesthetic wonder. His unerring attention to the details of surface produced fetishistic images in which the particularity of the female subject was secondary to the celebration of her mythical public image established on the grounds of her aesthetic preferences. The glitz of Boldini's paint harmonizes perfectly with the glitter of lavish costume to produce an image, the content and form of which are mutually reinforcing and thus easily enlisted by the collector for display as a fetish object. In Maurice's case, his accumulation of these painted fetish objects allowed him to fashion an environment at a geographic and conceptual remove from social codes that governed his life as a Rothschild. Boldini's paintings, then, were not simply decor. Rather, their richly embroidered surfaces contributed to a carefully crafted private stage against which Maurice could be nothing short of another person.

CONCLUSION

As Russell Belk and Melanie Wallendorf observe, "the worldly images of the collection are used to mediate images from everyday life with those that exist in the mythic realm. Thus, a collection can tangibilize the individuation process of constructing an identity through personal myth" (246). Baron Maurice de Rothschild's collection of Boldini paintings offers two views of his double life: as a member of the Rothschild family on one hand, and as a collector invested in the images of the *Belle Époque* on the other. First, and most obviously, Maurice's rejection of the rules of inherited taste allowed him to pursue interests outside the Rothschild paradigm. Rather than becoming simply another indiscernible layer of a homogenous Rothschild collection, the additions he made to the collections he inherited mark Maurice's collection as distinctly his own. Second, and most importantly for the purposes of this chapter, as we have seen, the iconography of his Boldini paintings make explicit reference to the preoccupations of *Belle Époque* Decadent culture in Paris and to Maurice's involvement in this world. Boldini's *à la mode* female portraits were quite obviously spaces of fashion in and of themselves, but in

Figure 4.5 Giovanni Boldini, *Portrait of the Marchesa Luisa Casati, with a Greyhound*, 1908, oil on canvas, (99 ¾" x 55 ¼").

the context of Maurice's collection, the appeal of clothing and costume is revealed as a far more complex social phenomenon that has been acknowledged to date. Maurice's patronage of Boldini considered in the context of the discourse of sexual deviance, dandyism, and Decadence in Paris at the turn-of-the-century forces us to extend our discussion beyond the implications of his taste alone, and to reevaluate the emphasis on fashion and costume in Boldini's works. We must consider Boldini's paintings of women not simply as expressions of traditional misogyny and celebrations of heteronormative sexuality, but also as examples of art that appealed to the equally (but differently) misogynistic tastes of a generation of dandies epitomized by Robert de Montesquiou, who fetishized and commodified the image of women, not as sexual objects, but as forms of aesthetic entertainment displayed and consumed by men like Maurice and Montesquiou. Installed at Pregny, these paintings were instrumental in constructing a social space in which Maurice could realize and indulge the "decadent" tastes and behaviors disallowed by his conservative family. If "a collection can tangibilize the individuation process of constructing an identity through personal myth," then Maurice de Rothschild's patronage of Boldini should cause us to rethink the role played by images like Boldini's in the formation of gender and sexual identity in the Decadent culture of the *Belle Époque*.

ACKNOWLEDGEMENT

I am extremely grateful to Dr. Michael Hall for the research he generously contributed to the present essay, and to Jennifer Wulffson for her consistent support of an interest in this project, beginning at its inception in 2004.

NOTES

1. Translation mine: In front is Madame Casati with her grace/ her mystery, her dogs, her huge hat/ and her bouquet of flowers, all of which can be seen with a glance/ as long as the weather is clear, and it's a fine day.

WORKS CITED

Belk, Russell W. and Melanie Wallendorf. "Of Mice and Men: Gender and Identity in Collecting." In *Interpreting Objects and Collections,* edited by S. M. Pearce. London: Routledge, 1994: 240-53.

Christie's. *Fifteen Paintings by Giovanni Boldini Collected by theLlate Maurice de Rothschild.* Christie's New York (1 November 2006).

Garb, Tamar. *Bodies of Modernity: Figure and Flesh in Fin-de-Siècle France.* London: Thames and Hudson, 1998.

Gundle, Stephen. "Mapping the Origins of Glamour: Giovanni Boldini, Paris and the Belle Époque." *Journal of European Studies* 29, 115 (September 1999): 269–95.

Lottman, Herbert R. *Return of the Rothschilds: The Great Banking Dynasty Through Two Turbulent Centuries.* London: I. B. Tauris, 1995.

Matlock, Jann. "Masquerading Women, Pathologized Men: Cross-Dressing, Fetishism, and the Theory of Perversion, 1882–1935." In *Fetishism as Cultural Discourse,* edited by Emily Apter and William Pietz. Ithaca, New York: Cornell University Press, 1993: 31–61.

McPhearson, Heather. *Fin-de- Siècle Faces: Portraiture in the Age of Proust.* Birmingham: University of Alabama, 1988.

Munhall, Edward. *Whistler and Montesquiou: The Butterfly and the Bat.* New York: The Frick Collection, Flammarion, 1995.

Nye, J. A. "Michel Foucault's Sexuality and the History of Homosexuality in Modern France." In *Homosexuality in ModernFrance,* edited by Emily Apter and William Pietz). New York: Oxford University Press, 1996: 225–41.

Painter, George D. *Marcel Proust: A Biography.* New York: Random House, 1978.

Proust, Marcel. *Marcel Proust: On Art and Literature, 1896–1919.* New York: Random House, 1963.

———. *In Search of Lost Time. Volume VI, Time Regained and a Guide to Proust.* New York: Random House, 1993.

Part II
Cultures of Display

5 Fashion's Chameleons
Camouflage, "Conspicuousness," and Gendered Display During World War I

Alison Matthews David

> Other creatures grow their clothing on their individual bodies; scales, or
> bristles, fur or feathers—they have but one suit, self-replenished. They
> may clean it perhaps, but cannot change it—save . . . the chameleon.
>
> The human animal shows in its clothing as conspicuously as in
> many other ways, the peculiar power of extra-physical expression.
>
> —Charlotte Perkins Gilman, *The Dress of Women* (1915)

In his 1920 book, *Strategic Camouflage*, British artist Solomon J. Solomon
asked whether camouflage was unchivalrous. He concluded that it was not
because modern warfare demanded new tactics, including the use of camouflage (50–51). While traditionalists thought that using disguise and concealment in war was far from sporting, technology had changed the rules of
battle. Men no longer fought hand to hand, but were bombarded from above
by airplanes, gassed by invisible but deadly chemicals, or hit by shells shot
from miles away. Because their enemies were often unseen, armies sought
ways in which to gain the same mantle of invisibility as their opponents.

The result was the advent of camouflage, a word derived from a French
theatrical slang term meaning disguise or makeup. The French were the first
to form special regiments of *camoufleurs* during World War I, but other
countries soon followed. These men were portrait painters, set designers,
and landscape artists conscripted to experiment with camouflage on the
battlefront. Amongst their inventions were *papier maché* observation trees,
netting to conceal gun emplacements, and screens to hide roads from aerial
photographers. Much of their work came in for considerable ridicule from
the press and public because it was often makeshift. The gender dynamics
of camouflage also influenced its mixed public reception. Even Solomon,
who was one of the first *camoufleurs*, called it a "Cinderella among the
military arts," clearly feminizing the role camouflage played in wartime.

While the majority of camouflage developed in World War I was designed
to hide large-scale landscape features and troop movements, this chapter
focuses on the earliest attempts at "personal" camouflage designed to conceal individual male bodies. While "camo" prints now abound on textiles

both military and civilian, early camouflage consisted in trimming head-gear with natural material and wearing hand-painted sniper suits or robes. The textile technology necessary to produce what is now known as "disruptive pattern material" did not yet exist.[1] I focus on women's millinery and men's headgear as a case study for larger issues of gender difference both on the home front and in the trenches. By reexamining discourses surrounding fashion and embodiment in both social and physical spaces, I hope to come to a fuller understanding of the complex interrelationship between ideas of visibility and gender in dress in the years leading up to and during World War I, a time when traditional gender roles were being contested in both sartorial and political terms.

The term camouflage provides a strong metaphor for two distinct but often overlapping concepts. These I term "social" and "physical" camouflage. Social camouflage is the process of using clothing in order to blend seamlessly into the social landscape, to put it simply, to wear the right clothing at the right time and in the right place. In the nineteenth and early twentieth centuries, strict clothing etiquette governed the behavior of members of the middle and upper classes, who were expected to appear in appropriate dress and accessories according to the time of day and social occasion. As Brooks Picken attested:

> You must realize that if you are going out to business you should not dress as you would if you were going to a church gathering; nor should you, if you are going to an elaborate dinner party, wear a shirtwaist and skirt, as you may be privileged to do at a simple home dinner with your own family or with intimate friends (9–10).

This etiquette was further complicated by the increasing number of young women "going out to business" who needed office-appropriate attire for their jobs. To enable women to dress for different occasions, Picken devoted ten pages to tables on "correct dress for business, outing and the home in spring, summer, and autumn/winter," as well as dress for special functions such as an informal dinner at a restaurant or hotel, or a formal outing to the theater, a concert, or a lecture (49–81). To flout strict social conventions regarding dress made a person instantly conspicuous or easily visible, an effect that might or might not be desired. Though men needed to engage in rituals of social camouflage as well, the more limited style options at their disposal made it much easier for them to assemble an appropriate wardrobe than their female counterparts.

For both men and women, social and physical landscapes were inextricable: fashionable people had to negotiate the demands of the spaces and places in which they played out their lives. These settings might include such varied terrain as country estates, opera houses, and city streets, which demanded hunting gear, evening wear, and street wear, respectively. Men and women used fashion to negotiate their social topography, but they were subject to different sartorial rules, particularly in terms of their literal visibility. This is where physical camouflage enters the picture. Physical camouflage refers to elements of clothing which physically affect a viewer's perception of the human body in its environment and might include the color, silhouette, cut, and construction of garments. By environment, I mean the literal spaces which that clothed body inhabits. I explore the gender dynamics of both social and physical camouflage through the idea of "conspicuousness" or visibility, a concept which recurs in period discussions of fashion, naturalism, and military strategy.

Men were generally less "conspicuous" in their dress than women. In the Edwardian era, middle- and upper-class men dressed in tailored clothing in a muted color palette. The result was a definite silhouette with crisp, clean lines, unbroken by ornament or decoration. The practicality of their dress allowed them to move more or less comfortably in the public and private spaces of their habitual physical landscapes. They were even permitted a greater freedom to expose their bodies if the context demanded it. The feminist author, sociologist and dress reformer Charlotte Perkins Gilman published a series of articles in 1915 entitled *The Dress of Women,* which criticized gender inequalities surrounding the etiquette of dress and modesty in public spaces:

> A man may run in our streets, or row, visibly, on our rivers, in a costume—a lack of costume—which for women would be called grossly immodest. He may bathe, publicly, and in company with women, so nearly naked as to shock even himself, sometimes; while the women beside him are covered far more fully than in evening dress (11).

By contrast, women were expected to both dress modestly and be visually appealing, but only if they did not make a spectacle of themselves. By the end of World War I, women were still being admonished to negotiate the contradictory imperatives of alluring men while remaining inconspicuous in a manual on how to dress "distinctively." As Mary Brooks Picken writes in *Secrets of Distinctive Dress* (1918): "A really well-dressed woman is never conspicuous nor uncomfortable no matter where she may be" (4). But, she reminds women that "[t]o be attractive is to be pleasing in face and figure, and you owe it to your self to emphasize to the utmost every good point you possess, be it big or little" (13). For women, social camouflage did equate with invisibility. In fact, women were expected not only to bear the burden of displaying their husbands' wealth, but also to vie for prestige in social settings through their appearance, dress, and grooming. In his famous *Theory of the Leisure Class* (1899), Thorstein Veblen expounded at length on how the adornment of both the female person and her environment was an expression of women's inferior economic power and her social status as a man's chattel.

The late nineteenth-century Aesthetic Movement had carried this injunction to beautify women's dress and domestic spaces to an extreme. Mrs. Haweis compared the need for a woman to consider her own complexion in choosing a "background" to the ways in which animals cleverly harmonized with their homes:

> There can be no doubt that people look different in different rooms. A pale person in a pale room is obliterated, whereas in a deep or richly coloured room, the paleness might become enhanced and beautified. A person of high colour in a room the colours of which do not properly contrast with her own, is lost and wasted, while with different surroundings her colour may be improved and softened. . . . Brown creatures live in rosy homes, white creatures cull hues from the rainbow, and snooze in delicate beds of mother-of-pearl (205–06).

Women were reminded to be constantly aware not only of what kind of picture their own dress made but how it looked against a series of shifting backgrounds, taking into account home décor and varying lighting conditions. If a lady succeeded in harmonizing with her surroundings both physically and socially, she had successfully managed her sartorial presentation. This aesthetic advice found echoes in later writings on animal mimicry, notably the artist and naturalist Abbott Thayer's 1909 book *Concealing-coloration in the Animal Kingdom,* which was used as a military camouflage manual during World War I.[2] Thayer constantly adopted clothing metaphors when referring to the ways in which animals used "obliterative" patterns to blend into their surroundings. The overall aim of the book was to "clear the way to a more general understanding and more intelligent study of the relations between animals' costumes and their environments" by looking at how animals used color and pattern to escape observation (10).

In the animal kingdom, the male animal was often more brightly colored and conspicuous than his female counterpart; the difference in plumage between the resplendent peacock and his drab peahen was a perfect example. A 1909 *Vogue* cover went so far as to suggest that women were the real peacocks of the human realm by illustrating a peacock and a peacock-gowned woman with identical silhouettes and color schemes gazing at one another across a sundial (18 March 1909). As Gilman remarks of her female contemporaries: "Our position is analogous to that is a pea-hen who has somehow secured the gorgeous tail-feathers of her mate, and is strutting about to attract him—a thing any pea-hen would be ashamed to do" (68). Amongst social Darwinists like Veblen and Gilman studying the human realm, physical adornment was read as the sign of a lower degree of evolution. This belief was very entrenched during the late nineteenth and early twentieth centuries. According to Gilman: "This savagery, this use of the body itself as medium of decoration, is show in that still enduring habit of women, once belonging to the ancient Briton, the naked redman, or African—painting the skin" (81). An 1897 caricature ironically entitled "Civilisation!" makes a visual equivalence between the plumed, bead-encrusted, fur-clad, and floral-patterned dress of a tribal chief and a fashionable woman (Gordon 268). Clear visual contrasts in sartorial display led male commentators and feminist writers alike to brand women's lack of modernity in dress, as evidenced by their love of adornment, as regressive. In *Le vrai et le faux chic* (1914), the French caricaturist Sem judged that "progressive" men's dress echoed the bold, streamlined lines of the modern automobile, while "backwards" women still arrayed themselves in irrationally elaborate costumes: "It is singular that women hunt out such excessively complicated ornaments, at the exact moment when men's suits tend towards the most absolute clarity" (n.p.).[3]

SILHOUETTE AND GENDER

As the 1909 *Vogue* cover suggests, silhouette or "line" was another important way of making rapid visual gender distinctions. Before the war, one's silhouette clearly marked one's gender. Two plates from the Parisian luxury publication the *Journal des Dames et des Modes* clearly illustrate the contrast between fashionable European men's and women's fashions on the eve of World War I (Figure 5.1). Both are socially camouflaged, in that the woman on the left wears an appropriate dress for a garden-party while the man standing outdoors is dressed for travel.

Figure 5.1 "Garden Party Dress in White Muslin and Orange Liberty" and "Overcoat for Travel by Mr. Marcel Lus," *Journal des Dames et Des Modes,* 1914. Courtesy of the Royal Ontario Museum Library, Canada.

Though a woman might wear tailored clothing for walking or sport, her dress was markedly different from that of a man of the same class. As the woman in this fashion plate demonstrates, feminine dress often consisted of soft, colorful fabrics such as gauzy silk chiffons and tulles. Lace in particular was very popular at this period. She might ornament her dress with jewelry, beading, sequins, feathers, and flowers, adding complexity to her toilette. As in the garden party dress of flowing white muslin, the resulting silhouette stresses transparency and layering. This woman's outline shifted and changed with the breeze. In addition, women changed the shapes of their dresses and bodies using corsets and foundation garments to keep up with constant changes in women's fashions. As Brooks Picken commented, fashion consisted of changing silhouettes and "new lines" (5). Women's bodies and dresses marked them as shape-shifters compared to their stolid and seemingly solid male counterparts.

GENDER IN THE TRENCHES

The gender dynamics of masculine dress carried over to military uniforms in the early twentieth century. In the eighteenth and nineteenth centuries, ornamental, even gaudy uniforms in all of the hues of the rainbow had been the norm (David 2003). Colonial warfare had taught European armies to tone down the color schemes of their uniforms. The red-coated peacock of the British armies, for example, had doffed his plumage to become a drab khaki-clad "mudlark" (Newark 45). The animal metaphor was no accident, as military strategists used ideas of animal camouflage and books such as Thayer's 1909 *Concealing-coloration in the Animal Kingdom* to help disguise troops. As Gilman wrote in 1915: "Only now are we beginning to wear the plain, inconspicuous khaki, or dull grey, since concealment has been expensively proved to be more profitable than ostentation. Our soldiers are now clothed in a 'protective mimicry' worthy of nature's best efforts" (12).

In earlier periods, the brilliant colors of uniforms had helped armies distinguish friend from foe through thick clouds of gun smoke. The advent of smokeless gunpowder and more accurate weapons made traditional military uniforms, with their sparking gold braid, elaborate plumes, and rainbow hues, into lethal liabilities. British conflicts in India and South Africa led to the widespread adoption of the color khaki, which means "dust" in Urdu, for overseas service in 1896, and by 1902 it had replaced scarlet as the official combat uniform color (Newark 45–46). Germans tested and adopted equally camouflaging uniforms in the neutral "field gray" or *feldgrau*.

With uniforms, governments are able to impose social and sartorial frameworks for interpersonal relations, which would be impossible with mere civilian dress (Craik 5). In principle, if not always in practice, uniforms leave little room for the expression of individuality. In this sense, they are the most extreme form of social camouflage. To be correctly uniformed is to fit perfectly into a set social group—in this case the regiment, battalion, and in a larger sense, the nation for which the soldier fights. Conscripted men had little choice in the matter: their uniforms were issued to them. Uniform etiquette (which occasions called for battle dress? mess dress? undress uniform?) was complex, but the codes were transparent. To wear the wrong uniform at the wrong time or in the wrong place was to incur military discipline. Officers who purchased their own uniforms might enlist their tailors and play a bit more with the rules and regulations to stress their individual style but overall social strictures governing "appropriate" dress were at their clearest for uniformed men. Unlike most civilian women, a soldier could be confident that he was not "conspicuously" dressed in relation to his peers. His social camouflage was perfect.

In terms of physical camouflage, the World War I uniform was better than its predecessors, but when it was tested in actual warfare, unexpected problems presented themselves. Its neutral color palettes were generally appropriate for muddy trench conditions, but its crisp, clean tailored silhouette, the hallmark of masculine dress, proved problematic in the field. Color was an element of disguise, but line and silhouette were even more important in escaping observation, particularly when a body was in movement. Abbott Thayer, who devised a camouflage uniform consisting of a Norfolk hunting jacket with multicolored pieces of fabric pinned to it as a prototype, observed that "khaki-colored uniforms, although they readily blended with sand, were insufficient camouflage. A monochrome shape is too easy to see" (White 295). Even when they wore khaki, officers were targeted by German snipers because their legs, clad in distinctive riding breeches and knee-high boots, were thinner than those of the trousered and ankle-booted soldiers (David 2006: 134). The same items of equestrian-inspired clothing, which would have been ideal social camouflage on the polo or hunting fields, were not effective physical camouflage on the battlefront.

As the targeting of commanding officers suggests, sniper fire was a particularly lethal and demoralizing tactic already perfected by the German army at the beginning of World War I and quickly adopted by the Allied forces, which began to train specialized units of scouts and snipers (Gilbert 50–52). I focus on disguises used by these new fighters, the only combatants who used sophisticated "personal" camouflage during World War I. The sniper used his accurate weapon to pick off his opponents from hiding spots on the ground or in trees. His activities recalled the big-game hunter, and there is considerable evidence that many snipers saw themselves in this role. One of the pioneers of the technique during World War I, Major Hesketh-Pritchard, was a genteel British-born traveler, big-game hunter and cricketer, as well as the author of such classics as "Through the Heart of Patagonia" and "Through Trackless Labrador." He introduced the use of armor-piercing bullets and elephant guns into the army. In his book *Sniping In France,* the officer wrote that "[s]niping in a dangerous sector . . . was really neither more nor less than a very high-class form of big game shooting, in which the quarry shot back" (37). Sniping offered soldiers a chance for individual action, if not true glory. Like the World War I flying ace, the sniper acted alone or with one scout, his activities independent of the massed troops huddling in the trenches. Because he did not have any other protection, his life could depend on the ability of his suit to hide him from enemy observation. He used suits or robes which helped him blend in to the landscape by breaking up his silhouette.

Like a woman, he had to think about the aesthetics of the physical space he occupied and be constantly aware of the picture his body made (or did not make) from different angles of observation. As one manual advised in terms that echo Haweis' exhortation to women to think of the ways in which they were framed by their surroundings: "In occupying any cover, be careful of your background" ("Periscope" 64). It prescribed dress in the following terms: "You must have a veil or mask over your face; cover your head with the same material if you take your cap off. You must also wear gloves; woolen khaki ones are the best . . . Your buttons must be painted, or covered with a khaki-covered material" (63). These injunctions, which amount to sartorial surveillance, echo the often bossy tone of women's advice manuals. Nowhere was this rapprochement between sniper's dress and women's fashions clearer than in the solutions that snipers developed to camouflage their heads.

HATS

One item of dress was crucial in war: headgear. The conditions of trench warfare made soldiers' heads especially vulnerable to bullets and shrapnel flying low over the ground (Disruptive Pattern Materual 150). Like their clothing, men's headgear had a crisp clear outline. Though by the end of the war most armies had issued protective helmets, traditions of civilian dress still persisted. In particular, British officers kept their hats with wide, flat tops. This design was to prove fatal to them because it made them perfect targets for enemy fire (Figure 5.2).

Hesketh-Pritchard observed that the British were easier to see than the Germans:

> . . . not because of khaki . . . but because the tops of the British caps were all of so much larger area than the German. . . . Any flat surface worn on top of the head is certain to catch every bit of light, and a flash of light means movement, and draws the observer's telescope as a magnet draws metal. The ideal army, could I clothe it, would wear a very curious shape of cap, with certainly an UNEVEN outline.

But I do not need to labour this point, You have only to look at the photographs contained in this book to see what a terrible handicap a definite outline is (142).

Many officers exchanged these caps for their slightly less visible soft undress caps when on the front lines, though these too caught the light. A definite outline, a traditionally masculine attribute, proved a deadly handicap in battle. Luckily, innovative soldiers were used to constant change in their regulation headgear. As costume historian James Laver observed, in the nineteenth century there had been "almost as much change in cavalry headgear as in women's hats" (18). In the context of the battleground, the military tactician had to look to these very same hats, if only indirectly, as inspiration for new and "curious" shapes of caps with "uneven" outlines.

Charlotte Perkins Gilman began her chapter on hats by stating that "[i]n no one article of dress is the ultra-feminine psychology more apparent than in the hat" (61). While a woman's choice of hat might not be a matter of life and death, it was an essential part of her social camouflage. No part of a woman's attire sent clearer and more easily visible signals about her taste, wealth, and personality. So important was the hat that Brooks Picken describes it as forming portable frames for the face which

Figure 5.2 "The Fatal Cap" from Major Hesketh-Pritchard, *Sniping in France,* c. 1920.

the wearer could use to create a "desirable background" when she was away from home:

> We talk of clothes making a background for us, of having our dresses made of a color that harmonizes with our individuality, and even of having our coat linings of such a color that when they are thrown back on our chair, they add to the background of the picture. But do we realize fully the value of the right hat—the individual hat, the hat that makes a background for our eyes, our face, our hair? . . . We must expect a great deal from our hats. They must make a frame for the face. . . . If we are not in our homes, then our hats must be intimate enough to make a desirable background (Picken 64).

Edwardian "picture hats," as they were called, were remarkable for their size, exuberance, and wealth of trimmings. Men complained that they could not see over women's heads at the theater and decorative effects often included whole stuffed birds perched on their wearer's heads. Gilman railed against the clear differences in design between men's and women's head coverings:

> In the matter of hats, the scope of masculine expression is not large. A hat he must have, of severe and simple outline. . . . The top-hat has always its clear distinction, the crisp straw in summer, the hard hat with the latest roll brim—there is little to boast of (62).

However, a woman's hat was "not simple and distinct in outline; and, need it be said?—it is not restrained in ornament" (Gilman 62). For Gilman, women's hats were ridiculous and served absolutely no purpose at all. I would argue, however, that snipers profited from lessons learned indirectly from prewar millinery designs. A woman's "garden" hat from about 1910 from the collection of the Royal Ontario Museum is typical of hats of this era (Fig. 5.3). The green hat, covered in artificial leaves, pink roses, and little white flowers, had exactly the principle of the broken outline, naturalistic materials, and potential for blending into the landscape that was to be adopted by the *camoufleurs* when hiding snipers. As the image on the bottom from "Scout-Sniping" suggests, men were expected to trim themselves in grass, leaves, and even flowers when the local landscape demanded it. The caption even notes that man number three on the right by the telephone pole has not succeeded because "the flowers are partially withered, and, being unnatural, do not conform to the freshness and lay-out of the other flowers close at hand" (facing 48). Snipers certainly covered their heads, which were the most visible and vulnerable parts of their bodies. Various devices were invented, from the simple but terrifying cowls that looked much like an executioner's hood, ridiculous straw and hay confections, worn over a regulation uniform.

These hoods disguised and distorted the shape of the human head in the same manner as women's hats of the period. As Charlotte Perkins Gilman said, women's hats seemed to be "[t]he invention of some malicious caricaturist" and noted that "[w]hen a man puts on his wife's 'Easter bonnet,' big hat with flowers and ribbons, or small hat with some outsquirt of stiff or waggling decoration, he looks contemptible or foolish" (63). Yet this unconventional and feminized decoration of the head with straw, leaves, and even flowers saved lives on the battlefield. Public perception of the sniper picked up on the potential ridiculousness of the sniper's disguises. In a popular song entitled *Camouflage, or the Tale of the Sorrowful Sniper,* a Cockney sniper is dressed for battle in a "coiffure" "trimmed" with grass and hay like a ladies' bonnet and "painted" with green makeup:

> So I trimmed myself in straw, with a grass and 'ay couffur
> And I clothed myself in faggots wot a pal 'ad (that a pal had),
> And the sergeant took a brush and some green and sticky slush
> And 'e painted me all over till I couldn't raise a blush
> And I looked just like a vegetable salad (Wilton 1918).

Despite his deadly skill, in popular opinion the suited-up sniper was a not a hero in the conventional sense. Clothed in sniper suits which were often spattered with paint, he looked like a clump of vegetation or a "salad." He cloaked himself in the painted disguises of theatrical set designers and adopted the broken outline typical of women's fashions. This feminization is clear in "Hide and Go-Seek-A-Hun," an article which appeared in American *Vogue* (1918) about the Woman's Reserve Camouflage Corps (1 July: 58+). While the male recruits were set to work "modeling aeroplanes and ammunition wagons and guns to scale and camouflaging them," the female volunteers "specialized on that branch of camouflage which seemed to be particularly a feminine task," in other words designing sniper robes. Although they were artists, sculptors, or professional photographers, as women they "were also more or less familiar with materials and they knew . . . how much tension a dome fastener will stand, and whether it was or wasn't superior to a button or a hook and eye when the time came for getting in and out of one's clothes in a hurry" (86). Another now-lost painting shown at a special exhibition of works by *camoufleur* artists at the Royal Academy of Arts in 1919 was entitled "Dressmaking for Snipers." Had the production of sniper suits been perceived as a masculine occupation, the title would have included the word tailoring rather than dressmaking (Wardle no.141). Women's supposedly innate knowledge of clothing design and appearance was framed as a positive attribute, which made them natural *camoufleurs* and the snipers natural objects of their arts.

Figure 5.3 (a, b) Top: Woman's garden hat, c. 1910, Courtesy of the Royal Ontario Museum Collection and Veronika Gervers Fellowship. Bottom: "Three Men Dressed to Conform to Local Conditions." New recruits unsuccessfully attempting to camouflage themselves by placing flowers in their hats. From *Scout-Sniping* by "Periscope," 1918.

WOMEN IN UNIFORM

The flip side of this feminization of the sniper was the much more generalized masculinization of women's civilian and uniform dress during the war. Women deliberately muted their fashionable dress as a form of both social and physical camouflage. War altered the female wardrobe in important ways. The demands of a more active lifestyle brought the practical masculine tailored suit back into fashion. In a 1917 article in *The Queen,* the author of "The Indispensable Tailor Suit" noted that suits in solid colors including the military-inspired navy blue serge were fashionable and did not draw too much attention to their wearers:

> It would seem that Dame Fashion hath her uses, even in this most practical of times. . . . Just now, however, like the wise dame she undoubtably is, she is not exactly obtruding her presence, the merest whisper of her forthcoming schemes being liable to call down such a chorus of abuse and protest for the more rabid anti-fashion folk, that she is fain to find some more subtle means of imposing her will . . . (186).

Because war work forced women to live in new social and physical environments, they had to adapt their clothing to unfamiliar activities and spaces. Many women did adopt uniform dress for their war duties, and these were not always viewed with approval. In many ways, seeing a woman in masculine tailored khaki was as troubling and potentially ridiculous as seeing a sniper disguised in feminized robes and headgear. The uniformed woman's physical camouflage was effective—she was theoretically wearing a neutral color cut into a practical silhouette. Color, however, always has symbolic properties and khaki was "sacred to those for whom it forms a shroud . . . it is the garb of the fighting man who goes out to war for England, home and his women-kind; and it should not be donned lightly" (Grayzel 194). When worn by women, the same color which made men into socially accepted and celebrated fighters became a source of criticism. Some perceived that women wearing khaki were "rendering it ridiculous by adopting it for themselves and playing at soldiers" (Grayzel 193). Part of the problem, I argue, was not the masculine color itself, but the background it was worn against, namely the home front or behind the lines rather than the actual battlefields of Europe.[4] The largely negative response reserved for women in khaki proves that the gendering of space and place are just as crucial to the public reception of dress as cut, design, and color. Despite these criticisms, many women felt that their willing and patriotic participation in the war entitled them to equal rights and suffrage. While more attention has been focused on dress during World War II by scholars including Guenther and Veillon than during World War I, both large-scale conflicts were clearly pivotal in redefining social and sartorial rules for women.

Though nowhere near as severe as the rationing which occurred during World War II, reliance on dyes which had been manufactured in Germany and restrictions on wool consumption reduced the number of colors and fabrics available to consumers (Field 77). Field explores how striped dress became popular because less dye was required to manufacture textiles with alternating stripes of white and color. Many garments in the collection of the Royal Ontario from the period are constructed or lined with black and white or mauve and white striped fabrics. The optical illusions created by these striped and patterned garments have more in common with marine camouflage called dazzle painting, which attempted not to disguise but to distract enemy submarines from their true targets (Disruptive Pattern Material 164–1). In the postwar period, these changes were referred to as camouflage in dress design. This concept of camouflage, which was more in keeping with the reality that women in public were never truly invisible, entered the arsenal of women's techniques of bodily display. An image from 1922 entitled *Camouflage in Dress Design* illustrates this principle (Figure 5.4). Women had been encouraged to think about line and pattern in dress design before the war, but it was not called camouflage. The military sense of the term was coined during the conflict. In essence, this form of camouflage, which is physical, encourages a large woman to use vertical stripes to make her look thinner and a thin woman to use horizontal stripes to make her look broader. According to the caption: "Vertical parallelism offsets heaviness and creates illusion of greater length." In "a" the figure ostensibly looks broader because of the vertical stripes and floral pattern of the dress, in "b" she has overdone the use of stripes, but in "c" at the bottom of the image she has created a perfect visual harmony by the use of one broad tabard-like band of fabric flanked by small stripes on either side.

This form of optical illusion has more in common with the dazzle camouflage mentioned earlier, but the concept of using pattern in dress to deceive the viewer is merely an extension of earlier gender dynamics in dress which typecast women as shape-shifters and chameleons. What was new was the simplification of the actual cut and construction of dresses, which reached its apogee in the knee-length flapper dress of the 1920s. Because there was a shift from corseted dress which imposed an external structure, waist shape, and silhouette on the body to shorter and simpler dress structures and shapes, women were now expected to use pattern and color to create an internal structure and logic for their clothing. Dress now had to serve the role of both foreground and background. A 1924 advice book reads like a military camouflage manual, advising its plump or thin readers to use refracted light and color to create convincing illusions of an ideal size: "Softly curved and attractively plump becomes the thin person who calls to her aid the magic of certain colors. She realizes the value of reflected, broken, and refracted lights in rounding out her silhouette" (Story 99).

Elite fashion imagery also reflected this shift towards the camouflaged female body as an internally coherent visual structure. In a 1921 fashion

Figure 5.4 "Camouflage in Dress Design" from Louis Weinberg, *Color in Everyday Life*, 1922.

plate from the luxury publication *La Gazette du Bon Ton*, the illustrator Charles Martin makes a wry reference to military techniques (Figure 5.5). A woman who occupies most of the picture plane stands with her back to us. Her form is concealed in a woolly leaf and olive green "sports coat" imagined by the famous designer Paul Poiret. A large, floppy-brimmed hat trimmed with shells completely obscures her face, and we catch only glimpses of her ankles and the twig-like fingers emerging from her right sleeve. To all appearances she is a well-camouflaged, couture-clad tree. She

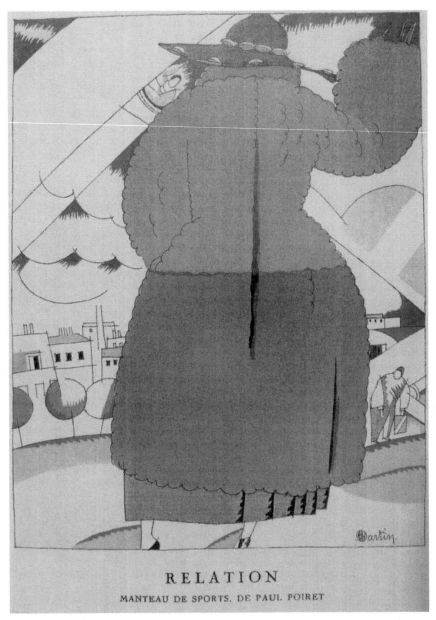

RELATION

MANTEAU DE SPORTS, DE PAUL POIRET

Figure 5.5 Charles Martin, "Relation: Sports Coat by Paul Poiret," *Gazette du Bon Ton,* no.1, Plate 6, 1921.

completely embodies camouflage and nature. Yet because of her sex, even her literally camouflaged body is designed to be highly visible. Scrutinized from all angles by the intersecting gazes of the viewer and two figures in the background, she is even under aerial surveillance. A plane flies overhead, a tricolor emblazoned on its tail. The pilot waves at the "tree" and she waves back at him. On the ground, an earthbound traffic controller gazes not up at his charge but at the fashionable spectator as well.

The subject is perfectly socially camouflaged: she wears an appropriate outfit for the activity she is engaged in—a sports coat for elite sporting activities. Yet in terms of her physical camouflage, this Daphne is literally grounded. Despite the uneven division of gender roles between active pilot and passive spectator, this woman of fashion has adopted several lessons from male dress—her felt hat, which resembles nothing so much as a scout's hat in silhouette, is eminently practical, unornamented, and crisp in silhouette. Gilman might have been reassured to read in a 1916 report on the state of the women's dressmaking and millinery industries that sartorial habits in terms of headgear were in fact changing in response to women's increased presence in the workforce. The author wrote that the mannish hat was increasingly worn for sports or ordinary street wear and that "[w]orking women of all classes are more frequently calling for the plain hat which can withstand each day's weather and still retain its good lines for a considerable period" (Bryner 48).

In his chapter on "Dress as an Expression of the Pecuniary Culture," Veblen suggested that the dress of the leisure classes at the end of the nineteenth century had to follow three cardinal rules: it must look costly, show by its design and ornamentation that the wearer was not engaged in productive labor, and be fashionable and up-to-date (104). The Great War did not succeed in completely overturning class and gender dynamics which were entrenched in prewar society, but it did help to transform the culture of women's dress. The twenties saw Chanel's "poverty de luxe" and stretchy jersey fabrics become the height of fashion; war work had proven that women could engage in productive labor and simplified cuts and styles made it more practical for women to keep abreast of fashion changes by making their dresses at home. Streamlined and more "masculine" dress, which was more practical than the prewar ankle-length skirt and starched white shirtwaist, had become acceptable social and physical camouflage for the increasing ranks of working women who, like the Reserve Camouflage Corps featured in *Vogue,* began to think of their roles in a broadened public sphere as an intrinsic part of their social and sartorial identities. As the author remarked: "Woman's place is in the home—that's so. But where is home, anyway? Mightn't it be in a foreign land, a trench or a hospital?" (87).

ACKNOWLEDGMENTS

I am grateful to the Gervers Research Fellowship in Textile and Costume History, which funded an archival research trip based on this project to study the collections of the Royal Ontario Museum, Canada, in 2004. At the ROM, Dr. Alexandra Palmer, Anu Liivandi, Karla Livingstone, Julia

Matthews, and Arthur Smith gave me invaluable help during the research process. In addition, I would like to thank Dylan Reid, Danielle Suppa, Caroline Evans, Barbara Burman, and Dr. Lesley Miller for their assistance and support.

NOTES

1. The first printed camouflage textile or *telo mimetico* was developed for tents and uniforms in Italy in 1929 (DPM 184).
2. In the preface to the postwar 1918 edition of Thayer's book, his son wrote: "Is this a 'war-book'? Yes and no. It was written eleven years or more ago, and first published in 1909; and it treats of birds and beasts and insects, not of ships and armies. Yet it has been one of the main foundations of a very important feature of present-day warfare, the French nickname for which is on everybody's lips today. 'Camouflage' has been largely built upon it."
3. *Il est singulier que les femmes recherchent des parures d'une complication aussi excessive, au moment précis ou le costume masculine tend vers une plus absolue nettete.*
4. Women did, of course, work as nurses and occasionally as combatants and many did lose their lives in the conflict, but nurses' uniforms were based on the modest dress of nuns and did not attract the same kind of negative attention as the khaki dress devised for volunteer corps.

WORKS CITED

Brooks Picken, Mary. *The Secrets of Distinctive Dress*. Scranton, PA: The Women's Institute of Domestic Sciences, 1918.

Bryner, Edna. *Dressmaking and Millinery*. Cleveland, OH: Survey Committee of the Cleveland Foundation, 1916.

Craik, Jennifer. *Uniforms Exposed: From Conformity to Transgression*. Oxford: Berg, 2005.

David, Alison Matthews. "Decorated Men: Fashioning the French Soldier, 1852–1914." *Fashion Theory* 7.1 (March 2003): 3–38.

DPM Disruptive Pattern Material: An Encyclopaedia of Camouflage: Nature, Military, Culture (Vol.1). London: DPM, 2004.

Field, Jacqueline. "Dyes, Chemistry and Clothing: The Influence of World War I on Fabrics, Fashions and Silk." *Dress* 28 (2001): 77–91.

Gilbert, Adrian. *Sniper: One on One, the World of Combat Sniping*. London: Sigwick & Jackson: 1994.

Gordon, Rae Beth. "Fashion and the White Savage in the Parisian Music Hall." *Fashion Theory* 8.3 (September 2004): 267–300.

Grayzel, Susan. *Women's Identities at War: Gender, Motherhood, and Politics in Britain and France during the First World War*. Chapel Hill: University of North Carolina Press, 1999.

Guenther, Irene. *Nazi Chic?: Fashioning Women in the third Reich*. Oxford and New York: Berg, 2004.

Haweis, Eliza. *The Art of Beauty*. (1878). New York: Garland, 1978.

Hesketh-Pritchard, Major H. *Sniping in France*. London: Hutchinson, c. 1920.

"Hide and Go-Seek-A-Hun." *US Vogue* (1 July 1918): 58+.

"The Indispensable Tailor Suit." *The Queen* (10 February 1917): 186.

Laver, James. *British Military Uniforms*. London: Penguin, 1948.

———. "War and Wellingtons: Military Footwear in the Age of Empire." In *Shoes: From Sandals to Sneakers,* edited by Giorgio Riello and Peter McNeil. Oxford: Berg, 2006: 116–37.

Newark, Tim. *Camouflage*. London: Thames & Hudson, in association with the Imperial War Museum: 2007.

"Periscope." *Scout-Sniping*. London: Gale and Polden, 1918.

Gilman, Charlotte Perkins. *The Dress of Women: A Critical Introduction to the Symbolism and Sociology of Clothing,* edited by Michael Hill and Mary Jo Deegan. Westport, CT: Greenwood, 2002.

Sem. *Le vrai et le faux chic*. Paris: Succès, 1914.

Solomon, Solomon J. *Strategic Camouflage*. London: John Murray, 1920.

Story, Margaret. *How to Dress Well*. New York: Funk and Wagnalls, 1924.

Thayer, Abbott. *Concealing-coloration in the Animal Kingdom*. New York: Macmillan, 1909.

Veblen, Thorstein. *The Theory of the Leisure Class*. New York: Dover, 1994.

Veillon, Dominique. *Fashion Under the Occupation*. (trans.) Miriam Kochan. Oxford and New York: Berg, 2003.

Wardle, Bernard Arthur. *Exhibition of Works by Camoufleur Artists with Examples of Camouflage at the Royal Academy of Arts*. London: 1919.

White, Nelson. *Abbott H. Thayer: Painter and Naturalist*. Hartford: Connecticut Printers: 1951.

Wilton, Pauline. *Camouflage, or the Tale of the Sorrowful Sniper*. London: Reynolds, 1918.

6 Making the Princeton Man
Collegiate Clothing and Campus Culture, 1900–20

Deirdre Clemente

The intellectual intersection of gender identities and fashion has, in the past two decades, become surprisingly well trod. Scholars from a variety of disciplines, ranging from anthropology and art history to economics and material culture, have studied how clothing shapes self-image and, more broadly, speaks to socioeconomic, cultural, and political affiliations. The nuances of dress silently broadcast one's own adherence to or rejection of society's definitions of masculinity and femininity. Yet, with all of the trail-blazing scholarship published in the last two decades, the study of clothing remains, for the most part, the study of women's clothing. If "clothes make the man," then why has the majority of scholarship focused on women? (see Breward; Cole; Deslandes; Martin and Koda).

Trends in men's clothing, though undeniably less capricious than those of women's, reveal much about a given era's notions of masculinity. In *Fashion as Communication,* Malcolm Barnard argued that "fashion and clothing are instrumental in the process of socialization into sexual and gender roles; they shape people's ideas of how men and women should look" (117). Yet, beyond the shifting boundaries of gender roles, clothing is a powerful analytical tool used to give insight into broader and more concrete social, economic, and political change.

This chapter examines clothing as a harbinger of changing definitions of American masculinity in the first two decades of the twentieth century. At the center of the analysis is the clothing worn by the students of Princeton University between 1900 and 1920. During this period, the all-male university, known for its upper-class, homogenous student body, became a premier source for menswear trends. The "collegiate style"—one that would ultimately give the fashion world saddle shoes and cuffed jeans—came to prominence in the years studied and would dominate men's clothing trends in the wake of World War I. The students of Princeton were instrumental in redefining the American man as youthful, leisure-focused, and casually yet carefully dressed.

The focus of this chapter is twofold. First, it aims to answer the question, "why Princeton?" That is, how did the social and cultural climate of the Princeton campus produce a style of dress that was imitated not only by other college students, but by young men across the country? The answer lies in the institution's unique student culture. In an era when the issue of higher education was center stage in an ongoing national discourse, Princeton and its Ivy League counterparts were perpetually in the public eye. However, unlike Harvard, Yale, and Columbia, Princeton was an insular institution, tucked away in New Jersey swampland. As America at large watched from the sidelines, a vibrant and self-regulated student culture emerged at Princeton, and the correct clothing was needed to participate. For example, sportswear in the form of varsity sweaters and golf knickers became an emblem of active or feigned participation in the campus's avid sports culture. Unapologetically homogenous, Princeton was a rich boy's school; in the period studied, more than eighty percent of the students came from elite private schools. Fashion flourished in this well-funded and fertile environment.

The second aim of this chapter is to understand how Princeton's elaborate social hierarchy served as a means of turning a Princeton boy into a Princeton man. This well-adhered-to "pecking order" actively controlled the clothing of all students. Freshmen were forced by convention—and roving bands of sophomores—to wear a specified uniform, consisting of a black sweater, corduroy pants, and black shoes. A rigid code of "appropriate" attire for newcomers was published yearly in the handbook distributed to the freshman class. Each class was allowed more and more freedom, and, by the spring of their senior year, students earned the right to wear the coveted beer suit—a white canvas suit perfect for protecting Brooks Brothers jackets from leaky keg taps. Clothing worn at Princeton served as the prototype of collegiate clothing precisely because the students presented a unified front to America at large. By regulating the clothing of underclassmen and indoctrinating them into the ranks of a Princeton-defined masculinity, students developed "the Princeton style."

Between 1900 and 1920, the campus of Princeton emerged as the style center for America's young men. The University's rise to prominence heralded dramatic shifts in the country's notions of masculinity. The stodgy Edwardian father, whose wardrobe was as fixed as his stoic expression, was passing gracefully from the scene. In his place developed a distinctly different portrait of the American man. The students of Princeton University in the first two decades of the twentieth century took an active role in shaping these new standards of masculinity.[1]

"A PASTORAL PARADISE AMONG THE JERSEY SWAMPS": SEPARATENESS AND SELF-REGULATION AT PRINCETON

The location of Princeton University itself fostered an environment ripe for an active campus culture, as it was isolated, and, in the words of one editor of the yearbook *Bric-A-Brac,* "a pastoral paradise among the Jersey swamps." Most young men stayed in the same dormitory for all four years, leaving campus only to eat at a private eating club or one of the town's many student-focused sandwich shops, such as the famed Renwick's.

While the vast majority of students' time was spent on campus, many upperclassmen did venture off campus on the weekends. Poet and alumnus of the Class of 1917, John Peale Bishop wrote in *The Smart Set,* "The outside world did exist—for weekends and eventually for more troublesome purposes" (55). One early account published in the *New York World* in 1883, "How the Rich Students at Princeton Enjoy Life," noted how "[w]hen they want a fine, fourteen-carat spree the boys jump over to New York or Philadelphia." Cars were allowed on campus until 1927, and trains provided easy access to the outside world. On these sojourns to nearby cities, the Princeton boys dined, danced, and developed their reputation as well-dressed dilettantes.

The physical layout of the campus was a key contributor to the insular nature of Princeton. Its aesthetic was imposing and heralded as the archetype for other campuses to follow. An editor of the *Princeton Alumni Weekly,* a publication founded in 1900, wrote in 1957 that "Princeton looks more the way a college ought to look than any other institution in America" (6). Large walls and iron gates cut the campus off from the comings and goings of the main thoroughfare, Nassau Street. Gothic-inspired buildings, complete with towering spires and crouching gargoyles, lined long quadrangles. An air of organization prevailed.

In his study on masculinity on the Oxford and Cambridge campuses between 1850 and 1920, historian Paul R. Deslandes wrote that "manhood was acquired in this setting not only on the playing fields and in college rooms but also in Oxford and Cambridge thoroughfares and alleyways" (85). Such was also the case with Princeton, as its many steps, open lawns, and campus hangouts were the perfect locale for watching other students. Amid constant scrutiny, upper-class men were determined to bring newcomers into the fold via monitoring and harassment for actions or attire deemed inappropriate.

It was in this secluded world that students became their own judge and jury; one hallmark of the University was self-regulation by the students. During the period studied, Princeton students ran most extracurricular events with little to no input from University administrators who took a decidedly "hands off" policy to monitoring campus culture. Student publications were written, edited, and sometimes printed by students. Team sports and associated trips were planned by students. Musical and theatre groups such as the Glee Club and The Triangle Club planned and orchestrated their own touring schedules. These groups became ambassadors of the Princeton style. The *Princeton Alumni Weekly* announced that "[t]he musical clubs practice for three months in order to make a few appearances in starched shirts and to 'advertise' the University" (1904: 371).

The most telling example of this self-regulation was in the adherence to and respect of the institution's honor code. In an atmosphere marked by an unwavering nonchalance to all-things-academic, cheating was one exception, as students viewed it with disdain. *Scribner's Magazine* published an article on student life at Princeton and wrote of its honor code: "A student caught by his fellows cheating at examinations loses his social status, is disgraced, and, as a matter of fact, has to retire from the University" (June 1897: 673). Decades later, the honor code was still intact and holding sway. A sociological study of student life on American college campuses used the Princeton honor code as an example of how enduring such self-regulation could be: "One student generation transmits (such codes) to the next, and they are unreflectively accepted and obeyed. This is control by indoctrination." The article continued, "indoctrination is supplemented by other variety of regulation: informal gossip, initiation practices and other more of assimilation" (Cowley and Waller 136).

In such a watchful environment, clothing took on a heightened meaning, as it was readily visible to the judging eyes of those students higher up on the pecking order. Amory Blaine, the main character of the novel *This Side of Paradise,* written by Class of 1917 alumnus F. Scott Fitzgerald, felt he was being watched from the moment he stepped on the Princeton campus. Fitzgerald wrote of Amory:

> Several times he could have sworn that men turned to look at him critically.
>
> He wondered vaguely if there was something the matter with his clothes and wished he had shaved that morning on the train. He felt unnecessarily stiff and awkward among these white-flannelled, bareheaded youths who must be juniors and seniors, judging by the *savoir faire* with which they strolled (43).[2]

At Princeton, Amory "tried conscientiously to look both pleasantly blasé and casually critical, which as near as he could analyze was the prevalent facial expression" (44). With time, Amory would become the watcher, not the watched. In their senior year, Amory's pal Tom D'Invilliers became disillusioned by the critical and snobbish air of Princeton. Tom declared: "I want to go where people aren't barred because of the color of their neckties and the roll of their coats." Amory quickly replied: "You can't Tom. Wherever you go now you will always unconsciously apply these standards of 'having it' or 'lacking it.' For better or worse, we've stamped you. You're a Princeton type" (94).

Popular novels such as Fitzgerald's and the earlier *Princeton Stories* (1899) by alumnus and founder of the *Princeton Alumni Weekly,* Jesse Lynch Williams, touted the University as the progenitor of men's fashion. Magazines, such as *Scribner's, The Saturday Evening Post,* and *Ladies*

Home Journal profiled life on the Princeton campus. Axtell wrote that students, "tried to fashion a recognizable 'Princeton style," whose distinctiveness some popular magazines were all to ready to certify" (311).

"APPEARING 'TOO RAH-RAH' NO LONGER SEEMS TO TERRIFY THE MODEST": CLUBS, SPORTS, AND SPORTSWEAR AT PRINCETON

The upper-class, homogenous nature of the student body was essential in the establishment of Princeton as the soothsayer of collegiate clothing. Social scientists and historians have long recognized the interaction between fashion and social stratification. Thorstein Veblen's *Theory of the Leisure Class* (1899) was a particularly pertinent study of how and why the upper class used fashion to display their wealth. Aside from an atmosphere where men were perpetually watched and judged by their peers, Princeton was "more than any other institution of its kind in the United States, [the] unconquered citadel of the elite" (Schreiner 8). Writer Upton Sinclair, who penned *The Jungle* (1906) in a tarpaper shack a few miles from the campus, contended that "Princeton is the first school of snobbishness in the United States amid an education system that suppresses individual opinion and exalts false social standards" (*The Daily Princetonian* 11 October 1926: 1).

Extracurricular activities were an essential element of undergraduate life at Princeton and participation was equated with masculinity. Historian Anthony Grafton has asserted that "[m]anliness, at Princeton, meant class spirit, accomplishment in athletics, the *Princetonian* or other student-run activities and sociability on Prospect Street" (484). Hence, club- and organization-associated regalia played a pivotal part in illustrating that one was a Princeton man. Most clubs and organizations had badges, pins, and hatbands as symbols of belonging.

Commonly, the University's signature orange and black were used on such regalia and also for general attire. *The Daily Princetonian* reported in 1910 that "[o]range and black is distinctly the style. The fear of appearing 'too rah-rah' no longer seems to terrify the modest. Instead, there is an honest wearing of honors won" (15 October 1910: 3). The colors themselves were relatively new during the period studied; orange was selected in 1867 as "a symbol of freedom, enlightenment and progress" and black was added in 1874.

Some of the most coveted emblems of association were those of the sports teams. In *American Manhood: Transformations in Masculinity from the Revolution to the Modern Era*, E. Anthony Rotundo notes how athletics had a "special significance for the redefinition of manhood at the turn of the century" (239). Again, by wearing clothing associated with sports teams, students laid additional claim to the image of the physically fit Princeton man. Blazers, complete with a team crest, were standard fare and worn with pride. The tradition began with the crew team and was extended to other teams. An exceptionally important sports emblem was the varsity sweater, as "on each campus, special deference was given to those who wore the varsity sweater" (Thelin 166). At Princeton, the varsity sweater took several forms during the period studied from a turtle-necked, ribbed cable-knit to a boat-necked version; all varsity sweaters were black with a large "P" in the center of the chest.

From 1900 to 1920, Princeton athletics were a matter of national attention. Baseball was the first organized sport at Princeton when the Nassau Baseball Club formed in 1858, but it was football that became its most followed. In 1869, the University's team played neighboring Rutgers and, within a few decades, Princeton's football team was dominating the sport. Rugby, crew, tennis, golf, swimming, and track and field were also popular and respected campus activities.

The social status of sports and its players gave rise to sportswear on the Princeton campus. Emerging trends at Princeton set the pace for the rest of collegiate fashion. Remarkably, in an era when sportswear was rigidly confined to the time when one was actually playing sports, at Princeton, sportswear was round-the-clock attire and students wore it to study and to socialize. Sportswear provided the opportunity to claim participation in a manly activity and redefine the rules of men's dress. In doing so, students unwittingly shaped menswear styles for the coming century.

Golf wear served as the most telling example of the adoption of sportswear. The sport was incredibly popular at Princeton and "golf, with links to wealth, heritage and clubs, has served as a fertile ground for sportswear styles" (Martin and Koda 123). Golf clothing was popularized early at Princeton and was worn even in cold weather. An article in *Scribner's Magazine* noted how "[i]n the winter of 1895 the prevailing costume was a golfing suit of rough tweed, with heavy corduroy waistcoat, or a sweater" (June 1897: 679). More than two decades later, Princeton men were still dressing in relaxed golf wear. *The Daily Princetonian* noted in 1923 that "[e]ven those men who do not play golf or tennis prefer this style for regular campus wear" (15 September 1923: 3). Amid the strict social standards for appropriate place for sportswear, Princeton men took to such casual clothing and implemented it into their wardrobes on a year-round basis, a harbinger of the casualization of menswear.

Knickerbockers, later shortened to be called "knickers," were one of golf's biggest contributions to the aesthetic of the Princeton campus, and the below-the-knee, tweed pants were a common sight by the second decade of the twentieth century. Such was not the case with other non-collegiate locales, where knickers were not popular attire until the early 1920s. Fashion historians claim that "golf was never able to transfer knickers to town," but in the sports-crazed culture of Princeton, athletic-inspired clothing was a sign of belonging (Martin and Koda 143). Knickers were also the privilege of the upperclassmen; freshman and sophomores were strictly forbidden from wearing them. This was also the case with white flannel pants worn to play tennis. Underclassmen were not permitted to wear white flannels, until such rules were relaxed in the early 1930s.

A second example of menswear trends to emerge from athletics was the sports shoe (Pattison and Cawthorne 86). While many men at the turn of the century wore ankle-length boots, a lower cut, more casual shoe emerged in response to the popularization of golf. The most common form were brogues. Originally heelless, the brogue originated in Scotland and Ireland and was worn by field and bog workers in the 1700s. The shoe's signature holes, called brogueing, allowed water to seep out of the shoe in an effort to keep workers' feet dry; hay was stuffed into the shoe to prevent foot irritation. For this practical reason, golfers took to brogues, and fringed tongues were added for additional waterproofing. With time, the holes assumed a merely decorative purpose. The golf craze of the Guilded Age brought brogues into the wardrobes of many American men.

Also significant was the rubber-soled athletic shoe. High-top, canvas versions made by companies such as Spalding were not worn off the basketball court during the period studied, but a dressier rubber-soled shoe made of white buckskin was the shoe of choice for tennis players. These shoes were commonly sighted on Ivy League campuses in the first years of the twentieth century, and by 1915 had taken on black or brown accents. By the early 1930s, these two-toned shoes were known as saddle shoes, and by mid-decade were ubiquitous for college students across the country. Princeton and other elite colleges were instrumental in popularizing sports shoes. The trade publication, *Boot and Shoe Recorder,* suggested how "[s]tyle ideas developed in the colleges have played and are playing a tremendously important part in influencing the trend of men's shoe fashions generally" (21 September 1929: 34). Princeton men and the like were unarguably trendsetters and responsible for breaking down many of the established rules of seasonal dress. The magazine asked: "Who was it that started this business of wearing oxfords the whole year round? The college man" (21 September 1929: 99).

The insular nature of the campus, the students' ability to self-regulate, the homogenous composition of the student body, and the pronounced emphasis on sportswear, all contributed to the development of Princeton as the arbiter of collegiate clothing in the first two decades of the twentieth century. Perhaps the University's most significant attribute was its elaborate social hierarchy that enabled, through four years of college, to turn Princeton boys into Princeton men.

"ABIDING BY THESE CUSTOMS STAMPS THEM AS TRUE PRINCETON MEN": CLOTHING AND THE SOCIAL HIERARCHY AT PRINCETON

Youth and youthfulness were important tenets of a new masculinity to emerge after 1900. The contemporary press of the era often commented on the youthfulness of Princeton students: "The students of Princeton struck me as being more boyish than elsewhere. They seemed like Peter Pan not quite grown up and not quite wanting to." The newspaper then commented on "the air with which they wore their yellow slickers," a campus sartorial staple. It wrote of the demeanor: "It is the natural indifference of irresponsibility and careless boyishness" (*The Independent* 1909: 474). The student culture of Princeton encouraged juvenile pranks, competitive games, peer-pressure, and devote loyalty in male–male friendships. Above all, it stressed initiation into the ranks of the student body.

As with many college campuses, hazing or "horsing" freshman was elaborate and unrelenting at Princeton. It often involved gangs of sophomores making newcomers act out silly scenarios such as "milking" a bicycle or belly dancing for the amusement of the crowd. Freshmen were forced to push past crowds of sophomores in order to get into the gym to elect their class officials. The freshman class picture was known as the "flour picture," as the sophomore class perched on the building above them and dumped flour on their heads as the camera snapped.

A particularly enduring form of "horsing" was the annual cane spree when the freshman class was forced to wrestle with the sophomore class for control of canes, intricately carved with the names and dates of previous bouts. The tradition began in the early 1860s and grew out of upperclassmen's annoyance of freshman using walking canes as fashion accessories. Open bouts were scheduled yearly until 1881 when each classed picked representatives to wrestle in three different weight classes. Despite attempts to organize according to weight, the crowds often jumped in on the action; broken bones and bruises were commonplace. Clothing was often ripped off bodies, and accounts of nearly naked students abound in the student press coverage of the matches.[3]

The cane sprees were but one example of an intricate and enforced set of rules the Freshman Handbook, which was published yearly by the Philadelphian Society. The handbook for 1914–15 warned: "You will be expected to adhere rigidly to these rules." Freshman could not smoke on campus, sit in particular areas, enter certain restaurants, or even walk on "upperclassmen-only" walkways. Most significant and telling of the campus's social hierarchy were the many regulations on clothing. Regulating what freshman could and could not wear was part of their initiation into a campus culture that stressed the importance of clothing; obeying the rules was part of freshmen's process in claiming their rights as Princeton men.

The goals of these regulations were multifaced. Axtell wrote, "Freshmen were obliged to wear a standard uniform designed to tame their coltish exuberance, develop class spirit, and honor the seniority of all upperclassmen, particularly the sophomores, who were delegated the duties of campus-cultural enforcement" (321). From the turn of the century to about 1915, the uniform consisted of a black turtleneck sweater, black corduroy pants without cuffs, black shoes, and a black tie. While sophomores and upperclassmen wore bright yellow slickers, freshmen could only wear black ones. Freshmen were not allowed to wear colored garters or patterned hosiery. Sophomores commonly forced them to roll up their pants to check that the rules were being followed. Freshmen could not wear the school colors, as students had to earn the right, nor were vests, knickers, and white flannels permitted.[4]

Freshmen were not obliged to follow the dress code when they walked on campus with out-of-town visitors, at Yale football or baseball games, or on Sundays. One freshman documented the relief in his weekly column, "Diary of a Freshman," featured in the *Princeton Alumni Weekly*. He wrote: "On Sunday I had the luck of being asked to dinner, so for once I got out of my freshman clothes and sported a loud tie, socks and hat. I went so far as to replace my black garters with pale pink ones" (7 October 1914: 48). A similar relief was felt on the last day of class at the end of freshmen year. The first thing students did was change their attire. Harrington Green (Class of 1911) wrote to his parents: "We have had a great time. Regular caps, loud ties, soft shirts, trousers rolled up and last but not least, smoking our pipes on campus" (Harrington Green Papers, Princeton University Archives, letter dated 8 April 1909, Box AC018, Folder 3).

While the purpose of the uniform did not change between 1900 and 1920, the garments associated with it did. In 1916, the black corduroys and sweaters were discarded, and freshmen were allowed to wear regular trousers with cuffs and soft-collared shirts. The reaction to this loosening of the rules was dramatic. A column entitled "Undergraduate Week" in the *Princeton Alumni Weekly* commented that when the Senior Council passed the resolution to allow for the change, "[a]ll the wise ones on campus shook their heads with a 'what-are-we-coming-to' expression" (18 October 1916: 63).

The deregulation of the freshman uniform resulted in a flurry of letters to the editors of *The Daily Princetonian* late in 1916. These letters illustrate that the upperclassmen viewed such regulations as important markers of manhood, and that the relaxing of standards was interpreted as "feminizing" the student body. One letter asked for editors to clarify "the exact date on which Princeton became coeducational." Another complained that changing such rules "may readily result in self-interest, effeminacy, and lack of respect for college traditions." In the mid-1920s, however, many of the dress regulations faded due to lack of enforcement and growing freshman insurgency.

One regulation that endured from the 1890s until the mid-1950s was the requirement to wear a black beanie, called a "dink." As with freshman regulations on behavior, such hats were very common for freshman at other colleges around the country. Thelin notes that "[h]azing included being made to wear class 'beanies' (often known as 'ducs') and to adhere to various rules of conduct" (174). Dinks changed in size and shape over the course of their tenure at Princeton. Early in the century, they looked like skullcaps, and by 1914, dinks resembled berets. In the 1920s, they had a similar appearance to sailor hats; in the 1930s, the shape of the dink called to mind a Yamika and it was worn on the back of the head.[5]

Freshmen who broke the dress code were often physically punished. One account in the alumni newsletter observed how "[o]ne freshman assayed to wear a shirt with a soft collar to the 'flour picture,' but needless to say that he did not wear it home" (7 October 1914: 45). Freshmen who wore clothing or accessories that were too showy were also punished. In 1903, John Carson wrote to his parents of a freshman whose Class of 1907 watch fob was too prominently displayed. The sophomores attacked him. Many freshmen claimed to have valued such "horsing" because it united them as a class. One account reported how "The horsing [he] received from the sophomores was the first thing [he] had in common with [his] classmates" (*Princeton Alumni Weekly* 5 May 1915).

Sophomores were indeed responsible for making the freshmen respect Princeton's ever-evolving "traditions," but they themselves were not allowed to wear whatever they wanted. Again, dressing overly fashionable or wearing elaborate jewelry attracted too much attention to oneself; most sophomores avoided doing so in efforts to ingratiate themselves with upperclassmen who would be offering bids to join private eating clubs. Sophomores were not allowed to wear white flannels or knickers, a privilege reserved for those higher up on the pecking order.

As juniors, Princeton students could dress as they pleased. One tradition held to mark their status was the yearly Junior High Hat parade. Juniors donned top hats and canes and marched down Nassau Street in an elaborate procession watched by other students and locals. Such dress hats were strictly forbidden for all underclassmen, and the Junior High Hat parade served as an important rite of passage.

In an effort to assert their ultimate seniority, seniors created the infamous beer suit in the spring of 1912. These white, canvas suits, consisting of overalls and a loose-fitting jacket, called to mind the apparel of workmen. The University went on record in the 1930s to claim that the suits were worn in protest to the rising price of fabric following World War I. However, the suits were popularized nearly a decade before; students claimed that, as the name suggests, the utilitarian suits were worn to protect students' clothing from spilled beer. The first suits were embellished only by a black stripe on the arm; the following year had two stripes. In 1922, students silk-screened a cartoon representing their class on the back of the jacket. To this day, each class created and voted on a design. These cartoons have documented the events shaping Princeton's campus culture including wars, campus policy, social trends, and inside jokes undecipherable to those who are not in-the-know.

"MANHOOD HAS A HISTORY": CONCLUDING COMMENTS

The study of the interplay between campus culture and clothing at Princeton is, on the surface, an interesting glimpse into American cultural history. The insularity of the campus, the self-regulating and elite nature of the student body, the importance of extracurricular activities such as sports, and the widespread acceptance of sportswear shaped an environment where clothing took on heightened meaning. The strict social hierarchy created and enforced by students *for* students did much to create a standard style for the public image of the Princeton man. This image was heralded and endorsed by mass-circulated magazines and clothing manufacturers who borrowed the University's name for everything from shoes to shirt collars.

But how the students of Princeton University came to serve as the progenitor of the collegiate style goes beyond a nuanced look at an era long past. As Rotundo has commented in his seminal study *American Manhood,* "[m]anhood can be shaped and reshaped to the human imagination; that is, manhood has a history" (1). How young men chose to dress during a period of profound economic, social, and cultural developments in the United States tells us much about an emerging definition of masculinity, one that would become increasingly prominent in the decades to follow. The image of the youthful, leisure-focused American man to come to prominence in first half of the twentieth century was profoundly shaped by the students of Princeton University during the period studied. In an era of Birkenstocks and business casual, clothing remains today a powerful lens for examining social and cultural change. The emergence of Princeton as a progenitor of men's fashion is but one example of how the study of clothing can add texture and tangibility to American history.

ACKNOWLEDGMENTS

Research for this project was funded by The Friends of Princeton University Library. The author would like to thank Steve Schlossman and Scott Sandage of Carnegie Mellon University for their help and encouragement. Also, James Axtell provided everything from research assistance to editing advice. His expertise added much to the chapter.

NOTES

1. Redefining masculinity during this period was not a passive development but an active process. Gail Bederman wrote in *Manliness and Civilization: A Cultural History of Gender and Race in the United States, 1880–1917,* "Men were actively, even enthusiastically engaging in the process of remaking manhood" (Chicago: University of Chicago Press, 1995).
2. It should be noted that Fitzgerald did not graduate from Princeton, but during the period studied, the University considered any student who came as a freshman to be an alumnus.
3. Horsing was officially abolished in 1914. Cane sprees continued into the 1950s.
4. It should be noted that other Ivy League colleges had similar clothing restrictions, though these were not as diligently enforced or enduring as those of Princeton. For example, sophomores at Columbia in 1902 handed out to freshmen their "sophomore orders," in which they forbid new students from using walking canes, wearing golf trousers, or sporting prep school hats.
5. A yamika is a small circular hat worn by Jewish males.

WORKS CITED

Admissions Office Records. "Princeton University's Analysis of the Freshman Class 1920." Princeton University Archives, Box 3, Folder 12.

Axtell, James. *The Making of Princeton University: From Woodrow Wilson to thePresent.* Princeton: Princeton University Press, 2006.

Barnard, Malcolm. *Fashion as Communication.* London: Routledge, 2002.

Bederman, Gail. *Manliness and Civilization: A Cultural History of Gender and Race in the United States, 1880–1917.* Chicago: University of Chicago Press, 1995.

Boot and Shoe Recorder (21 September 1929): 34–35.

Breward, Christopher. The Hidden Consumer: *Masculinities, Fashion and City Life 1860–1914.* Manchester: Manchester University Press, 1999.

Bric-a Brac, Student Yearbook, 1958: 225.

Carson Brothers Papers. Princeton University Archives, Box 1, Folder 3.

Cole, Shaun. *"Don We Now Our Gay Apparel": Gay Men's Dress in the Twentieth Century.* New York: Berg, 2000.

Cowley, W. H., and Willard Waller. "A Study of Student Life." *The Journal of Higher Education* 6.3 (March 1935): 132–42.

Deslandes, Paul R. *Oxbridge Men: British Masculinity and the Undergraduate Experience, 1850–1920.* Bloomington: Indiana University Press, 2005.

Fitzgerald, F. Scott. *This Side of Paradise.* New York: Pocket Books, 1995.

"The Freshman Handbook." Official Publications Collection. Princeton University Archives, Box 8.

Grafton, Anthony. "The Precept System: Myth and Reality of a Princeton Institution." *Princeton University Library Chronicle* 64.3 (Spring 2003): 467–503.

Harrington Green Collection. Princeton University Archives, Box AC-018, Folder 3, letter dated 19 January 1908.

"How the Rich Students at Princeton Enjoy Life." *New York World* (21 October 1883).

Martin, Richard, and Harold Koda. *Jocks and Nerds: Men's Style in the Twentieth Century.* New York: Rizzoli, 1989.

Pattison, Angela and Nigel Cawthorne. *A Century of Shoes.* Secaucus, NJ: Chartwell Books, 1997.

Peale, Bishop John. *The Smart Set* (June 1917): 55–61.

Pendergast, Tom, *Creating the Modern Man: American Magazines and Consumer Culture, 1900–50*. Columbia, MO: University of Missouri Press, 2000.

"*Princeton Boys Dress in a Uniform.*" *Life* (6 June 1938): 31.

Rotundo, E. Anthony. *American Manhood: Transformations in Masculinity From the Revolution to the Modern Era*. New York: Basic Books, 1993.

Schreiner, Samuel A., Jr. *A Place Called Princeton*. New York: Arbor House Press, 1942.

Scribner's Magazine (June 1897): 663–92.

Stearns, Peter N. *Be a Man! Males in Modern Society*. New York: Homes & Meier, 1979.

Thelin, John R. *A History of American Higher Education*. Baltimore: The Johns Hopkins University Press, 2004.

The National Clothing Retailer (7 July 1927).

Turbin, Carol. "Fashioning the American Man: The Arrow Collar Man, 1907–1931." In *Material Strategies: Dress and Gender in Historical Perspective*. Malden, MA: Blackwell, 2003.

Veblen, Thorstein. *Theory of the Leisure Class*. New York: MacMillan Company, 1911.

7 Elegance and Spectacle in Berlin
The *Gerson* Fashion Store and the Rise of the Modern Fashion Show

Mila Ganeva

> At the beginning of Jäger Street in Berlin, facing the Werderschen Market, stood the designer house *Gerson*, a synonym for elegance and good taste. As a child [in the 1880s] I was always thrilled when my mother said: "I must go to *Gerson*," because it meant that I could accompany her. Throughout my life, the *Gerson* fashion store remained a source of entertainment and diversion. . . . Over the decades I witnessed all its transformations and got to know personally the owners from the family Freudenberg. However turbulent the changes in my own life—whether I was able to order clothes for hundreds of marks before the war [World War I] or could afford only a modestly priced simple dress after the war—I always followed the slogan: "I must go to *Gerson*" (Vallentin 44, 49).[1]

This reminiscence from 1925 by the then well-known journalist, Frieda Vallentin, is representative of the ways in which middle-class Berliners have continuously perceived *Modehaus Gerson* (Gerson store) as a prominent institution of public life and an inviting, personable space of entertainment for people of different social strata and generations. By the 1920s, *Gerson* was not only an undisputed leader in design and sales of mass-produced stylish attire, it was also at the forefront of all forms of the spectacularization and marketing of fashion. In addition to being the premiere exporter of off-the-rack clothes to France, the Netherlands, and the United States, the German fashion company knew how to entice and entertain its local clientele too. At its premises, fashion teas (*Modentee*) and formal fashion parades (*Modeschauen*) were held at least once a week. Star actresses such as Anna May Wong, Grete Mosheim, and Maria Paudler became its exclusive clients and top models: they promoted its fashionable clothes from the silver screen, the theater stage, and the pages of high-circulation fashion magazines. Finally, it was the full array of costumes provided by *Gerson* that constituted the appeal of popular Weimar films such as *Der Fürst von Pappenheim* (*The Prince of Pappenheim*, 1927, dir. Richard Eichberg) and *Die Frau von vierzig Jahren* (*The Woman at the Age of Forty*, 1925, dir. Richard Oswald).

During the Third Reich (1933–45), the once glamorous Berlin fashion trade that *Gerson* was part of was destroyed, the Jewish-owned stores expropriated, and the owners forced into exile or sent to camps. The scant visual and written records about the industry either vanished in the Allied air raids on Berlin or were scattered to various archives. Thus, despite its former glory and international reputation, the company quickly fell into oblivion. This chapter sets out to retrace *Gerson's* involvement in the creation, distribution, and spectacular display of fashion in Germany in the second half of the nineteenth and the early twentieth centuries (1850–1933). It analyzes diverse archival materials recording the company's presence in the public sphere—from magazine articles, advertisements, and photographs to feature films and newsreels documenting fashion shows and mannequin contests—to demonstrate how various fashion displays were carefully staged to achieve maximum effect on a broad, middle-class, mostly female audience. It was due, in large part, to *Gerson's* efforts and ingenuity that fashion in early twentieth-century Germany became a prominent visual medium of its own right that shaped the experience of modernity for the masses.

THE BEGINNINGS OF THE MODERN FASHION STORE

In many ways, the story of the *Gerson* store is emblematic of the amazing ascent of Germany's garment industry, known as *Konfektion*, from around 1840 till the mid-1930s. Located in the capital city of Berlin, in a central part of town around *Hausvogteiplatz* that became famous as the capital's fashion district, German *Konfektion* rose as both a rival and counterpart to French *haute couture*. Most salons in Berlin were as much geared toward creating their own lines of high-end fashion as they were emulating Parisian styles and adjusting them for a mass clientele. Since it was known that the fashion-conscious public liked to take its cues from France, the German companies sent designers to Paris to observe what women were wearing in fashion shows, on the streets, at the races, and in the theatre. Upon their return, expensive *haute couture* creations were transformed into affordable, mass-produced, off-the-rack garments of French flair that were not only sold locally but exported to many countries, including France. As an essential branch of German economic life, *Konfektion* became both significant in size and very profitable. By the mid-1920s, after decades of steady expansion, the number of clothing businesses in Berlin, most of them Jewish-owned, reached nearly 800. The Berlin fashion industry employed a third of the city's work force, sold merchandise in big department stores throughout the country, and exported its goods all over Europe and the Unites States (Guenther 78–85; Wagner; Waidenschalger 1993).

Most founders of garment companies in Berlin around 1840—Herrmann Gerson, Valentin Mannheimer, Rudolph Hertzog, David Leib Levin, Salomon Blumenreich, Aaron Nathanson, Moses Löwenstein, and the members of the Wertheim family—were Jews and often recent migrants from Eastern Europe. In their pursuit of economic opportunity, they took advantage of a variety of favorable social and political factors in the 1830s—abundant and cheap work force, civil rights, economic freedom, and a rapidly expanding garment market. The Prussian Emancipation Edict of 1812 explicitly stated that Jews from Brandenburg, Silesia, Pomerania, and East Prussia, as well as those already residing in Berlin, were regarded as nationals and Prussian citizens. As a result, many poorer Jews from these provinces, especially from Posen, where they were still without rights and civil status, promptly moved to the city in search of employment. The sizeable influx of Jews included many garment and button peddlers, home seamstresses, and tailors with experience in the hand-manufacture of uniforms for the Prussian army (Makela 184–86). It was in that same period, between 1820 and 1840, that Berlin recovered from the Napoleonic Wars, developed as a modern metropolitan center, doubled its population from 200,000 to 400,000, and became the fourth largest city in Europe after Paris, London, and Vienna (Ribbe 87). Thus, when the need arose for the city's swiftly growing middle-class population to be dressed appropriately, quickly, and cheaply, the founders of *Konfektion* businesses embraced the advance of new industrial technologies and adopted the rationalized manufacturing process for men's and women's attire.

The history of the *Gerson* store dates back to 1836. Born in Königsberg as Hirsch Gerson Levin, the founder Herrmann Gerson (1812–61), along with his brothers, settled in Prussia's capital in 1835, where only a year later he opened his first fashion store not far from *Hausvogteiplatz* (*Juden in Preussen* 73). From its very conception, the *Herrmann Gerson* store considered the effect of fashionable garments as tied to the spaces in which they were displayed and sold. It is noteworthy that from 1836 to 1849 Gerson rented space on the ground floor of Berlin's *Bauakademie* (School of Architecture), which at the time was a newly erected, modern multipurpose public building, designed by the famous architect Karl Friedrich Schinkel (*Berlin und seine Bauten* 285–86). The *Bauakademie* was centrally located just around the corner from the Royal Palace, not far from a busy market place and a shipping dock on the river. In 1849, Gerson decided to move the business to a building of his own, a specially constructed neoclassical edifice from the late Schinkel era, designed by Theodor Stein (Waidenschlager 2001: 21). This "landmark" building, the first of its kind in Berlin, featured four stories: the first two combined a huge sales floor with an atrium, the third story had apartments for the owners and work space for about forty seamstresses, and the fourth housed storage space and living quarters for the delivery personnel. The new building, especially its large display windows and spacious atrium with a skylight (a glass rotunda) that illuminated the sales floor, presented a unique architectural and social attraction to Berliners (Osborn 57). In its grandeur, the *Gerson* establishment was also considered "a true precursor of the famous Berlin department stores" *Wertheim, KaDeWe,* and *Tietz,* those spectacular temples of consumerism and venerable institutions of modernity that were built later in the nineteenth century (Gay 183).

According to contemporary newspaper accounts, the new *Gerson* building immediately drew throngs of visitors, even in the bitter aftermath of the unsuccessful revolution of 1848, which ended in bloody street fights just a block away from the store. Not all of those visitors who came in the first days after the store opened were necessarily customers, but rather curious window-shoppers who flocked to mill around in search of affordable entertainment. As an anonymous eyewitness wrote in a report for the *Berliner Modenspiegel* in 1849, Berliners were "welcomed personally by the owner, Herrmann Gerson, and lead to admire the goods on display," as well as the innovative selling practices, whether or not they could afford any of the elegant clothes on offer (Waidenschlager 2001: 22). The unique attractions described in the press included an enclosed chamber with mirrors (*Spiegelkabinett*), illuminated by a single gas flame so that the female clientele could evaluate the effect of certain fabrics by candle light. Attached to the merchandise were large price tags, another novelty for that time, so that customers did not have to ask every time about the cost of an item. Visitors were also impressed by the personnel: between fifty and sixty sales assistants, many of them young women, were employed in the new store. *Gerson* also hired accountants, salesmen, seamstresses, and designers, which comprised a staff in total of 150 to 200 people. In addition, close to 1,000 tailors worked as outside contactors for the company (Bruer 255; Waidenschlager 2001: 23).

In the second half of the nineteenth century, *Gerson* was the biggest fashion establishment in Germany, and its brand name became synonymous with exquisite elegance. The store served as an exclusive supplier (*Hoflieferant*) to Queen Elisabeth of Prussia, the Tsar of Russia, and the Queen of Sweden. It also employed a "living model" with the exact proportions of the Empress Augusta Victoria: Charlotte Krüger, a humble Berlin woman, was specially selected to demonstrate clothes whenever the company gave a presentation at the royal court (Dähn 169). And while the royal clientele received *Gerson*'s representatives at their own living quarters, the middle classes paid visits to the salon to experience fashion and shop in a yet newer and even more lavishly outfitted building. The 1849 shop was partially torn down, and a new edifice designed by Felix Wolff with "a monumental façade" and "huge display windows" sprang up in 1889 (Dobert 140).[2] The building complex, which included workshops and a warehouse, took up the whole block and stood there until it was torn down after receiving heavy bomb and fire damage in World War II (Maciuika 344).

THE FASHION SHOW

In addition to the opulent buildings that it occupied, what distinguished the *Gerson* company most was its status as a pioneer in the way in which it revolutionized the public presentation of fashion and emphasized the element of spectacle in all its enterprises. More often than not, the cues for innovation came from French *haute couture* and its main players with whom *Gerson* maintained strong ties in a pronounced effort to keep its audience attuned to a cosmopolitan spirit even during periodic nationalist or anti-Semitic backlashes.[3] For example, while the invention of the live mannequin is credited to Paris couturier Charles Worth, who used his wife Marie Vernet as a house model in his newly founded salon in 1858, *Gerson* was the first among its competitors in Germany to employ living mannequins in its daily sales practices. In an attempt to attract a growing middle-class female clientele to the store, *Gerson* introduced the *Vorführdamen,* specially trained young women who would put on dresses and paraded in front of clients. More colloquially, these models were known as *Gelbsterne* (or "yellow stars") and most Berlin companies in high fashion as well *Konfektion* started employing them. The designation *Gelbstern* was derived from the then newly standardized sizes symbolized by stars (blue, yellow, white, green, and red) that were made out of fabric and attached to the sleeve of a dress, jacket, or coat as the clothes were displayed in the *Konfektion* store. The yellow star represented body measurements considered ideal in late nineteenth and early twentieth centuries—110 cm around the hips and 44 cm at the front of the chest—and, according to contemporaries, served to reinforce the "fashion trend against voluptuous body forms and toward de-materialization of femininity" (Loeb 72–73).[4]

When the new store opened its doors in 1889, its interiors, too, reflected *Gerson*'s ambition to change the ways in which fashion was presented to and experienced by the public. In an 1892 sumptuously illustrated article in the magazine *Moderne Kunst,* writer Paul Dobert reviewed the novelties that the store had to offer to its customers. After touring the three-story building using an elevator to get to the top level, Dobert noted that there was no other establishment in Berlin that housed such a variety of fashionable garments for the broadest clientele:

> For the first time ever, the German audience enters a house of fashion which covers a spectrum of products as multiple and various as can be found in any of the famous Paris bazaars. The fine and opulent design of the building makes it a jewel of the Empire's capital (138).

One of the most spectacular spaces, according to the reviewer, was the floor on which products of the *Konfektion* were displayed on live models and tried on by customers. The floor included a spacious hall for the public presentation of dresses and numerous private fitting rooms. The visitor was impressed by the interior arrangements of these spaces flooded in light that came through the building's tall windows and was reflected in numerous mirrors. The fact that the interior design of this floor with its large display hall (*Vorführraum*) was commissioned to a then well-known decorative painter artist and Art Déco designer associated with the German *Werkbund*, Alfred Mohrbutter (1867–1916), only confirmed *Gerson's* alignment with the most progressive aesthetic practices of the time (Figure 7.1).[5] Ultimately, fashion was envisioned as a multidimensional experience which included special arrangements, light effects, and carefully choreographed movements.

This new phase of *Gerson's* development, which began around 1889, was also marked by the new European trend of "theatricalization" of fashion marketing. As late nineteenth-century stage productions in London, Paris, Berlin, and Vienna discovered the dramatic potential inherent in the act of putting on different clothes, theater became a prominent space for sartorial display. Realizing the increased importance and accessibility of fashion to the middle classes and in order to attract a wider female audience, dramatic productions began to mimic the presentational practices common in the *haute couture* salons. Plays were written that consisted of nothing more than a series of dramatized fashion *tableaux:* the primary focus was on the performative aspect of wearing clothes and the meager

Figure 7.1 The display hall ("Vorführraum") of the *Gerson* fashion salon in 1912. Designed by Alfred Mohrbutter. Permission of the Granger Collection.

plots were usually secondary to the goal of having the lead actresses appear in as many different outfits as possible. The distinction between actresses and models collapsed as fashion and theatre merged symbiotically into the new genre of the "fashion play," a form of musical comedy that stormed the stages of the European capitals from the 1890s to 1914 (Kaplan and Stowell). At the same time, couturiers sought to advance their brands off the stage by luring the most popular among the actresses into becoming their exclusive customers. This was made easy by the fact that actresses, often poorly paid, were expected to supply their own costumes, almost always from their personal wardrobe, for plays set in contemporary times (Aschke 239–40).

In view of these new trends, *Gerson*'s new owner, Philipp Freundenberg, who presided over one of the store's most glamorous periods (1888–1919), considered a theater stage on its premises "an absolute must," especially if he wanted to sell outfits to actresses.[6] Dobert describes the stage as a "unique miracle of technology," with a tilting floor and variable lime lights in different colors. A few years later, this stage would be used for a performance of a new kind that owed much to the repertoire of theatrical display, namely the formal fashion show. The fashion show not only targeted the individual female clients entering the premises but was specifically organized for a selected audience of consumers and connoisseurs, female as well as male. However, while the turn-of-the-century theater embraced fashion display as a way to escape its elitist aura and broaden its popular appeal, the early fashion shows borrowed the requisites of pomp and exclusivity from the theater in an effort to legitimize its own high cultural status. Parisian Paul Poiret and London couturier Lucile (Lady Duff Gordon), who both claimed to have invented the fashion show after being inspired by contemporary theatrical performances, consciously styled their mannequin parades as dramatic plays. They even went on international "tours" with their troupes of mannequins (Kaplan and Stowell 117).

It is noteworthy that when French fashion reformer Paul Poiret "performed" with his troupe of mannequins in a dozen European cities between 1910 and 1913, one of his first stops in 1911 was Berlin (Loschek 22–24). He was invited there by the capital's premier *Konfektion* retailer *Gerson* (Figure 7.2). Keenly aware of current international trends and oblivious to local, often nationalistically flavored calls to liberate Germans from the domination of French fashions, *Gerson*'s new owners, Philipp Freudenberg (1833–1919) and his sons Hermann and Julius, had strong personal ties with the famous Paris couturier. They not only invited Poiret repeatedly to Berlin for shows and lectures, but also actively supported reforms in design, production, and public presentation of fashion that would make it part of German women's everyday lives.[7]

As it turned out, Berlin's metropolitan public was also eager for fashion as a form of entertainment. On its initial visit in Germany in 1911,

Figure 7.2 Poiret's Fashion Show hosted by *Gerson* and covered in great detail in the press. *Illustrierte Frauen-Zeitung* 1 December 1911: 42. Permission of Kunstbibliothek, Staatliche Museen zu Berlin.

Poiret's show became the object of mass fascination and intensive scrutiny. The observers were thrilled by the new, corset-free dresses as well as by the novel form of their public presentation. As one magazine reported: "[Poiret's creations] were demonstrated not on wax dummies . . . but by live mannequins, *one almost wants to call them actresses*" (von Suttner 42). While only a select few were invited to attend the fashion show, the public at large followed enthusiastically the Parisian mannequins at every step in the city and read reports in the press about their diets, street clothes, and the exact measurements of their bodies (Dähn 144–45). The excitement at the first day of presentations reached such heights that Poiret wrote to his wife in Paris: "You could have counted the people who came this morning only by the thousands, and a few minutes ago, when the afternoon show was over, an entire crowd, delirious with joy acclaimed your little sweetheart with an enthusiasm unprecedented in Berlin" (White 72).

By hosting Poiret's first show in Berlin, *Gerson* enhanced its reputation not only as a leader in the sale and export of mass-produced clothes, but also as a trend setter in the practices of public display of fashion in turn-of-the-century Germany. Beginning in 1910, *Gerson* as well as numerous other stores in Berlin held regular formal fashion shows with living mannequins (on a few occasions during the week), at a fixed time in the afternoon and in specially designed salons that resembled a theater space: there was an elevated stage or a dramatic staircase, curtains and seats for the members of the audience who were either invited or payed admission. Many of the shows were mere walkabouts during which an orchestra played and refreshments were served, a popular practice of the "fashion tea" (*Modentee*) that persisted well into the 1920s, as is evident in scenes of Walter Ruttmann's 1927 film *Berlin: Symphony of a Great City*).[8] However, in an attempt to outdo the competition, other fashion shows employed simple scenarios and models who already had some stage coaching (Evans 278). Moreover, as some commentators noted, the fashion show turned into an elaborate spectacle, often "complete with lectures, dances, poetry and music presentations; the audience [was] treated with tea and cookies and well-known actors [were] hired to announce the prices during the mannequin parade" (Ledermann 6).[9]

Fashion display in Berlin of the 1920s reached new spectacular heights during the annual fashion contests, the so-called *Modekonkurrenzen*. At these pageants, the most graceful model would be selected who, according to the magazine *Elegante Welt*, personified the "ideal fashionable woman for our times: not too thin and not too sumptuous, partly gamin and partly lady, refined and natural at once" (Könniginnen der Mode 12 January 1927: 38). It was the fashion industry's professional association, *Der Verband der deutschen Modenindustrie,* which inaugurated the tradition of the fashion competition during its annual ball (*Modenball*).[10] Held at the Symphony Hall in Berlin in December 1925, the fashion ball was widely covered by all the media—from the daily newspapers to the specialized fashion magazines to the newsreels at the movies. The selection of the best model event mixed elements of the beauty pageant, upscale fashion show, and revue kick-line, and was thus attractive to the masses of newspaper readers and moviegoers. The first "fashion queen" (*Modekönigin*) was Sonja Sovanowitsch, a mannequin at the Berlin salon *Heß* who was proclaimed "Sonja I." She was followed the next year by *Gerson*'s top model, sixteen-year-old Hilde Zimmermann

Figure 7.3 Fashion queen and *Gerson* top model Hilde Zimmermann in *Elegante Welt* 12 January 1927: 37. Permission of Kunstbibliothek, Staatliche Museen zu Berlin.

(*Elegante Welt* 12 January 1927: 38). Both Sovanowitsch and Zimmermann were featured in traditional royal vestments—a crown and a velvet ruby-colored cape donned over the typical mid-1920s outfits—on the cover pages of the respective January 1926 and January 1927 issues of *Elegante Welt* (Figure 7.3). The images were accompanied by the following commentary: "Our republic has already accepted the fact that it has a queen again, a queen of beauty and fashion" (*Die drei Kleider Sonjas* 13 January 1926: 12).[11] By the end of the decade, fashion shows and contests of all kinds, as well as occasions to observe fashion and be on display, had become so ubiquitous and frequent in the German capital that the press gave up its efforts to cover them all. "The Berlin fashion season has gone mad, it is not a season any more, it is a permanent wave," admitted the German edition of *Vogue* in 1928 (24).

FILM AND FASHION

Perhaps the most dramatic change in the display of fashion in the first third of the twentieth century was precipitated by the Berlin *Konfektion*'s alliance with another modern medium, film. The trendsetters in the garment industry soon realized that while the formal fashion shows had an elitist flair—they were performed for a limited audience of a select few—fashion shows within films could reach thousands of middle- and lower-class women in the movie theatre. The leaders in the film industry, almost from its very conception, grasped the opportunity to attract larger audiences by transforming film into a spectacular site for the display of fashions. In tandem, film and fashion in Germany in the 1910s and 1920s not only satisfied the audiences' desire for entertainment and visual pleasure, but also managed to seduce female viewers into believing that their own fantastic transformations were somehow possible. The main agents of that seduction were of course the actresses who effectively doubled as models presenting the latest fashions on the screen as well as on the pages of illustrated magazines. In a 1919 interview for *Elegante Welt*, Danish star Asta Nielsen, who had just resumed filmmaking in Berlin after the war, publicly declared her conscious involvement in the promotion of clothes and trendy appearances from the movie screen: "A well made film must, in any moment, have the effect of a good fashion magazine. This fact is being realized quickly in countries, where fashion is taken seriously. Today's actresses pay special attention to this aspect of film" ("Asta Nielsen ist wieder in Berlin" 18 June 1919: 7). And, indeed, while watching a film with lavish fashion displays, women were virtually given practical lessons on how to sew and wear their own fashionable dresses while also being lured to the stores to purchase cheaper knock-offs of the exclusive fashions they saw on screen. Popular film became something like the double of *Konfektion:* both media broke down the aura of the unique high fashion item into the multiplicity of mass-manufactured products and images. Both also epitomized many of the commercial, cultural, and national tensions of early twentieth-century modernity between creativity and business, elitist exclusiveness, and mass appeal and individuality and uniformity.

The merger of the *Konfektion*'s business interests with the mass audience's growing appetite for new forms of entertainment was most evident in the rise of a new subgenre of silent film, *Konfektionsfilm* or the fashion farce

(*Konfektionskomödie*). Fashion farces were among the first longer and commercially successful feature movies produced in the 1910s, including the first films that featured Ernst Lubitsch, initially as the lead actor, and later as actor and director: *Die Firma heiratet: Drei Kapitel aus dem Leben einer Probiermamsell* (*The Perfect Thirty Six: Three Chapters from the Life of a Mannequin*, 1914, dir. Carl Wilhelm), *Der Stolz der Firma. Die Geschichte eines Lehrlings* (*The Pride of the Company: The Story of an Apprentice*, 1914, dir. Carl Wilhelm); *Schuhpalast Pinkus* (*Shoe Palace Pinkus*, 1916, dir. Ernst Lubitsch) and *Der Blusenkönig* (*The Blouse King*, 1917, dir. Ernst Lubitsch). Set in Berlin's fashion district and featuring characters such as smart and dazzling mannequins and shrewd salespeople, these films established a notion of an early German comedy associated primarily with specific fashion situations: masquerades, cross-dressing, infatuation with appearances and mix-ups, and transformative effects caused by clothes. Throughout the 1920s and well into the 1930s, German fashion comedies continued to proliferate and exhibit alluring locations, events, and products associated with the modern lifestyle of the metropolis including designer salons, upscale department stores, fashion shows, and stylish clothes.[12]

One of the very few fashion farces that enjoyed great popularity in the 1920s which has survived is *Der Fürst von Pappenheim* (*The Prince of Pappenheim*, 1927, dir. Richard Eichberg). The audience was guaranteed not to be disappointed, since all the costumes were provided by Berlin's best-known designer house, *Gerson*, as it was boastfully announced in the program for the film's premiere. The film offered the type of entertainment that the mass audience craved: a runaway princess (played by Mona Maris) who works incognito as a top fashion model in an upscale Berlin fashion house, as well as a former mannequin (Dina Gralla) who married a count and as a result could afford all the clothes that her heart desired. It also features hilarious cross-dressing scenes in which the male shop assistant (Curt Bois) parades in front of an admiring audience as a masked mannequin in a dazzling evening gown. In addition to the ostentatious fashion show in an upscale hotel, the film's plot calls for several routine in-house presentations of clothes for individual clients (Figure 7.4).

This 1927 comedy serves as one of the best examples of the intermedial and intertextual connections between the institutions of cinema and fashion. The explicit and implicit fashion shows incorporated in *Der Fürst von Pappenheim* fulfilled multiple overlapping functions. First, they most obviously provided an occasion for direct product placement, and, needless to say, designer houses such as *Gerson* frequently took advantage of this opportunity (the source of the costumes was listed in the credits). Second, the display of fashion became one of the paradigmatic cinematic moments in which the female body was transformed literally into a spectacle, with the camera closing in on the new, fetishized forms: slender torsos and exposed legs. At the same time, the fashion shows within this and other fashion farces constituted significant breaks

Figure 7.4 The Prince of Pappenheim (1927). Permission of Deutsche Kinemathek.

in the flow of the narrative during which the spectators were offered glimpses at the earlier "cinema of attraction" preserved fragmentarily in the fabric of 1920s popular, story-based cinema (Gunning).[13] Third, fashion farces like *Der Fürst von Pappenheim* played a role in shaping notions of modernity, especially for the audience of increasingly mobile and often working lower- and middle-class women. As a peculiar mix of narrative and spectacle, the fashion farce guided its viewers through sartorial practices that could be relevant, with some adaptation and modification, to their own everyday lives. After all, the New Women of the 1920s, as recent studies have pointed out, were not only projections of the mass media, but also "real" subjects, actively involved in the creation of their own modern image.[14] They were employed outside of the home and possessed some, albeit limited, leisure time and money to spend. Those who worked office jobs and were present in the public realm, were particularly interested to know what the up-to-date fabrics, designs, and haircuts were, how makeup and lipstick were applied, and what clothes were appropriate for different occasions. By going to the movies, female viewers were able to satisfy their curiosity in the cheapest and most immediate way. In other words, cinematic fashion farces served, as one contemporary observer noted, as "a live fashion magazine," as a compendium of suggestions, tips, and updates disseminated to a mass audience at no extra charge (Moreck 239). In short, they offered fantasies beyond reach, but they were also a source of practical, usable advice.

* * *

The crash of the stock market in 1929 and the ensuing economic crisis forced the *Gerson* fashion house to file for bankruptcy in 1932. At that time, it was owned collectively by the Freudenberg family and Rudolf and Herrmann Meyer. In 1935, when the business was bought out by an "Aryan" owner and promptly renamed "Horn," all Jewish employees were fired. By 1936, the former owners (the Freudenbergs and Meyers) managed to leave Germany for Belgium and Holland; their fate after this year is unknown. After the war, the *Horn* fashion salon reopened in West Berlin's premier avenue, *Kurfürstendamm,* where it remained for over forty years until it closed in 2003.[15]

A visit to the former center of fashion in Berlin, *Hausvogteilplatz* and the surrounding streets, would now reveal the void left by the demise of the garment industry in the course of the 1930s and 1940s. The first wave of intimidation was followed by organized boycotts, lootings, and finally by the so-called "aryanization" of the fashion business: all Jewish-owned salons were "bought out" for under market price or simply turned over to new, German proprietors. By 1936, the term *Konfektion* itself was banned and the Jewish owners, labeled *Konfektionsjuden,* were forced into exile or arrested (Barkai 126–28). With the advance of the war, most of the old buildings disappeared in the air raids of Berlin and modern ones were erected in their place in the decades following 1945. Whatever old edifices were spared by the bombs, they no longer housed any of the fashion stores so popular in the 1920s.

The vibrant scene of fashion display has been now replaced by subtle markers of remembrance that hardly disturb the quiet surface of the city plaza. Climbing up from the subway station *Hausvogteiplatz,* a visitor to today's Berlin notices the plaques on the vertical surface of the stairs: they list the addresses the defunct Jewish businesses that once crowded the area and the names of the owners, many of whom perished in the Holocaust. Once standing in the middle of the *Hausvogteiplatz,* one is greeted silently by three mirrors, slightly tilted toward each other (Figure 7.5).[16] This memorial offers the contemporary visitor an appropriate opportunity to establish an imaginary connection to the ephemeral fashion displays of the past as fashion itself has left barely any material traces. Looking at ourselves reflected in the three mirrors makes it clear that the resurrection of the history of *Hausvogteiplatz* and the *Gerson* fashion house is possible only if one crosses the surface of the mirror into the ghostly space of archival photographs, old films, and yellow-stained magazine pages.

Figure 7.5 Memorial "Fashion Center Hausvogteiplatz" designed by Berlin artist Rainer Görß and unveiled in July 2000. Author's own.

NOTES

1. All translations from German are mine unless otherwise noted.
2. Another innovation that increased *Gerson*'s public visibility and reinforced its alignment with modernity was the fleet of horse-drawn carriages (and later the first Mercedes automobiles) with the sign "Herrmann Gerson" prominently displayed on the side that crisscrossed the city to deliver the purchased goods to the customer's homes ("Aus den Archiven des Hauses" Gerson-Brevier 1:1, 1928; Waidenschlager 2001:62).
3. For a detailed discussion of anti-semitic tirades against *Konfektion,* see Westphal 21–29; Makela.
4. Translation mine. For more on the history of the fashion model in the 1920s and its representation in the press and literature, see Ganeva 2005.
5. Hermann Freudenberg, *Gerson*'s co-owner at the time, was a powerful ally of *Werkbund* founder Hermann Muthesius and his friend, Alfred Mohrbutter, who was known not only as a painter but as a fashion designer as well. Freudenberg was also a prominent supporter of the commercial and cultural policies of the German arts and crafts movement of 1890 to 1920; see Jessen 3–8.
6. The company's founder Herrmann Gerson died, fairly young, in 1861. The business was then run by his brothers until 1888 and soon afterwards sold to Philipp Freudenberg and his sons Albert, Hermann, Julius, and Siegfried.

Throughout the years after the founder's death, the name "Herrmann Gerson" or "Gerson" for short, was preserved and the subsequent owners built on the reputation of the original label.

7. In his autobiography, Poiret wrote extensively of his travels to Germany before World War I and of his visits with the Freudenberg family where he felt particularly welcomed and appreciated: "It was they [the Freudenbergs] who first brought me to Germany, and I was surprised to find them so extremely 'Parisian'" (Poiret 157–59).

8. For images and a detailed description of a "fashion tea" organized by *Gerson,* see Feiner.

9. Ledermann complains that is had become impossible for the smaller stores to keep up with the cost of such lavish spectacles. As a result, an "Anti-Fashion Show League" was founded which organized a boycott of all fashion shows during the fall of 1927.

10. The professional association was founded by eighteen of the biggest and most prominent Berlin *Konfektion* companies in 1915 as an off-shoot of the *Werkbund*'s Commission for the Fashion Industry (*Ausschuss der Mode-Industrie*). Its first president for many years until his death in 1924 was *Gerson*'s co-owner Hermann Freudenberg. See Wagner 121; Maciuika 210–11.

11. The third fashion queen was again a *Gerson* model, Tutti Fertig, as seen in an advertisement in *Gerson-Brevier* 1.1 (1928): 73.

12. For a complete list of German fashion farces and extended analysis of this subgenre, see Ganeva 2007.

13. I am drawing here from Tom Gunning's influential argument that preclassical cinema, which he called "cinema of attraction," had a tendency to engage in direct address with the viewer. See Gunning.

14. For some representative studies of the position of the New Woman in Weimar Germany, see Grossmann, von Ankum.

15. For all information about the fate of the *Gerson* business after 1933, I am thankful to Heike-Katrin Remus at Stadtmuseum Berlin with whom I was in e-mail communication in 2005.

16. The signs on the steps and the mirrors are part of the memorial "Fashion Center Hausvogteiplatz" designed by Berlin artist Rainer Görß and unveiled in July 2000.

WORKS CITED

Aschke, Katja. "Die geliehene Indetität: Film und Mode in Berlin 1900–90, Betrachtung einer medialen Symbiose." In *Berlin en vogue: Berliner Mode in der Photographie,* edited by F. C. Gundlach and Uli Richter. Berlin: Wasmuth, 1993: 233–76.

"Asta Nielsen ist wieder in Berlin." *Elegante Welt* (18 June 1919): 7.

"Aus den Archiven des Hauses Gerson." *Gerson-Brevier* 1:1 (1928): 62–64.

Barkai, Avraham. *From Boykott to Annihilation: The Economic Struggle of German Jews 1933–43.* Translated by William Templer. Hanover: University Press of New England, 1989.

Berlin: Sinfonie einer Großstadt, Berlin: Symphony of a Great City, 1927, dir. Walter Ruttmann.

Berlin und seine Bauten (Vol.2). Berlin: W. Ernst & Sohn, 1896.

Bruer, Albert. *Aufstieg und Untergang: Eine Geschichte der Juden in Deutschland 1750–1918.* Cologne: Böhlau, 2006.

Dähn, Brunhilde. *Berlin, Hausvogteilplatz: Über 100 Jahre am Laufsteg der Mode.* Göttingen: Musterschmidt, 1968.

Der Blusenkönig. The Blouse King. 1917, dir. Ernst Lubitsh.

Der Fürst von Pappenheim, Prince of Pappenheim, 1927, dir. Richard Eichberg.

Der Stolz der Firma. Die Geschichte eines Lehrlings. The Pride of the Company: The Story of an Apprentice, 1914, dir. Carl Wilhelm.

"Die drei Kleider Sonjas." *Elegante Welt* (13 January 1926): 12.

Die Firma heiratet: Drei Kapitel aus dem Leben einer Probiermamsell, The Perfect Thirty Six: Three Chapters from the Life of a Mannequin, 1914, dir. Carl Wilhelm.

Die Frau von vierzig Jahren, The Woman at the Age of Forty, 1925, dir. Richard Oswald.

Dobert, Paul. "Im Reiche der Mode." *Moderne Kunst* 7.11 (1892/93): 137–40.

Evans, Caroline. "The Enchanted Spectacle." *Fashion Theory* 5.3 (2001): 274–97.

Feiner, Ruth. "Modentee bei Gerson." *Gerson-Brevier* 2:3 (1929): 32–34.

Ganeva, Mila. "The Beautiful Body of the Mannequin: Display Practices in Weimar Germany." In *Leibhaftige Moderne: Körper in Kunst und Massenmedien 1918–1933,* edited by Michael Cowan and Kai Sicks. Bielefeld: transcript, 2005: 152–68.

———. "Weimar Film as Fashion Show: *Konfektionskomödien* or Fashion Farces from Lubitsch to the End of the Silent Era." *German Studies Review* 30:2 (2007): 288–310.

Gay, Ruth. *The Jews of Germany: A Historical Portrait.* New Haven: Yale University Press, 1992.

Grossmann, Atina. "Girlkultur or Thoroughly Rationalized Female: A New Woman in Weimar Germany?" In *Women in Culture and Politics: A Century of Change,* edited by Judith Friedlander et al. Bloomington: Indiana University Press, 1986: 62–80

Guenther, Irene. *Nazi Chic? Fashioning Women in the Third Reich.* Oxford: Berg, 2004.

Gunning, Tom. "The Cinema of Attractions: Early Film, Its Spectator and the Avant-Garde." In Early Cinema: Space, Frame, Narrative, edited by Thomas Elsaesser. BFI, 1990: 56–62.

Jessen, Peter. "Nachruf für Hermann Freudenberg." *Mitteilungen des Verbandes der Deutschen Moden-Industrie* 6.1 (1924): 3–8.

Juden in Preussen. Edited by Ernst G. Lowenthal. Berlin: Dietrich Reimer, 1982.

Kaplan, Joel, and Sheila Stowell. *Theatre and Fashion: Oscar Wilde to the Suffragettes.* Cambridge: Cambridge University Press, 1994.

"Königinnen der Mode." *Elegante Welt* (12 January 1927): 38.

Ledermann, Martin. "Die Modenschau—in erledigtes Kapitel? Führende westdeutsche Konfektionshäuser gründen eine 'Anti-Modenschau-Liga.'" *Der Konfektionär* (19 October 1927): 6.

Loeb, Moritz. *Berliner Konfektion.* Berlin: Hermann Seemann, 1911.

Loschek, Ingrid. *Mode im 20. Jahrhundert: Eine Kulturgeschichte unserer Zeit* (5th ed.). Munich: Bruckmann, 1995.

Maciuika, John. *Before the Bauhaus: Architecture, Politics, and the German State, 1890–1920.* Cambridge: Cambridge University Press, 2005.

Makela, Maria. "The Rise and Fall of the Flapper Dress: Nationalism and Anti-Semitism in Early-Twentieth-Century Discourses on German Fashion." *Journal of Popular Culture* 34.3 (2000): 183–208.

Moreck, Curt. *Sittengeschichte des Kinos.* Dresden: Paul Aretz, 1926.

Osborn, Max. "Alt-Berlin als Geschäftsstadt." In *Berlins Aufstieg zur Weltstadt: Ein Gedenkbuch herausgegeben vom Verein Berliner Kaufleute und Industrieller aus Anlaß seines 50jährigen Bestehens.* Berlin: Reimar Hobbing, 1929: 23–96.

Poiret, Paul. *King of Fashion: The Autobiography of Paul Poiret.* Translated by Stephen Haden Guest. Philadelphia: J.B. Lippincott, 1931.

Ribbe, Wolfgang. *Geschichte Berlins: Von der Frühgeschichte bis zur Industrialisierung.* Munich: Beck, 1988.

Schuhpalast Pinkus, Shoe Palace Pinkus, 1916, dir. Ernst Lubitsh.

Vallentin, Frieda. "Ich muß zu Gerson: Erinnerungen an das Modehaus." *Gerson-Brevier* 2.3 (1929): 44–49.

Vogue. Deutsche Ausgabe (9 May 1928): 24.

von Ankum, Katharina (ed.).*Women in the Metropolis: Gender and Modernity in Weimar Culture.* Berkeley: University of California Press, 1997.

von Suttner, M. "Berliner Modenrevüen: Sechs Poiret Kleider der Modenschau bei Herrmann Gerson." *Illustrierte Frauenzeitung* (1 December 1911): 42.

Wagner, Gretel. "Die Mode in Berlin." In *Berlin en vogue: Berliner Mode in der Photographie,* edited by F.C. Gundlach and Uli Richter. Berlin: Wasmuth, 1993: 113–46.

Waidenschlager, Christina. "Berliner Mode der zwanziger Jahre zwischen Couture und Konfektion." In *Mode der 20er Jahre,* edited by Christine Waidenschlager and Christa Gustavus. Berlin: Wasmuth, 1993: 11–24.

———. "Aus den Anfängen der Berliner Konfektion." In *Berliner Chic: Mode von 1820 bis 1990,* edited by Christine Waidenschlager. Berlin: Stiftung Stadtmuseum Berlin, 2001: 11–24.

Westphal, Uwe. *Berliner Konfektion und die Mode 1936–39: Die Zerstörung einer Tradition* (2nd ed.). Berlin: Edition Hentrich, 1992.

White, Palmer. *Poiret.* New York: Clarkson N. Potter, 1973.

8 The City Boutique
Milan and the Spaces of Fashion

Francesca Muscau

Milan is a city of display windows. . . .

—Caroline Klein (2005)

SPACE, GAZE, MONEY

In the early 1980s, Milan was the stage of a youth phenomenon that many Italians still find intriguing today. A small group of teenagers, collectively called the *paninari* after the café *Al Panino* where they used to meet, created a strict fashion system that identified a social hierarchy as much as it organized the city space. This group appropriated the area around *San Babila,* a few minutes from the *Duomo* Cathedral, as its headquarters together with the just-mentioned café.[1] When the *paninari* phenomenon exploded, a new category of young individuals, perceived as careless and hedonistic, was born. Nobody in Milan had expected such a trend.

The phenomenon of the *paninari,* with which I chose to start my chapter, provides a striking example of the peculiar interaction between the space of Milan and its fashion practices. The cultural phenomenon of the *paninari* exemplifies the vital relationship that the city of Milan has established with fashion and its need for display and surveillance.

Many Milanese—intellectuals and non—still find it odd to this day that a phenomenon like the *paninari* should have taken place. In doing so, they ignore the long history of the Milanese urban culture and subcultures in which identity has always been deeply indebted to both the display of one's own self as a commodity and the careful monitoring of one's own lifestyle and outfit. If we want to understand the connection between Milan and the space of fashion, then the *paninari* provide a neglected cultural window and an intriguing perspective from which to begin the exploration of such a link.

Since the 1960s, *San Babila,* the already mentioned *paninari*'s place of choice, had been the meeting point of the right-wing Milanese youth, yet this historical connection was not the sole reason that the area had been chosen. Its proximity to the first fast-food restaurant in Milan, *Burghy,* whose American symbolic value the young gang embraced, was equally pivotal.

The *paninari* (literally meaning "sandwichers") were defined by their uniform: *Armani* Jeans, *Timberland* or *Frye* boots, *Americanino* tops, *Burlington* checked socks, and *Naj-Oleari* handbags for the girls. They skiied in the winter in determined areas (strictly wearing a *Moncler* feather down jacket), holidayed in the summer in Liguria (*Lacoste* t-shirts, *Vans* shoes and *Marina Yachting* garments were then *de rigueur*), and belonged to the gang that met in the allocated places in the city (Figure 8.1).

Everything about the *paninari* typified the self-conscious display of new money which the 1980s brought to Italy, and which manifested itself in careful, neurotic attention to appearance (*paninari* sat under sunlamps compulsively at the *Rino Beauty Center* in the exclusive *via Montenapoleone,* which became a no-go area for non-*paninari*). It should be pointed out that if you tried to copy the look without having been sanctioned by the original group, you might end up being aggressively bullied.

Each *paninaro* monitored the other carefully for the correctness of "the look." In such a world inspired by television commercials, every eye was a camera and every glance a video. Display of one's own perfect outlook

Figure 8.1 Paninari in the Piazza San Babila, Milan, ca. 1983. Courtesy of IL Corriere della Serra Archives.

was therefore fundamental: *paninari* could be found around *San Babila* most days, after school hours, sitting on their motorbikes (the *Zundapp* 175 was the favorite, though not necessarily the only, choice), which provided an in-between place, linking the inside space of the café or favorite shops to the outdoor environment of the city. It was in these "non-places" as Marc Auge' defines them, in these "transitional . . . areas that facilitate the movement of bodies as well as the constant flow of information in and around urban space" (in Quinn 26) that the *paninaro* semiotic was most efficiently conveyed.

Weekends were mostly spent in the appointed clubs of choice, dancing to the beat of British pop music. The *paninari,* in fact, snubbed Italian music and were eventually repaid for their Brit-pop devotion by the band Pet Shop Boys, who wrote the famous, homonymous anthem song *Paninaro.* The *paninari* made the most of the theatrical power of Italian architecture: the piazza and the café were the stages on which they consciously acted. In fact, most of Milan city center from around 1981 to 1988 became neatly demarcated by the areas which the youth movement had elected to be their own: the aformentioned *Rino Beauty Center* in *via Montenapoleone,* the Italian-style McDonald restaurants, *Burghy,* and the *Doria* gym near *San Babila.* Importantly, *paninari* wore their clothes as much as they wore the city, both of which were irremediably entwined with their (carefully manufactured) identity and lifestyle.

On the weekends, the (much) less trendy youth of the Milanese suburbs would make the journey from the outskirts of the city into its elegant center, lured and fascinated by the glamour of the *paninari,* in the secret hope of catching a glimpse of the "real thing" as well as new style hints and gaining the hopeful validation of their own look from which as suburban dwellers they felt (and were) inevitably cut off. This would at the same time appear to satisfy a scopophilic pleasure which was encouraged by the *paninari* themselves, who were always ready to point out to perfect strangers whether they were "in" or "out" with the look. Yet, while the *paninari* seemed to be "policing" youth urban style effectively, they also appeared to resent the "mimicking" of their own "original" appearance.

It wasn't long, however, before different youth groups started challenging the self-professed cultural supremacy of the *paninari,* and gang fights, which took place mostly outside schools, became the norm. At the time, the *paninari* prided themselves on being entirely apolitical, revolting against the overpoliticized 1970s. Yet, the social conflicts that had scarred Milan in the previous decade, when the extreme-left terrorist group "The Red Brigade" had committed a number of high profile homicides and when a second wave of the students' movement was still causing social unrest, had not disappeared, they had simply taken different shapes, finding different outlets of expression in which fashion had come to play a crucial role. The *paninari* were initially labeled "right wingers,," then more aggressively as "fascists," until, eventually they themselves ended up accepting and endorsing this most stigmatic of political labels.

It needs to be stressed that the *paninari* were identified by both their look *and* the Milanese areas they patrolled and controlled. They indeed dressed the city, parts of which they treated as their personal living rooms, and in which they paraded as if living-mannequins in shop windows. They were certainly looked upon and coveted like beautiful objects by most young outsiders.

Their insistence on display appeared to be provocative, stressing an exclusivity which was nevertheless visually highly accessible since the *paninari*'s success was founded, as a group, on being looked at and consequently envied in public spaces: a strategy which allowed them to delimit visual codes, living areas, and even language (the group spoke a peculiar jargon that was mostly unintelligible to the uninitiated). Their language paraphrased the fast, slogan-like, artificial, and overconfident dialogue of TV commercials. The *paninari* longed to live as characters in such commercials: perennially carefree, beautiful, young, tanned, and successful. In the *Paninaro* music video shot by the Pet Shop Boys, the group reached its cultural apotheosis. In it, the *paninari* were finally represented precisely for what they longed to be: representations.

Language, urban space, and the dressing of the body are all major features in determining human identity, which explains why the *paninari* appear as a complete urban subculture and not just a trendy fad.[2] We cannot but agree, therefore, with Anthony Quinn when he states that "fashion space is intensely cinematic . . . a synthesis between fiction and realism. In the fusion between them, the act of shaping and forming social identities is constructed and performed" (36).

THE CITY OF MONOCHROME

In his highly fascinating analysis of architecture and fashion, Quinn affirms that "fashion is a representation of what inhabited space can mean, to the wearer as well as to the onlooker" (27). Quinn is keen to establish a close correspondence between the spatiality of architecture and that of fashion, claiming that we inhabit spaces as much as we inhabit clothes. This is particularly evident in the postmodern megalopolis, like New York and London. It is in the analysis of urban space, in fact, that the closest synergies between fashion and architecture can be detected. Clothes are, ultimately, the most intimate expression of architecture, while acting at the same time as boundary or threshold between our embodied selves and the world.

While not a megalopolis, Milan, one of the key cities of the fashion industry in the world, the queen of *prêt-à-porter,* at least until the turn of the twenty-first century, established in the nineteenth century an intriguing relationship between the spaces and practices of fashion. To the foreign visitor, Milanese fashion, whether it is related to art or sport, food or lei-sure time, appears to be at the heart of the inhabitants' sense of self. As the capital of the Italian financial and "creative" industries, from advertising to PR, from design to broadcasting, from banking to law, Milan seems to demand a heightened level of attention where appearance is concerned. Milanese fashion therefore, exists in excess of its industry, pervading the spaces of existence itself, regulating the daily routines of self-expression and self-presentation.

My study analyzes the relation between Milanese fashion and its living space. *Living* is here indissolubly entwined with the mapping and the signi-fying of a *space,* which is in turn conceived in its broadest and most inter-active sense: as a category in creative synchronicity with existence. Space is what allows existence to take *place* yet it is also the "work in progress" of a life and its embodied subject, the category in and through which cul-tural meanings are both created and negotiated, since life does not unfold in "a void that could be colored by diverse shades of light, [but] inside a set of relations that delineates sites which are irreducible to one another" (Foucault 22).

Generally, Milan is considered an ugly city. For John Foot, Milan is "a non-cinematic city" which is "flat . . . without a river" and where "the light is often bad" (71). Foot remarks how,

> Milan is a grey city, a black-and-white city where only occasional co-lours are allowed to spring out—the pinks of the Duomo . . . the bright blues of spring. Milan is best remembered as grey, in black-and-white . . . [It] is universally recognized as an ugly city—by residents and non-residents alike (Foot 4).

Of this greyness, worsened by the perennial winter fog which the sun rarely manages to penetrate, the Milanese have made a signature feature, embracing a monochromatic world of understated elegance. The natural darkness that pervades the city seems to have led both to the privileg-ing of artificial illumination and to the creation of an infinite number of extremely sophisticated shopping windows, which infuse such grey space with a phantasmagoria of colors. Yet, this same greyness appears to have led the Milanese world of fashion to espouse an aesthetic of containment rather than extravagance, measure rather than excess.

Alessandro Zaccuri interprets the Milanese obsession with "beauty" as the eternal challenge of the city against the natural elements, and which expresses itself in a certain "desire for immateriality" (33). Milan is "the city that longs to be beautiful like the Armani models . . . but which always needs to brush her hair instead, to wear slightly less tight denims or a foun-dation that could cover her wrinkles" (67).[3] The very fact that here Zac-curi employs a fashion metaphor to describe Milan illustrates the extent to which fashion monopolizes the Milanese psyche. For Zaccuri, Milan is a place ashamed of its body (which he implicitly parallels to ugliness); it is a city that has done everything to become immaterial but which, nevertheless, over and over again, finds itself immersed within vulnerability (that is, materiality itself).

The glamorous space of the historical center, which has kept its compact medieval and circular structure, and which appears to compensate for the lack of "natural" beauty and light, is the one that gives Milan its world identity; it is built precisely on a notion of "lustrous immateriality," to paraphrase Zaccuri, and is in strong contradiction with the greyer, uglier, and "material" space of the suburbs. The dialectic that exists between center and periphery, immateriality (i.e., alluring commodity, city lights, high class) and materiality (raw matter, gloom, working class) does not necessarily always generate frustration and resentment among most Milanese (even though the social phenomenon of the *paninari* was precisely constructed on this dialectic as much as the political tumults of the 1970s). It seems, nevertheless, to have provoked an even more persistent aesthetic approval for the exquisiteness of the city center, a more intense longing for the artificiality of the shopping windows' manicured appearance and an inexhaustible admiration for synthetic lights as the only consolatory surrogate for the city's lack of beauty.[4] In fact, Milan is the only city in Italy in which fashion billboards have become cultural landmarks: "in Milan, Missoni and then Armani have led the way with radiant artificial models on . . . billboards the size of buildings, which have surprisingly become even more important as city landmarks than any new architecture, however radiant it may be" (Frisa 384).

Alternatively, the monochromatic Milanese environment has led Milan to develop innovative projects like Gio' Ponti's famous Pirelli skyscraper near the city's central train station. The building appears as a monument to modern simplicity and industrial economy. It also appears to be made only of metal and glass, giving it an illusion of slimness and razor-like consistency. Importantly, everything inside the tower was the product of careful design "furniture, lighting, clocks and lifts" (Foot 118), testifying to that connubial link between life and style which has always been at the core of the Milanese notion of existence and self.

Whether *in spite of* or *because of* such landscape features, since the 1980s Milan has been commonly known as one of the international capitals of fashion. Yet the relationship of the city with spectacle and display, which constitute some of fashion's major features, can also be traced back to the development of the city in the eighteenth and nineteenth centuries, when wealthy patrons privately helped to develop Milan into a version of their living room. In 1816, Stendhal wrote that *"Milan est la ville d'Europe qui a les rues les plus commodes et les plus belles cours dans l'intérieur des maisons"* (Stendal 41).[5] At the same time, the city of Milan has always prided itself as being at the forefront of technological innovation and urban development compared to the rest of Italy.

Elena Papadia writes how

> in 1833, Milan was the first city in Europe to provide regularly organised electrical lighting. Lightning did not start in the streets, but in the theatres and in the shops instead, in particular in the Manzoni theatre and in the Bocconi's brothers store in which the shopping windows started to be illuminated following the criterion of theatrical illumination (24).

Shops like the Bocconi's store (which would later be famously renamed the *Rinascente* by the poet D'annunzio), together with theaters like the *Manzoni* and to a large extent *La Scala* as well, were largely the product of private investment. The Milanese commercial and industrial classes, which included a certain branch of the aristocracy (like the Visconti di Modrone who in the late nineteenth century owned textile factories), can be seen, therefore, to have propelled from an early stage the development of the city and to have profited from property speculation. This is why Milan, at the end of the nineteenth century, was "the only 'European' city that . . . Italy could flaunt as such" (Papadia 24).

The happy union between industry, commerce, and urban development has been a key factor in the "private" development of Milan, which was a city that while in Italy, always looked beyond the Alps for guidance and inspiration and longed to be part of a more "industrialized" and "modern" European society. The Bocconi brothers' store, for example, was the first attempt to introduce ready-to-wear and rationalized mass production to a nation whose economy was still largely agricultural and preindustrial. Nicola White notes how "in the nineteenth century, textiles played a vital pioneering role in the revolution of industrial production [and] the Milanese cotton industry is generally regarded as the first-factory based industry in Italy" (20).

In the interwar years, the imposition of the fascist autarkic regime had helped Italian fashion, to a certain extent, to gain confidence in itself and its own resources, while the subsequent partnership in the post-World-War-II era between Milan and its surrounding industrial area, the *Brianza,* contributed to the development of the design industry of which the Pirelli tower was an innovative result. Because of this long-term partnership, Milan has always embraced, more than cities like Florence and Rome, a rhetoric of modernity rather than one of nostalgia, which resulted in a futuristic and less languid approach to fashion. The minimalist black and grey Milanese fashion trademark is also reflected in many of the contemporary design choices for commercial venues like, for example, the MH Way shop. The brand, which possesses cult status in Milan, was created by Japanese designer Makio Hasuike, who opened his first designer studio in Milan in 1968. While MH Way specializes mostly in business and travel briefcases, its cult status was attained in the early 1980s in producing innovative bags meant to satisfy "architects, designers and engineers' needs as well as the needs of people who had to carry around and show drawings and projects" (http://www.mhway.it). The brand prides itself in creating "simple forms and very accurate details" (http://www.mhway.it), using a palette of mostly black and white. The MH team favored the same innovative essentiality of lines and colors in the creation of its shopping venues where steel and glass dominate.

The Milanese economic-aesthetic debt to its (now past) industrial economy can be also traced in the transformation of many former industrial areas into entertainment spaces like the *Magazzini Generali,* which used to be a warehouse and whose ample, austere space now hosts a club and various cultural events.

If, on the one hand, the commercial class was pivotal in shaping the city as a consumerist center, as a city of lights, at the same time many Milanese buildings dating from the seventeenth century had been built to link in a peculiar way the sheltered environment of the private home to the external space of public life. In the center of town, many palaces, in fact, possess private courtyards, which while being inaccessible to passersby, also theoretically link the indoor to the outdoor. Enclosed courtyards are in-between spaces, thresholds, where the inhabitants can be glimpsed while still being in the safety of their private homes. They are also voyeuristic places, hiding luxury while revealing just enough of it to make luxury visible and therefore coveted.

The center of Milan is a space rich in thresholds, with its porticos and arcades, and gives, at times, the feeling of an interior space with an open sky. The famous *Galleria Vittorio Emanule,* where the historic Prada shop, which opened in 1922, is located, is commonly called "the Milanese living room." The glass-roofed *Galleria,* which connects the main *Piazza Duomo* with *La Scala,* gives a feeling of being indoors and outdoors at the same time, and is paved with marble like most Milanese bourgeois apartments. To the same extent as Walter Benjamin's Paris, Milan's arcade is "a cross between a street and an intérieur" and the Milanese Galleria is equally "lined with the most elegant shops so that such an arcade is a city, even a world, in miniature" (Benjamin 37), providing the possibility of strolling in safety, while shopping and eating at the same time.

To testify to the importance of such a construction in the Milanese identity, in the big Armani centre in *via Manzoni* "the length of the building is bisected by what the designer and architect refer to as an internal street, a modern echo of Milan's glass roofed Galleria Vittorio Emanule" (Bingham 52). In the "block of gold" of the city center "pavements themselves were [and are] immaculately kept, with plants, carpets and other street-decorations" (Foot 128), reinforcing the bond established between the outdoor space of the streets and the indoor one of the living room.

The confusion between indoor and outdoor space, a feature that is considered quintessentially postmodern, has been intrinsic to the development of Milanese urban space long before postmodernism became part of the canonical theoretical lexicon. The relatively limited size of the city and the dominance of a bourgeois, even aristocratic, commercial class contributed to the development of unique public spaces in which many areas have been built up to resemble private rooms while, at the same time, private lodgings have been turned into commercial venues.

In particular, before other Italian regions, the Milanese aristocracy were involved in industrial production and, since space was at a premium due to the compactness of the city, they did not necessarily refrain from living in smaller buildings rather than in the imposing ones that could be found in Rome, Naples, and Palermo. Equally, beginning in the first half of the nineteenth century, the dwellings of choice of the bourgeoisie were large apartments, which whilst still impressive, were smaller than the aristocratic *palazzi*.[6] By necessity, where space is more constrained, life tends to be lived in larger measure outdoors, and hence the rite of the evening aperitif, which in Milan dates back to the late nineteenth century when Gaspare Campari, the founder of the famous brand of liqueur and himself a trained *liquorista* (liqueur maker), moved both his bar and home to the *Galleria*. His son Davide transformed the small family business into a full-fledged industrial enterprise. It is Davide who created *Campari Soda,* a premixed cocktail sold in the now celebrated cone-shaped bottle designed by the Italian Futurist Fortunato Depero (http://www.culturadelbere.it).

The evening aperitif was usually accompanied by a stroll and became a way to catch up with friends. Going out for an aperitif meant recreating the space of the living room where display, eating, and socializing were interconnected. It is a custom that is still very common and which is considered quintessentially Milanese. It comprises much more than just the social consumption of drinks since bars now include in the price a vast amount of food. The *paninari* themselves could have been seen as perpetrators of such Milanese custom, obsessively combining strolling, parading, and eating. The fashion sense of the *paninaro lifestyle,* in fact, moved beyond clothing not only to include which food one ate, but also what bar one went to, which motorbike one rode. All the aforementioned were equally determining factors of belonging to the group since one's own *life* was synonymous with one's own *style*.

Since the afternoon aperitif is equally a social occasion, food tasting, and fashion parade, it uniquely connects the fashion industry to the practice(s) of fashion. Certain bars will favor certain looks and crowds, while the drinking and the tasting always spills outside the allocated space of bars into the streets, courtyards, or sidewalks. The rapid exploitation of the connections such as these is evident in the collaboration between the most important designers and the food industry.

In a recent article in the *Guardian,* "Milan on a Plate," John Arlidge remarks that "designer branding doesn't end at the till in Italy's style capital—many labels now have their own restaurants and bars, too." Therefore, "the fashion industry has . . . expanded into corporate culture. They have become lifestyle producers, and are thus in a position to go beyond mere clothing to equip people with anything" (Arlidge).

In contrast to that which is often presupposed, Milanese commercial spaces have frequently adhered to, rather than opposed, the aesthetic of the private lodging where display and spectacle were no less important. Like their Parisian counterparts, Milanese high-class private spaces have always abounded in expensive furniture, glossy photographs, elaborate curtains and tablecloths, paintings and works of art, china, and crystal exhibited in glass cabinets. Some of the most famous architects that have been adopted by the Milanese bourgeoisie since the 1930s, such as Tomaso Buzzi (1900–81)—who was born in Sondrio but worked mostly in Milan collaborating with Gio' Ponti in the early phase of his career—espoused, like another eccentric architect of the time, the Turin-born Carlo Mollino, an aesthetic of "home as self-portrait." They both designed spaces "full or artifice, utilizing theatrical techniques, manifesting the claustrophiliac [*sic*] taste for the nest" (Frisa 404). The status and wealth of the bourgeois owners needed to be displayed with imposing antique and expensive furniture, paintings, lightning, and rugs, while drapes were often chosen to conceal walls, as if to "dress" the house, adding an extra tactile dimension which appears to "cite" the human body. Carlo Mollino, in a similar way to the Milanese Buzzi, "viewed the home as a background to life, a support and mirror of its inhabitant's psyche," treating the home "not exactly [as] a building, but as an experience" (Frisa 324).

What is important to highlight here is the fundamental importance given to the "dressing up" of the house over its functionality. Both architects in their projects for private dwellings commissioned by wealthy patrons "dandified" the house, which was then conceived as another form of affirmation of one's exclusive personal style so that the elegant vestment of the body becomes the extension of the elegant salon, which while private has to continue the public need for display of one's own luxury and wealth.

The shape of the Italian bourgeois apartment has always reserved a space for public decoration and display in the *salotto* or *soggiorno* (drawing or living room). Rarely used and often kept locked, such a room was a space for a space's sake, a small museum-like area that attested to the established status of the family. As Foot points out "the *salotto* had tended to be a no-go area, used only in special family occasions" (90).

Wealthier Milanese bourgeois apartments possessed a *salone,* a much wider room than a simple *salotto,* which attempted to mimic the aristocratic *palazzo* where ample, impressive spaces were purposefully created for entertaining on a large scale.

The *salone* was the most public of all of the private spaces, though the least useful, in which one received important guests and in which the best clothes were worn. It also provided a certain debutante-like training for the young ones of the family, who would learn to develop their social skills by interacting with people of older age under the vigilant eyes of parents. In this respect, the display function of the *salone* linked private to public life.

Such training in the display of one's appearance and wealth, fundamental to the upbringing of the upper classes, became a key feature of the fashion industry when, after World War II, the Italian aristocracy found itself greatly impoverished. Many aristocratic women in particular, like the Marchesa de Gresy or Simonetta Visconti, who dressed wealthy Roman women in the 1950s, did not eschew declassifying themselves by starting careers in fashion, a trade they saw as a potential for commercial success. These women "may have lacked technical knowledge, but they were seen as elegant, sophisticated and refined and they traded on their sophisticated notion of exclusive Italian good taste." They always operated on a small scale "from craft-oriented workshops" (White 38).

Such a tradition, which had much less aristocratic origins in Milan where the bourgeois Gigliola Curiel, Biki, and Jole Veneziani reigned supreme (each of whom always insisted in calling themselves "*sarte*" or "seamstresses," shunning the term "stylists"), was vital to the development of the Milanese fashion industry, which, in turn, found its apotheosis in the ritual of display at the first night of the season at *La Scala* where the link between the indoor and the outdoor spaces of spectacle became self-evident.

Since the eighteenth century, *La Scala* had represented one of the "salons de la ville" in the phraseology of Stendhal. Throughout the nineteenth century, the opera theater had become a second home for the aristocracy. Indeed, the aristocracy were accustomed to taking their dinner in the boxes of the theater. To attend a performance at *La Scala* meant to be part of the show. One went there to see and be seen: whilst music was one element, it was certainly not the only component of entertainment. The connection between *La Scala,* high fashion, and spectacle often had more direct links. Biki, the appointed designer of *la divina* Maria Callas, could count Puccini as her step-grandfather.

It is also interesting to note that the Milanese *via Montenapoleone,* the most elegant street of the "block of gold" (Foot 127), was originally almost entirely occupied by antique art and furniture dealers rather than fashion designers. Yet the substitution of furniture with fashion in the twentieth century is readily explicable: fashion continued the need for spectacle that was already at the heart of the wealthy way of life, while furniture, before the era of *prêt-à-porter,* already manifested the connection between fashion and space, the overlapping between the dressing of one's body and that of one's living space.

One of the most famous fashion designers in the Milanese postwar era, Jole Veneziani, whose nickname was "velvet paw" by reason of her dexterity with and love of furs, like Biki had located her atelier in *via Montenapoleone* from whose private, internal courtyard "there would rise a strong, extremely pleasant smell of caramel, a present from the Cova café-patisserie whose kitchen bordered on the courtyard." The atelier consisted of "a grey and gold huge seventeenth-century salon with painted panels, changing rooms with tall mirrors and heavy curtains that muffled voices and kept the choices of her incredibly jealous and competitive customers absolutely secret" (*Vergani* 1220).

Before Dolce & Gabbana revisited the concept, transforming a private aristocratic palazzo in *Corso Venezia* into a three-story commercial venue, much postwar fashion had linked naturally the semipublic space of the salon to that of the "fashion atelier," which was a space in between the public area of the shop and the private one of the dwelling.[7]

The fact that the salon in the Italian house was reserved for display was evident in its necessary separation from the kitchen, which had, as a paramount consideration, to be kept out of sight because it conveyed an unduly informal and intimate message. Until the 1980s, when the notion of open-space living started taking hold, the kitchen remained tainted as a working-class environment, embarrassing for the insight that it would provide into the more prosaic "materiality" of daily life.

It was often in the living room that the new technological instrument, the television set, was accommodated, a choice which logically continued the display-function of this area. The television, a media that through advertisement directly combines spectacle and consumerism, strengthened the connection between private lodging and commercial venues. Quinn rightly highlights that "the fashion industry exploits [the] media to instil the desire to be seen, be visible and even pursued. As the body becomes increasingly monitored by the fashion world, it creates a parallel culture of self-surveillance, in which individuals must also scrutinize themselves to monitor their social acceptability" (18).

The fact that Milan, thanks to the media-guru Silvio Berlusconi, became the city of private television, which was entirely supported by advertising, contributed to the perception of the city as one of commerce and fashion, feeding on a postcapitalistic, private economy of services. Berlusconi located his television headquarters in a small residential suburb on the outskirts of Milan called *Milano 2,* whose development he had financed in the late 1970s.

Milano 2 was a relatively new concept, albeit of North American inspiration: it was a space entirely and reassuringly "artificial," the antithesis of the working-class suburb. It sported a profusion of fake ponds and manicured lawns, a Disney-like atmosphere of enclosed living, total safety, and constant surveillance, while the Berlusconi logo (a revisitation of the aristocratic Visconti crest: a snake dragon embracing a newborn) was engraved everywhere. It is no surprise that the entertainment industry elected *Milano 2* as its location of choice. The creation of glamorous apartments within the development, many of which possessed spectacular features like ample balconies, further contributed to a certain blurring between the spaces of display, lifestyle, and commerce. Interestingly, it was in the TV studios of *Milano 2* that the first images of the *paninari* were broadcast to the majority of the Italian nation in the TV cult program *Drive in,* as if Berlusconi had been eager to appropriate as rightfully his own this youth movement in which fashion, new money, and display were deeply entwined.

If *Milano 2* had the ambition to become the postcapitalistic simulacrum of the "real Milan," attempting to dematerialize existence, to turn life into a glamorous commercial, in order to oppose the allure of the "other" more historical and necessarily more politicized (because bearing the weigh of history) Milan, old Milan itself had long ago inspired rather than learned the lesson of *Milano 2* by embracing the total commercialization of its own space. This is what *La Scala* and the *Galleria Vittorio Emanuele* already offered, and the process would be followed later by the big designer labels— Armani, Missoni, Versace—each of whom installed their headquarters in historical palaces of the city center, often locating them very close to their flagship stores.

In spite of the international reach of the Italian super-brands, it must be stressed that the fashion economy of Milan was mostly born on craft, on small family businesses that operated in intimate ateliers, which continued the humble seamstress's work undertaken in one's private (often working-class) dwellings, as in the case of Biki, Gigliola Curiel, and Jole Veneziani. Such an economy is not simply the anachronistic antecedent of contemporary global fashion, since it is from such a small family business structure that global luxury brands, such as Prada, have often been born.

Even today, the daily practices of the Milanese fashion crowd are not necessarily in tune with those promoted by the international corporate industry of "Made in Italy." The world-famous designers do not automatically dress the Milanese with the totality that is often believed. The boutique-like Milanese mentality endorses micro labels of limited local diffusion as much as its cherished world famous designers, of whom Armani and Prada are certainly the most "Milanese."

As I have pointed out, the specificity of a certain Milanese city space, architecture, and social structure has created a unique relationship between Milan and its *fashionistas,* which is often ignored by the outside world, and which, in turn, sees in Milan the solely (now declining) global capital of *prêt-à-porter.* This is why along with being the capital of international "Made in Italy," there exists a space of microfashion, which often pleasantly surprises the tourists and indirectly strengthens the perception of Milan as one of the world's capitals of style, giving the impression that the superbrands are, to a certain extent, only the tip of the iceberg, the corporate expression of a general widespread Italian creativity.[8]

The Milanese fashion industry, therefore, has always been a dynamic and fragmented environment where the "Esperanto of high fashion," to paraphrase David Gilbert, is always already mixed with "the local dialect" (Breward and Gilbert 12). Small niches of local designers and brands—from the currently cult-item *Gallo* socks to the historical *Panca*'s shoes, from *Valextra*'s luggage to *Boggi* shirts and ties—have created powerful microtrends (as in the case of the *Naj-Oleari* association with the *paninari* in the 1980s) and, while never crossing the Alps, have been very powerful for the local economy and the Milanese sense of self.

What such microfashions reveal is the expression of a more tightly personalized, certainly provincial, "piazza-informed" boutique culture that has interacted with and been produced by the boutique-space and the peculiar social structure of the city. We cannot underestimate such a powerful cultural feature of Milan even in the now predominant young world of Asian "fast fashion," corporate capitalism, and globalization. In turn, what this illustrates is that Milanese creativity, in spite of social rebellion and contradiction, revels in a perennial obsession with the ornamental detailing of appearance together with an equally obsessive need for its display.

NOTES

1. Interesting footages of the time can be seen at http://www.youtube.com/watch?v=7QQDdRdHvck
2. See Dick Hebdige, *Subculture,* for a careful theoretical investigation of the notion of subculture and its relation to both dominant and subordinate value systems.
3. All translations, unless otherwise indicated, are mine.
4. Elena Papadia, for example, remarks how, in the 1950s, to be a shop assistant at the department store *La Rinascente* gave the illusion "of accessing a world of elegance and refinement." Among other things, employees, "wore uniforms designed by Schiaparelli in Paris and were given a free weekly trip to the hairdresser's (114–15)."
5. "Milan is the European city with the most comfortable streets and the most beautiful internal courtyards."
6. See Giorgio Bigatti. *La Citta' Operosa*. Milano: Franco Angeli, 2000.
7. A certain commercialization of space was also customary within the more humble world of the artisans in whose small private dwellings their activities were mostly carried out (knitting, sewing, cobbling, etc.). See Giorgio Bigatti. *La Citta' Operosa*.
8. Kristie Clemens' letter to the Editor's in *Vogue Australia* (December 1999), for example, stated that in precedence to the catwalk, it was "more compelling . . . watching the utterly chic men and women of Milan going about their business."

WORKS CITED

Arlidge, John. "Milan on a Plate." *The Guardian* (May 2006).
Auge,' Marc. *Non-Places. Introduction to an Anthropology of Supermodernity*. London: Verso, 1995.
Benjamin, Walter. *Charles Baudelaire*. London: Verso, 1997.
Bigatti, Giorgio. *La Citta' Operosa. Milano nell'Ottocento*. Milano: Franco Angeli, 2000.
Bingham, Neal. *The New Boutique*. London: Merrell, 2005.

Breward, Cristopher and David Gilberd (eds.). *Fashion's World Cities*. Oxford: Berg, 2006.

Foot, John. *Milan Since the Miracle: City, Culture and Identity*. Oxford: Berg, 2001.

Foucault, Michel. "Of Other Spaces." *Diacritics* 16 (1986): 22–27.

Frisa, Maria Luisa, Mario Lupano, and Stefano Tonchi (eds.). *Total Living*. Milan: Charta, 2002.

Hebdige, Dick. *Subculture. The Meaning of Style*. London: Routledge, 2006.

Klein, Caroline (ed.). *Cool Shops Milan*. New York: teNeues, 2005.

Papadia, Elena. *La Rinascente*. Bologna: Il Mulino, 2005.

Quinn, Bradley. *The Fashion of Architecture*. Oxford: Berg, 2003.

Stendhal. *Rome, Naples et Florence*. Paris: Gallimard, 1987.

Vergani, Guido (ed.). *Dizionario della Moda*. Milano: Baldini Castoldi Dalai, 2003.

White, Nicola. *Reconstructing Italian Fashion. America and the Development of the Italian Fashion Industry*. Oxford: Berg, 2000.

Zaccuri, Alessandro. *Milano, Citta' di Nessuno*. Napoli: l'ancora, 2003.

9 Libertine Acts
Fashion and Furniture

Peter McNeil

In the years 2004 through 2006, the Metropolitan Museum of Art staged two major sequential exhibitions of costumes which attempted a new experience in the public gallery. *Dangerous Liaisons: Fashion and Furniture in the Eighteenth Century* and *AngloMania: Tradition and Transgression in British Fashion* interwove fashion, furniture, and period rooms to create a highly charged theatrical event for the viewing public. This chapter considers the different concepts of time played out in each exhibition, and the interdependency between a historical tradition and the contemporary fashion marketplace. Both exhibitions opened up many questions that might be fruitfully explored. What is the affinity between fashion, body, artifact, and space? Do developments in the history of furniture parallel developments in the history of clothing styles? Is furniture in fact more inventive in this period than costume in propelling the body in new directions? The chapter concludes with a consideration of the relationship between historical fashion, museology, display, theatricality, and the contemporary marketing of fashion in the twenty-first century.

DANGEROUS LIAISONS: FASHION AND FURNITURE IN THE EIGHTEENTH CENTURY (APRIL–SEPTEMBER 2004)

Sponsored by luxury brand Asprey and publisher Condé Nast, hosted as "The Party of the Year at the Metropolitan Museum of Art Costume Institute Benefit Gala" by Anna Wintour and Renée Zellweger, *Dangerous Liaisons* proposed to examine fashion's "aesthetic interplay with art, furniture, and the broader decorative arts between 1750 and 1789." It did so by creating a set of dressed and posed mannequins to animate and elucidate the spaces of the fabulous Wrightsman rooms, which constitute a design history lesson in elite rococo and neoclassical French interior architecture. In returning historical fashion to the museum room set—a feature of 1950s and 1960s contextual decorative arts exhibits including "Costume: Period Rooms Re-occupied in Style" (Metropolitan Museum of Art 1963–64)—the installation proposed the possibility of studying the tangible but challenging task of interpreting the links between the decorative arts of a discrete period.

The exhibition was entered through a dramatic upswept curtain, held aside by a voyeuristic couple dressed in eighteenth-century costumes. Their pose and dress indicated that this was a show about France and Francophile culture, wholly appropriate to the Wrightsman smorgasbord of eighteenth-century interiors. Unlike the English period rooms, the French series were arranged rather like a movie lot or a street. This encouraged and supported the viewer to organize his/her vision in a cinematic manner by following a series of highly charged moments drawn from literary vignettes and the poses and situations of eighteenth-century prints, notably Rétif de la Bretonne's "Monument du Costume" (1789, reproduced prints of the 1770s). Other situations were drawn from caricature, such as the scene in which a hairdresser climbs a library step in order to garnish a *montgolfier* or ballooning-style headdress.

Dangerous Liaisons employed synthetic-hair wigs to create a more "real" effect than we have seen in many recent exhibits of fashion. Some of the masterpieces of eighteenth-century hairdressing were wittily rendered, derived from the study of French portraits, journals such as *Galerie des Modes,* as well as the eighteenth-century treatise on hairdressing *L'Art de la Coëffure des Dames Françoises* (1768), a copy of which was displayed nonchalantly on one of the chairs. Many of the styles were exaggerated, however, which probably convinced a public already suspicious that this was an absurd age. The dressed figures—which flirt, faint, fan themselves, feign shock—enjoyed mixed success. Some, like the woman seated on a *chaise longue,* looked alert, natural, and thoroughly Enlightenment, and emphasized the new types of furnishing comfort offered by modern upholstery and seating forms.

In placing the mannequins in the Wrightsman Galleries, the curators were restrained by the limitations of display space and a preordained grouping of furniture and other decorative arts. Since museum-quality furniture cannot be photographed animated by real bodies, it was a salutary aim to reconsider the interaction of dress, body, textile, furniture, lighting, and space. Furniture is always designed with a body in mind—sometimes even absent ones. As Leora Auslander argues in her chapter "The Courtly Stylistic Regime," furniture for royal patrons in seventeenth-century France was so costly and impossible to emulate that its very presence could stand in for the body of the King (40–51). In "Architecture in the Bedroom," architectural historian Rodolphe el Khoury examines the *maison de plaisance* with its orchestrated progression of spaces of seduction, perfumed woodwork, dazzling optical effects, and progressively more comfortable and enveloping furnishings, set out in the libertine novel *The Little House* by J-F de Bastide. Such a path of pleasurable wandering and fantasy for the contemporary museum-goer was admirably suggested by introducing dressed mannequins suggestive of movement in the formerly fixed schema of the period rooms.

The exciting title of the Metropolitan exhibit, *Fashion and Furniture*, suggested examination of this most understudied aspect of design history. There are few studies of the relationship of dress, object, and spatial design in Enlightenment culture which go beyond stylistic history or generalized comments about the shift to informality or comfort. A notable exception is Mimi Hellman's essay on elite French furniture, sociability, politeness, viewing, and control, with its notion of eighteenth-century chairs, coffers, and tables as "visual and kinetic; objects [that] were not simply owned, but indeed performed" (417). She goes so far as to suggest that the proliferation and intricacies of furniture types "was linked to a growing impulse among elites to complicate and privatize the art of conduct" (437). Similarly, Dena Goodman sees the writing desk as more than a luxury item, but a new way of managing writing, display and discrimination (Goodman 74–75). Other useful models include Daniel Roche's magisterial study of material culture, Katie Scott's detailed work on the rococo interior, Carolyn Sargentson on the luxury trades, Piero Camporesi on food and lifestyle, and Yannick Chastang on marquetry furniture or "painting in wood." The room notes told us that *ancien régime* furniture became more accommodating of the body, but fashion "sought to shape and mould the body to prevailing ideals of beauty." This argument about comfort and "negligence" and the "natural" shape of the body was unclear. Was fashion constricting where furniture tried to "liberate" or modernize the actions and forms of the body?

Other analogies could be challenged. We were told that the latticework marquetry on a piece of marquetry and ormolu royal furniture by Riesener is synergistic with the latticework on a brocaded silk banyan and a muslin gown. Yet the origins of the latticework on the furniture probably lie in Japanese lacquer models, and the royal desk is of another order from the muslin gown. Marie-Antoinette had a separate wardrobe for use at the Petit Trianon, which was furnished differently from the royal apartments at Versailles. We were told that the *polonaise* dress in its transformative capacity parallels the transformative aspects of mechanical furniture (Figure 9.1). The idea is interesting but does it hold? In another example, a Chinese-painted silk was placed in a painted *boiserie* room whose sorbet colors echoed that of the dress fabric. But it might have been more useful to place this dress in the neoclassical bleached oval salon. The relationship of colors to notions of taste, harmony, and the composition of the dressed body in space is still little understood, despite the large amount of research available within the history of portraiture.

The exhibition raised many questions: Do developments in the history of furniture—the creation of new furniture forms such as the *bureau plat*, the *commode*, and the multiplication of seating types—parallel developments in the history of clothing styles? Is furniture in fact more inventive in this period than costume in propelling the body in new directions? Men's fashion has been depicted as more progressive than women's in the long eighteenth century (this is the argument of Anne Hollander's *Sex and Suits*).

Figure 9.1 Pierre Thomas Le Clerc (1739–85), *La Gouvenesse,* watercolor drawing, for *Gallerie des modes et costumes français dessinés d'après nature, gravés par les plus célèbres artistes en ce genre* . . . (Paris, les Srs Esnaults et Rapilly, 1778–87). Courtesy of the Martin Kamer Collection.

Decorative-arts historians, citing makers like Martin Carlin who worked for broker-entrepreneurs or *marchand-merciers,* argue that innovation in types and forms of furniture was more strongly marked in that produced "chiefly for use by women" (Darr 55). How do furniture and fashion together relate to theorizations of taste and desire? (el-Khoury 41). Was furniture more innovative in its techniques, production, and forms than fashion, because the King permitted foreign masters to practice outside the guild structure, and new demands of sociability required it? Does the shift from luxurious parquetry and marquetry inlays to large fields of rich brown or plum-pudding mahogany in the English taste echo the shift from heavily and dense brocaded silks to the use of painted Chinese silk, light spotted and striped silks and muslins? What analogy might be made between the specialization of the guilds that produced the silk, fly-fringe and ribbons for dress, and the carcase, inlaid or parquetry woods, ormolu mounts and silk-lined interiors for elite courtly furniture? It would also be interesting to consider the relationship of Japanese lacquer mounted in French furniture depicting landscape and architectural forms to the bizarre and rococo silks used for women's dress silks. Instead, the brochure notes referred very generally to the Chinese exoticism of a crimson lacquer (but unpictorial) royal desk.

The display of eighteenth-century clothes has a natural synergy with a mannered performativity. The theatricality inherent in aristocratic French life sanctions such a usage. At the Metropolitan, the clothes were viewed from a distance, on naturalistic bodies which emphasized the importance of codified gesture and that relationship of dress and body revolving around balletic gesture. The downside is that the details of the fabric and fabrication were impossible to see. Clothes such as these demanded and encouraged minute and careful attention as they glimmered in candlelight, brushed against Chinese silk upholstery, and rustled over ormolu mounts. The other pitfall of such an exhibit is that it presented a very limited narrative of historical dress, one dominated by rococo stereotypes. Yes, it was fun, but many of the public went away with their worst suspicions of this period confirmed. "That's all they did in the eighteenth century," said one bemused visitor of the libertine liaisons conducted by these highly sexed mannequins.

Should institutions with lesser resources attempt such an exhibition in the period rooms which abound in world museums? It is probably risky, but with the Metropolitan Museum of Art an important departure in costume installation has been made. The "specter" of this show is Debora Silverman's critique of Diana Vreeland's tenure at the Costume Institute, condemning her theatrical and ahistorical exhibitions, which blurred fashion magazine and photographic styling, department store display and museum exhibits. In a sense of *déja-vu,* American *Vogue* magazine covered the recent Metropolitan Museum opening and also featured contemporary dresses styled by Hamish Bowles in a *dix-huitième* manner. As all costume exhibits are fabrications anyway, and clothes require animation of some type to make sense, perhaps theatricality is necessary in the museum gallery. The nature of *popular* conceptions of eighteenth-century life, ideas about "life-style," and male and female sartorial systems within Sofia Coppola's artful film *Marie Antoinette* will provide fruitful research projects in the future. The exhibits and the film are surely related.

ANGLOMANIA: TRADITION AND TRANSGRESSION IN BRITISH FASHION (MAY–SEPTEMBER 2006)

Dangerous Liaisons laid the ground for a show at the Metropolitan Museum of Art that functioned as its pendant, the even more theatrical and dazzling *AngloMania: Tradition and Transgression in British Fashion.* The term "Anglomania" (*anglomanie*), which was used in the eighteenth-century periodical press to refer to broad-brimmed men's hats, pastoral modes of women's dress, as well as simple unmounted mahogany furniture, was first made popular in late-twentieth-century usage by Vivienne Westwood, whose collection of Autumn through Winter 1993 of that name clearly inspired the title of the Metropolitan show. This name continues to be used for Westwood's diffusion fashion range as well as her commercial perfume, whose publicity claims that it expresses "the duality of a woman picking up the best of different cultures." "Anglomania" also holds the sense of an "obsession" or orgasmic frenzy which is fitting for the fashion media as it suggests a crazed interest. Whether Westwood or the Metropolitan Museum of Art also intended it is as a joke on the cult of Englishness post-1980 (rather than post-1780) is unclear. In the New York exhibition, "AngloMania" was used as a shorthand for a particular type of Britishness in fashion characterized by playful historicism (Vivienne Westwood, John Galliano, Manolo Blahnik, Christopher Bailey, Philip Treacy, Stephen Jones) as well as dissent (Malcolm McLaren and Westwood in her punk phase, Alexander McQueen, Hussein Chalayan), with the dates 1976 through 2006. Most of these designers, especially jewelry designer Shaun Leane, cross these lines of historicism and subversion. The exhibition continued ideas established by Richard Martin and Harold Koda in their exhibition and publication, *The Historical Mode: Fashion and Art in the 1980s* (FIT 1989–90), in which they argued that "[a]n unremitting modernism—a long-standing cult of the new—has seemingly come to a rapprochement with memory and an alliance with history" (15).

Anglomania has now entered contemporary parlance, in part due to the publicity machine of *Vogue* magazine, which featured the stunning clothes worn by partygoers at the spectacular opening night. A new designation of the term—"AngloMania [*sic*]"—was constructed for the exhibition, one which marks it as a more contemporary expression but also artfully distinguishes it from the term found in historical sources and the Vivienne Westwood marketing. *AngloMania* also proposed a different concept of historical time and a different relationship between a historical tradition and the contemporary fashion marketplace. Unlike *Dangerous Liaisons, AngloMania* mixed British fashion of the past thirty years with eighteenth- and nineteenth-century prototypes, rather akin to Judith Clark's 2004 exhibition *Spectres*. The show proposed to consider the way in which British designers "have looked to past styles with an appetite that is as audacious as it is rapacious." The curator Richard Bolton used the garments and their staging to suggest themes such as the significance of historical fashion precedents for contemporary design, the long-term impact of national English "traditions" such as pastoralism and gardening, fashion practices such as dressing-up, balls, and dandyism, and the theatricality inherent in clothing as disparate as punk or Westwood's *couture* collections. This ambitious task was made possible by placing the garments in the context of already densely coded and furnished English period rooms, rearranged for the purposes of the exhibition.

In presenting over two years firstly a French-, and then an English-themed, exhibition, the Museum was creating a conversation which had a historical basis—the potential to consider the Anglo-French fashion relationship during the *ancien-régime*. But it also had a symmetry in terms of marketing. The meaning of these exhibitions is complicated by the fact that in both cases the opening event and accompanying publications were supported by luxury brand Asprey (for the French exhibit) and Burberry (for *AngloMania*), and publisher Condé Nast, and each hosted in turn as "The Party of the Year at the Metropolitan Museum of Art Costume Institute Benefit Gala." In using the term "AngloMania" (*anglomanie*), which refers to the French nation's "seduction" by soft, informal styles of English sporting and pastoral dress, did the exhibition in fact reinforce a notion of innate French superiority? Or in staging the English show as the *finale,* had English style triumphed in the contemporary imagination and marketplace? What role did the fashion worn by the celebrity visitors on opening night—styles by Alexander McQueen and John Galliano, working-class English-trained male designers now working for French houses—have on shaping popular conceptions of contemporary style? Did *AngloMania* suggest that the English nation now triumphed in style matters, or was it necessary to filter it through a French lens? References to sponsor Burberry's reinvention of the company as youthful and directional were clearly evoked.

Dangerous Liaisons had integrated posed and dressed mannequins surrounded by evocative props of the same date in a narrative structure. *AngloMania,* on the other hand, dispensed with any narrative and staged a series of *tableaux* in the newly restored English period rooms, which interconnect in more direct and intimate ways than the French galleries. In the English suite, apertures and doorways lead the visitor from a rococo space such as the Kirtlington Park Room (1748) to a reconstructed Robert Adam salon in the Lansdowne House Dining Room (1766–69). In the 1950s, curatorial decisions were taken not to replicate like spaces, so Kirtlington Park ceased to be for dining as it would compete with the Lansdowne. The effect of this was to make the visitor feel that they really pass through a mansion, whereas the Wrightsman rooms feel like a movie set. The irony of Vivienne Westwood's "Queen-ish Ensemble" from the *Harris Tweed* collection (Autumn/Winter 1987–88) or Alexander McQueen and David Bowie's collaborative "Union Jack Jacket" (distressed fabric, 1996–97) achieved their ultimate point once positioned in the grandeur of these furnished surrounds of the highest *bon ton*. Because one could see different facets of the English period rooms simultaneously, one could create a private set of narratives. *Tableaux* are designed to be taken in quite quickly as general effects. This seemed to be a new type of exhibition for dissemination in new media, as if it were for the net-generation, the sort of thing my fashion design students would enjoy. Like *Dangerous Liasions,* it was also a show that was very effective when activated by properly lit photography in the accompanying publicity, but *AngloMania* was much more about an immediate impression, image, and mood. It looked superb in the pod broadcast on the *New York Times* site—like the fashion Oscars. There was even an official Metropolitan Museum of Art podcast and audio file of John Rotten discussing fashion and society, and a CD *AngloMania: British Pop Music 1976–2006* was retailed by the museum. Due to the need to photograph the installation shots *in situ,* the accompanying catalogues were not available at the time of the exhibits. Thus, the viewer experience of the show was not mediated through the short catalogue essays and the large number of related documentary photographs (Bolton; Koda and Bolton). The latter photographs, which appeared flatter and more forensic than the theatrical lighting in the exhibition, do not reflect accurately the experience of the exhibitions. Rather, like the fashion parade, museum exhibits can be transient and ephemeral experiences, none more so than this pair.

AngloMania was more abstract and conceptual than *Dangerous Liasions,* in keeping with the styling and the topic—a brief which was not easily discernible without the program or a fashion knowledge. Whereas *Dangerous Liasions* was entered past a gesturing courtier, the visitor to AngloMania passed beneath a roughly stitched Union Jack, its fabrication a reference to punk, tradition, and subversion, echoed in the beautiful watercolor rendering of flags designed as prepublicity by Kinmonth Monfreda. Two male figures stood at the opening: a courtier with hair styled like an eighteenth-century "fribble" (an extreme macaroni) who perched on an artful but rough wooden tumbril, and a punk opposite astride a modern industrial scaffold. The mannerism of the caricatured eighteenth-century hair matched the "real" stylization achieved in the 1970s by punk. The opening sequence, then, set up a dialogue between men, which marked an important part of the exhibits, and not gallantry, as in *Dangerous Liasions.* Much of the weight of the fashion narrative in this exhibit is carried by men and by menswear. The exhibition mixed up servant and master in interesting ways as well as the "gender dimorphism" theme of fashion history, played out in ideas of uniform/uniformity (including spectacular livery) and hunting dress, versus the opulence of women in ball gowns.

Whereas both exhibitions were markedly spectacular and theatrical, AngloMania was styled more like a contemporary *défilé* or Barney's shop window than an eighteenth-century genre painting. It did this remarkably successfully and in so doing created installations that permitted the viewer to reimagine both clothing and spaces in new ways. Into this stately home were introduced accessories such as brilliant oversized abstracted flower hats by Philip Treacy after his Spring/Summer 2000 collection ("Paphiope-dilum *philippinense* Orchid Hat") and his Autumn/Winter collection 2001 through 2002 ("Venetian Mourning Hat"). They were installed above eighteenth-century Spitalfields silk dresses in order to underscore the English cult of nature and pursuit of botanical themes in textiles (McNeil and Leong). That clothes before the twentieth century did not have a type of modern "unity," being composed of separate but related elements such as stomacher, sleeves, cuffs, was one suggestion of this contemporary intervention. The Hussein Chalayan dress "Afterwords" of pink nylon tulle (Autumn/Winter 2000–01) surrounded by strewn rose petals was a stunning comment on the contrived naturalism of the English garden.

Elsewhere, mannequins in hunting clothes and contemporary fur fashion accompanied animals including a horse marching across table-like forms in dining rooms; they were literally put on a pedestal, which seemed like both the dining table that might have populated a later version of such a room, but also elevated them like haughty aristocrats. The conjunction of real fur in the contemporary Burberry Prorsum coat with archaic hunting was quite a riposte to the PETA antifur people. The curator also worked with the spectacular color palette and draperies of the portrait paintings in the room. There was even an "upstairs/downstairs" mood, with a stunning Worth gown c. 1888 trailing up and away from the servants, evoked by contemporary "rag" dresses such as the artful "Scrub Woman" (*Medea* collection Spring/Summer 2002), by Hussein Chalayan.

Perhaps the most extraordinary room was the Croome Court Tapestry Room (1771) hung with *Gobelins* tapestry of the highest pink key featuring birds in their reserves. The most Francophile space in the English rooms here received the most extravagant dress (Paris-made), and the most imaginative treatment. The room, the only one into which one could not enter, was viewed through two spectacularly dramatic roped doorways, and was occupied by a single black silk taffeta gown, "Maria Luisa," from Spring/Summer 1998, Christian Dior Haute Couture by John Galliano (British, born Gibraltar) crowned with a spectral raven headdress of black coq feathers by Stephen Jones, facing a console table brimming with Meissen ceramic birds. Tipi Hedren-like bird noises garnished the room. Surrealist fashion practice, Max Ernst, gala dressing, and Hitchcock were evoked, rather like a visual form of the late Richard Martin's writing about fashion. Harold Koda has expressly stated that the new curator Andrew Bolton has the "intellectual rigor" of Martin and is learning to "slowly understand the nature of our [USA] public" and their viewing habits (Drier 114). The

Croome Court Room had participated as a contemporary space before: it had been featured on the April 1986 cover of *Artforum* with a section of tapestry replaced by General Idea's "Le Fin" (1985). This *AngloMania tableau* was, in effect, an art installation.

AngloMania demanded a high level of viewer engagement with both currents of contemporary fashion and historical concepts. Another example of curator Bolton's intelligence and a nod to Richard Martin's superb writing on menswear occurred in the playful room of men's suiting, arrayed in the Lansdowne dining room. Courtiers, dandies, and punks from different centuries fraternized in this Adam space. Against the chill neoclassical statuary, which had been lit to project august silhouettes on the ceiling, new heads were introduced to the assembly in the form of punks with spectacular headdresses of cigarettes and newspaper made by Stephen Jones. The placing of the Duke of Windsor's blue-black tailcoat and vest by F. Scholte (British) in a room with punks and dandies was very clever, as the Duke's choice had been all about image and styling; he had preferred a blue-black evening suit as for the purposes of 1930s flash photography, a true black would not have looked as well. This ensemble created the sense of both a real and imagined dialogue of men's fashion across time. It was an effective *tableau* indicating that masculine status used to be demonstrated through extravagant clothing and was a class privilege, not effeminate. The mannequins also looked rather like the bored kids in aristocratic settings who feature in recent Burberry advertising. The inclusion of the Duchess of Cornwall's wedding hat by Philip Treacy on a console next to the mannequin representing the Duke of Windsor was a visual pun startling in its audacity; the current Prince of Wales may or may not enjoy the allusion to men who give up their thrones for more or less stylish women.

Historical fashion has been understood and reinterpreted in large part through representation such as painting. This is a product of the last 100 years of fashion history sanctioned in the early compilations which had line drawings, later 'improved' with color as printing improved, codified in models such as François Boucher's *A History of Costume in the West* (1965 French; 1966 English trans.), reedified in the Courtauld MA in the History of Dress model, in which fashion and its representations were the pivot. Now we are being asked to understand fashion through contemporary photographic and styling impulses. In both cases, the artifacts are not "speaking for themselves" as they are mute; their meanings are inferred and conferred through framing devices imposed by readers. Elsewhere, in the catalogue for *Dangerous Liasions*, Bolton wrote that his aim was to "associate disparate phenomena into a legible gestalt" (12). *AngloMania* then was part of the tendency to creatively recast the eighteenth century for today's audience and market. Even the taste for new opulence in interior decoration and the current shift from mid-century modern to new historicizing modes plays a role in the understanding and staging of the Metropolitan show.

The argument produced within *AngloMania* was primarily one generated via taste and aesthetics. Despite having some historical, and no sociological analysis, its argument about contemporary fashion was valid. In *AngloMania,* we learned more about how designers make use of oddments of the past in generating ideas for contemporary collections than we did about *anglomanie* or British fashion generally. Westwood's use and extrapolation of surviving garments and artifacts from the past—including images from high art painting, caricature, and prints that distill something about a period—was indicated as strongly here as in her own retrospective which has traveled around the world for the past few years. Her own position presented in interviews, that western fashion is a dialogue between England and France, between draping and tailoring, is another possible suggestion of the show. The exhibition also continued the legacy of Richard Martin's tenure at the museum, whose work on fashion had always emphasized that "[f]ashion is possessed and haunted by its acute sense of time" (Koda and Martin 15). The theatrical nature of these exhibits, often present in the display of fashion but here made overt by the context of artfully arranged period rooms, prompted reconsideration of the affinity between fashion, its bodily zone, and more general notions of space. As Katie Scott has argued more generally, "eighteenth-century images could engineer spaces, textual spaces, and were potentially objects . . . and spaces were viewed and felt respectively as images and enclosure (like clothing)" (Scott 2005: 139). *AngloMania,* informed by scholarship but delivered via the styling and media devices of the twenty-first century, indicates the competing demands of fashion delivered in the academy, the marketplace, and the museum. Fashion Studies is ideally placed to capitalize on the enormous popular media interest in dress, lifestyle, and fashion, most of which is marketing-led and unreflective. The enormous popular interest in dress, lifestyle and fashion offers opportunities for curatorial endeavour in the area of historical dress and also the possibility of interventions that make use of the past to help make the present 'strange'.

ACKNOWLEDGMENT

A version of this chapter was presented at the conference *Dressing Rooms: Current Perspectives on Fashion and Textiles,* Oslo University College, Norway, May 2007. A part of this chapter appeared in the exhibition review section of *Fashion Theory* 9:4 (2005): 477–85, and another in the special issue of *Fashion Theory* entitled "Museum Quality" (forthcoming, 2007).

WORKS CITED

Auslander, Leora. *Taste and Power: Furnishing Modern France.* Berkeley: University of California Press, 1996.

de Bastide, Jean-François. *The Little House: An Architectural Seduction*. Introduction translated by Rodolphe el-Khoury. Princeton: Princeton Architectural Press, 1996.

Bolton, Andrew. *AngloMania: Tradition and Transgression in British Fashion*. New Haven and London: Yale University Press, 2006.

Boucher, François. *A History of Costume in the West*, trans. John Ross, new ed. London: Thames and Hudson, 1987 [1st ed. 1966].

Camporesi, Piero. *Exotic Brew: The Art of Living in the Age of Enlightenment*. Translated by Christopher Woodall. Cambridge: Polity Press, 1994.

Chastang, Yannick. *Paintings in Wood: French Marquetry Furniture*. London: The Wallace Collection, 2001.

Clark, Judith. *Malign Muses: When Fashion Turns Back*. MoMu/ModeMuseum: Antwerp, 2004–05. Subsequently *Spectres: When Fashion Turns Back*. Victoria and Albert Museum: London, 2005.

———. *Spectres: When Fashion Turns Back*. London: V&A Publications, 2004.

Darr, Alan Phipps et al. *The Dodge Collection of Eighteenth-Century French and English Art in the Detroit Institute of Arts*. New York: Hudson Hills Press, 1996.

Drier, Melissa. "Haute Expositions, Harold Koda interview." *Acne Paper* (Autumn 2006): 108–14.

Goodman, Dena. "Furnishing Discourses: Readings of a Writing Desk in Eighteenth-Century France," in Maxine Berg and Elizabeth Eger (eds.) *Luxury in the 18th Century: Debates, Desires and Delectable Goods*, Basingstoke: Palgrave Macmillan, 2003: 71–88.

Hellman, Mimi. "Furniture, Sociability, and the Work of Leisure in Eighteenth-Century France.' *Eighteenth-Century Studies* 32. 4 (1999): 415–45.

Hollander, Anne. *Sex and Suits*. New York: Alfred A. Knopf, 1994.

Koda, Harold, Andrew Bolton, and Mimi Hellman."Introduction." *Dangerous Liaisons: Fashion and Furniture in the Eighteenth Century*. New Haven and London: Yale University Press, 2006.

———. *Gallerie des modes et costumes françcais dessinés d'après nature, gravés par les plus célèbres artistes en ce genre . . .* , Paris: les Srs Esnaults et Rapilly, 1778.

Les Gros, *L'Art de la Coëffure des Dames Françoises, avec des estampes, ou sont représentées les têtes coeffées, gravées sur les dessins originaux de mes Accommadages, avec le Traité en abrégé d'entretenir & conserver les Cheveux naturels*. Paris: Antoine Boudet, 1768.

Marie Antoinette. Coppola, Sofia, Dir. 2006. Columbia Pictures.

Martin, Richard and Harold Koda. *The Historical Mode: Fashion and Art in the 1980s*. New York: Rizzoli, 1989.

McNeil, Peter and Roger Leong (curator). *Everlasting: The Flower in Fashion and Textiles*. Melbourne: National Gallery of Victoria, 2005.

Rétif de la Bretonne. [N.-E.], *Monument du costume physique et moral de la fin du dix-huitième siècle, ou Tableaux de la Vie. Orné de figures dessinées et gravées par M. Moreau le Jeune et d'autres célèbres artistes*. Neuwied-sur-le Rhin: La Société Typographique, 1789.

Roche, Daniel. *A History of Everyday Things: The Birth of Consumption in France, 1600–1800*. Cambridge: Cambridge University Press, 2000.

Sargenston, Carolyn. *Merchants and Luxury Markets. The Marchands Merciers of Eighteenth-Century Paris*. London: Victoria and Albert Museum, 1996.

Scott, Katie. *The Rococo Interior: Decoration and Social Spaces in Early Eighteenth-Century Paris*. New Haven & London: Yale University Press, 1995.

———. "Introduction: Image-Object-Space." *Art History* 28.2 (2005): 137–50.

Silverman, Debora. *Selling Culture: Bloomingdale's, Diana Vreeland, and the New Aristocracy of Taste in Reagan's America*. New York: Pantheon, 1986.

Part III

Window Dressing and Boutique Culture

10 Dressing Rooms
Women, Fashion, and the Department Store

Louisa Iarocci

This chapter examines the representation of the fashionable woman as clothing fixture and modern body in American department stores at the turn of the century. I argue that in the most public and private spaces of the store—the shop windows and dressing rooms—the female body was constructed as the ideal fashion figure, at once public commodity and object of desire. The seemingly opposing spatial enclosures defining the "face of the store" and its most inner sanctum marked the critical moments of initiation and submission in the ritual of shopping enacted as commercial exchange and consumptive fantasy. Within these interstitial spaces, the fashionable woman was displayed in varying stages of dress and undress and was thus activated as the embodiment of fashion as a fluid exchange between clothing and its wearer, and the individualized body and consumer society. The narratives of concealment and exposure of the modern female body that take place in the department store position women as the artifact and fetish of fashion, at once fixed commodity and mobile consumer.

FASHION AS SPATIAL PRACTICE

An ever-growing body of interdisciplinary scholarship has, for the last thirty years, been examining fashion as a historical and cultural phenomenon, seeking to rescue its material artifacts from the inconsequential and its social practices from the faddish. The historicizing of the adorned body has been taken beyond the cataloguing of dress styles and the profiling of style makers to be revealed as a defining form of social expression and capitalist process (Perrot xi–xiii). This chapter seeks to build on this project by considering fashion as a "hybrid subject" that, in its material products and social practices, participates equally in systems of mass production and of modern consumption (Leopold 101). In this way, I argue that fashion can be understood as a spatial practice, wherein its places of manufacture, display, and exchange are considered not as backdrops, but as active participants in the exchanges between human agents and their material artifacts. Clothing can be thus seen as the mediator between the body and space, in intimate contact with the flesh that it covers and at the same time projecting a visual and gestural code that identifies and locates the wearer in their lived environment (Craik 4). The emergence of the fashionable woman in the turn of the century department store becomes just one example of how bodies, clothing, and places intersect in the operations of making and selling that constitute fashion as a dynamic spatial continuum in which material and cultural practices are intertwined (Entwistle 209–10).

THE BUSINESS OF FASHION

This representative figure of modernity must then be seen as the embodiment of collective developments in manufacturing and marketing in the United States in the second half of the nineteenth century. The practice of "fashion" was defined as ambiguously as it is today, the "glitz" of the stylish image rendered in the pages of women's magazines that defined desire and an elusive standard of taste in dress. Monthly publications like *Godey's Lady's Book* (1830–98) became leading authorities in women's dress, featuring color plates which portrayed stylish figures in intricately rendered settings (Daves 163). These fanciful illustrations reflected the more substantive economic role that fashion had taken on in the United States economy. Since the Civil War, the manufacture and trade of dry goods, including textile fabrics, clothing, and related articles of dress, had become a driving force in the massive shift from domestic manufacture to large scale mass production in the latter part of the nineteenth century. In his *Dictionary of Dry Goods* of 1892, George C. Cole attempted to comprehensively catalogue the products and processes which constituted a complex and far-reaching industry that outranked all other forms of manufacture in the nation both in terms of capital investments and establishments and employees. Included among the various technical descriptions of fabrics, trimmings, accessories, and procedures is a lengthy entry on the term "Fashion." Cole declared it to be a principle lacking in both definition and in intelligence, but nevertheless "the arbitress of weaver and buyer, and the terror of wholesale and retail buyers, and yet their main dependence for profits" (131). While quite vehement in his condemnation of the vagaries of *"la mode,"* he nonetheless found hope for the redemption of this "fickle, capricious and egotistical" practice in its concrete forms of expression. Clothes— given their own separate entry in the dictionary—are noted to be necessary and beneficial to both the individual and society for reasons of health, comfort, and financial and social status, even bestowed with the potential to "better humanity." The skilled and capable buyer is charged with the task of educating and guiding "the woman of taste," who, by "acknowledging her deficiencies, can construct her dress to emphasize her finest points," and thus become "the merchant's best advertising medium" (Cole 113).

READY-MADE FASHION

The conversion of fashion from volatile shifts in taste to guaranteed business profits was seen to be at the core of the dry goods business, as the stylish dress costume was remade into the stock sales garment. In the early part of the nineteenth century, the bulk of clothing was still custom made-to-measure, the product of home sewing and/or professional tailors and dressmaking shops, depending on the status of the consumer. After the Civil War, the manufacture of ready-made clothing developed rapidly with the expansion and reorganization of labor and production as well as the acceleration of innovations in technology, from sewing and cutting machines to drafting systems and graded patterns. While still including custom tailoring and second-hand clothing, by the mid-nineteenth century, factory-produced clothing dominated the menswear trade. Ready-to-wear men's and boys' coats, trousers, and suits can be seen as social expressions of individual status and national identity both in terms of industrial prowess and democratic freedom (Schorman 112; Zakim 4, 99). However, distinctly segregated by gender, the manufacture of women's ready-made clothing lagged behind for practical and less tangible reasons. It was not until the 1880s when select items of outerwear which did not require an exacting fit (coats, cloaks, or mantles), articles that were adjustable (corsets and collars), and specialty items that were difficult to sew at home (gloves and hosiery) first became readily available in the United States (Ley 8). Tailored suits, shirtwaists, or blouses followed soon after, but it was not until the second decade of the twentieth century that dresses were mass-produced in a range of affordable styles and sizes (Green 23). In the next few decades, these ready-to-wear items came to dominate the American apparel industry, able to respond more quickly to changes in style, and thus, theoretically, democratizing fashion by making it readily available to a mass audience. But the challenge remained of how to produce standardized women's clothing that was up-to-date in style, well-fitting, and of sufficient quality to make it saleable as an appropriate vehicle of fashion (Ley 8). The centralization of this endeavor—in an institution that was both distribution center and style maker—was critical to resolving the paradox of, on the one hand, selling fashion as an elitist and individualized mode of dress, while on the other, satisfying consumer demand with a plentiful stock of sales goods (Green 22; Porter-Benson 106–10; Zakim 69).

THE MODERN STORE

The path the ready-made garment took from factory to warehouse to store and home made use of networks of production and distribution already in place in the American dry goods business, but also forged new channels of movement (Scranton 464–65). The mass production of finished garments introduced a new layer of complexity to the traditional craft of tailoring in the mechanization of cutting, pressing, and sewing and its reorganization of labor in response to demands for accelerated production and greater uniformity of size and quality (Raff 9–10). The wholesale and retail marketplace was undergoing similar substantive changes both in scale and organization in order to handle the growing volume and bewildering array of consumer goods continually evolving into evermore specialized product lines. The process of delivering ready-made clothing to its intended wearers involved a new host of intermediaries variously involved in the production and marketing of clothing. As a result, the lines between manufacturers, dealers, warehouses, and shops becoming increasingly blurred (Raff 10). Overshadowing the independent shops of tailors, dressmakers, and milliners in number and scale were the new larger clothing businesses that had made their presence known in downtown commercial streets and in the pages of city directories since mid-century. This eclectic collection of urban establishments selling clothing direct to the public formed a diverse and fluid marketplace from which the premiere retailing institution would emerge in the late nineteenth century.

The accomplishment of the modern department store was in establishing a distinctive and permanent identity for itself, one that drew upon its internal organization, its selling practices with the public, and its physical presence in the urban fabric of major American cities. This retailing institution represented the concentration and consolidation of mass-produced consumer products by carrying a wide variety of personal and household goods that were offered at low, fixed prices. Narrow profit margins were made possible by bulk purchasing and rapid turnover in sales (Chaney 22–23). At the same time, the establishment presented itself as offering a personal level of service by systemizing business principles that privileged the buyer with promises of no pressure to buy and no-hassle returns. In its organization, the store further adopted the role of the specialist. The store was subdivided into discrete "stores," or departments of goods, run by a manager with intimate knowledge of his or her line. Each "store," however, remained under the larger control of the hands-on owner-patriarch (Raff 9–10). From its inception, store owners and their biographers defined and promoted their enterprise as both a unique form of trade and as a cultivated experience. This modern institution embodied the industrial warehouse in its abundance and profusion of goods and labor, and yet was rooted in the traditional notion of the shop as the home of owner, who, along with his store family, served as the purveyors of fine goods and arbiters of taste.

The effort of the department store to present itself as distribution center and fashion house was most evident in the product line that would define it from its inception: ready-made clothing. Even as it continually expanded its range of offerings to include newly available personal and household products, this retailing business remained inextricably linked to the textile industry from which it had arisen. Many department stores evolved from the large scale clothiers dealing in men's wear, well-established in urban centers since mid-century, who took advantage of their client base and central locations to diversify their offerings and services (Zakim 38). Other predecessors were the popular dry goods stores and specialty shops that carried the various fabrics, notions, and apparel items that constituted the raw materials of finished dress for female consumers. But women's ready-to-wear clothing came of age within the department store as this product and its hallmark institution worked together to stake out new positions in the marketplace. As the selling of cloth was subordinated to the selling of clothing, the primary task of its retailing centers shifted as distribution of a finished product took precedence over the production of raw materials. The process that men's ready-to-wear had undergone in acquiring respectability now fell to women's wear—a task now intensified by a greater emphasis on aesthetics and style versus functionality and economics (Stubbs 198). The department store became a central player not only in making women's mass-produced apparel readily available to the public but also in selling it as exclusive fashion (Porter-Benson 108).

The architecture of the department store made manifest its evolving role as the center of the exchange of a product newly defined as both commodity and craft. Drawing on the typology of its retailing predecessors, this commercial institution sought to bring together the scale and organization of the spaces of mass production and the aesthetics of particularization involved in selling consumer goods directly to the public. Like the modern factory that was the site of origin of its products, the department store had to accommodate and convey abundance and flexibility in order to facilitate a continual flow of mass quantities of goods, people, and credit through its premises. At the same time, operating as an amalgam of individual departments, this institution sought to articulate itself as an aggrandized collection of shops that served as the business "home" of a personalized seller of distinctive products and services. The tension in striking a balance between industrial efficiency and a more idiosyncratic individuality manifested itself in the exterior form and interior layout of this urban building type. The department store adopted an increasingly sophisticated vocabulary in its exterior shell of brick and stone in order to convey an impression of permanence and continuity in the urban fabric and yet act as a highly visible and distinctive sign for individual businesses. Within this solid shell, expansive and well-lit floor spaces provided the *tabula rasa* for the continually shifting definition of "shops" without walls, conveying the sense of freedom of movement that reflected the modern ethos of trade. Developments in building construction such as cast iron and steel framing, plate glass windows, and skylights facilitated the sense of the infiniteness of this new space of commerce through which the shopper could wander and drift (McDonald 233). Increasingly complex elements like arcades, grand stairs, elevators, and even escalators, pinpointed and highlighted the key points of vertical and horizontal movement throughout the premises, reflecting the emphasis on the efficient circulation of people, goods, and cash.

SHOPPING

The department store embodied a distinctly different kind of shopping experience often described as a more open and anonymous process liberated from the physical constraints and social expectations in the intimacy of small shops. With its accelerated pace and heightened spectacle, this commercial institution certainly sought to function as a continuation of the public street, but one in which the occupants could be identified as either sellers, buyers, or even goods (Zakim 100). But if social boundaries were blurred to accommodate the expanding scale of modern selling and dynamic flow of its consuming crowd, retailing space was even more rigorously controlled (McDonald 233). The delineation of the main selling floor by product type and customer service that was critical to the store's identity was accomplished by more subtle spatial means: solid partition walls were replaced by columns and other display fixtures. But certain specialty departments and luxury amenities like restrooms, restaurants, and art galleries were wholly separated in distinct enclosures, evoking the more domestic confines of the shop and the intimate exchanges conducted there. This play between openness and enclosure was evident in the insertion of discrete architectural elements in the open selling floor that acted as defining spatial markers in the shopping expedition, providing fixed points to ground and orient the mobilized shopper. The shop window was the most visible and public of these, occupying the ambiguous realm between exterior and interior that allowed it to participate in the public realm of the city street while being physically located within the proprietarial domain of the store. Supplanting its original role as a source of illumination for the interior, the shop window became the first and most public place for display, the critical point of visual entry into the store and point of initiation into the shopping ritual (Breward 1999: 129).

SHOW WINDOW

The shop window became the "show window" in the department store and was recognized very early on as one of the primary tools in the retail businessman's repertoire of advertising devices. In the flood of trade literature dedicated to the retailing industry that began in the late nineteenth century, window trimming quickly emerged as a leader and a specialized form of visual merchandising. Journals like the *Dry Goods Economist* devoted increasingly more space to the design of store windows. In 1897, L. Frank Baum began a monthly trade journal called *The Show Window* (1897–1903), devoted to this new profession which would form the basis of his voluminous textbook, *The Art of Decorating Dry Goods Windows* published in 1900. But there were even earlier, less discussed publications on the subject such as J. H. Wilson Marriott's *Nearly Three Hundred Ways to Dress Show Windows: Also Suggestions and Ideas for Store Decoration* (1889), George Cole's previously mentioned *Dictionary of Dry Goods* (1892), which included a lengthy appendix on "Window Trimmings," and Frank Carr's *The Wide Awake Window Dresser* (1894). Directed towards business owners and specialists in this emerging field, these lengthy handbooks set guidelines for the emerging field of window trimming as it evolved from an expedient method of heaping goods to a systemized practice based on business and artistic principles (Leach 106–07; Marcus 19; Schneider 8).

These early books are a curious hybrid of technical manual and artistic treatise, providing practical advice in the effort to legitimize the business as a scientific profession, but at the same time setting forth the principles and tenets that sought to establish it as an art. After an introductory chapter on "Color Harmony," Carr's *Wide Awake Window Dresser* is divided into chapters categorized according to the display of various categories of retail merchandise, from notions and fancy goods to furniture and crockery. But the most attention is given to the display of the fabrics that were the heart of the dry goods business as well as the raw materials of fashionable wear. Textiles were classified according to their material type (such as crepes, linens, silks, and cottons) and increasingly by their final use, for example, tennis "suitings" and mourning wear. Particular attention was given to the "art of draping," which consisted of the arrangement of fabrics into decorative patterns by hanging, swirling, pleating, and gathering them into folds, puffs, pleats, and other forms for display in store windows. Loose fabrics were draped over various kinds of display stands and forms, from drums to rectangular boxes, producing an eclectic collection of veiled sculptural "dummies." The evolution of these window displays evidences a gradual evolution from tiered two-dimensional arrangements to more three-dimensional ones where goods were assembled to form a large fan, star, or sunburst, and even the Brooklyn Bridge constructed of rolls of flannel blankets or spool cotton (Baum 239; Carr 234; Cole 529–31). Smaller articles like handkerchiefs and notions were particularly well- suited to these kinds of novelty arrangements. Other examples, like the pipe organ of ribbon, emphasize the effort to aggrandize items that were smaller in size and price in order to capture the viewer's attention against the widening expanse of the window background (Cole 543). Even more ambitious efforts found in early manuals turn the display into a naturalistic *tableau* as in the

Lover's Window, the balcony scene from Romeo and Juliet constructed in handkerchiefs, and the Indian Wigwam, a camp scene in the woods featuring a flannel teepee containing the body of a "full-fledged" native (Cole, 544, 548–49).

"FEMALE FORM DIVINE"

Even if these early novelty scenes only occasionally included human actors, the female figure quickly emerged as the primary vehicle for the display of fashionable clothing and a central component of the show window compositions. The early manual writers affirmed the advantages of using human forms as "higher forms of artistic window dressing." George Cole observed that the living "[m]odel or figure" in the show-room and the factory was of great importance, noting that the "female form divine," representing a woman of "natural grace and fine physical proportions," was crucial for the proper fitting of ready-made clothing and successful selling (78). This idealized female body was in the early stages of being recreated in the form of the naturalistic "waxen figure" that would make it the most effective fixture for the display of clothing and for the staging of fashion. Even though women's wear had already emerged as a distinctive category at the turn of the century, it still con-sisted largely of the raw materials of fashionable dress, like the loose fabric goods, and small scale specialty accessories required to complete a finished ensemble like gloves, hosiery, and corsets. The techniques used to display women's dress in show windows reflected this formative state in the production of ready-to-wear fashions in the late nineteenth cen-tury. The female form taking shape in the display windows of depart-ment stores was assembled piece by piece from the various body parts associated with available fashion accessories. "Box dummy" forms— plain, rectangular boxes used as stands for skirt drapings—formed an abstracted version of the lower half of a gowned female body. Corsets, which required a proper fit and called for a certain level of modesty, were displayed on bust forms consisting of the upper torso with or without a head. Hat forms that sought to place emphasis on the head consisted of frame hat stands or even more abbreviated upper torsos. Even the displays for cloaks and suits—garments that were emerging as ready-made items—employed three-quarter female forms or full-length figures that were often headless. A view of the Window Trimmers Department by Frank L. Carr shows a female model being assembled from a collec-tion of body parts consisting of skirt "dummies" on the far left, bust forms with and without heads on the upper shelves to the right, hands and wigs under the glass display case and even an apparently displaced head (Figure 10.1). In this behind-the-scenes view of an expansive, neatly organized work studio, the professional window trimmer is presented as

Figure 10.1 "The Window Trimmers Department," *The Wide Awake Window Dresser,* 1894. Courtesy of The Seattle Public Library.

expert manager and gifted artist, shaping his attractive creation from the various trade fixtures and body parts at his disposal.

This portrayal of the fashionable woman as a work in progress, the incomplete product of the manipulations of male merchandisers and embodiment of the larger state of clothing production, is also evident in more publicly visible displays in department stores. Early window displays of women's wear make evident that the image of fashion was in a formative state, reflected in the fragmentary state of the female body, which was its primary vehicle. Displays of accessories like millinery and hosiery often used partial female forms interchangeably with stands and geometric forms, appearing to be less interested in the naturalistic portrayal of the female model than with the impression of variety and abundance. The female form was consistently dissected, mirrored, multiplied, and stacked in numerous different poses and configurations to sell it alongside the commodities it supported, often subsumed in the cacophony of patterns of the objects displayed (Figure 10.2). Early manual writers did stress the advantages of using more naturalistic figures in their staged productions, noting that the more "lifelike and beautiful the figures the greater their value in display" (Carr 25). Commenting on "the fad of using human forms" in 1900, L. Frank Baum described a window

Figure 10.2 "A Corset Window," *The Wide Awake Window Dresser,* 1894. Courtesy of The Seattle Public Library.

display in which "in a handsomely dressed room, a lady, dressed in style costume, sits or walks about, showing off her gown to advantage . . . in a handsomely dressed room" (149–50). But even in this kind of "high artistic display," he suggested that this lady could display show cards, identifying the goods and prices she is wearing. Even if these price tags disrupting the illusion of the scene would become increasingly rare with more veristic scenes, the fashionable woman never fully relinquished her role as commodity. Baum also described a particular illusion window called the "Vanishing Lady," in which the head and bust of a "beautiful young lady" was supported on a pedestal with her lower half concealed from the audience (82–84) (Figure 10.3). The girl was then raised and lowered by a device beneath the stage, reappearing each time with new fashion accessories. In her analysis of the trick films on which this illusion was based, Lucy Fischer argues that the female subject was "conjured as a decorative object," her body dematerialized and decorporealized by the display of power of the male magician (341). The twist in the show window version of making this model only temporarily invisible and having her perform an endless striptease of dressing and undressing foregrounds the mutable nature of fashion embodied in the transient and incomplete state of the woman's body (Culver 106–07).

DRESSING ROOMS

If the show window was the most visible display of the most private side of the fashionable woman as clothing fixture and object of desire, its apparently opposing enclosure within the department store was the dressing room. In these most private spaces embedded within the public space of the store, fashion was rendered as a more active exchange between the clothing product and the female consumer, now facilitated by the intermediary figure of the seller. When precisely designated enclosures were provided in department store interiors for the explicit purpose of allowing women to try on clothing and/or observe them on living store models is not known. But the provision of these dressing rooms can be seen as a continuation of the fitting rooms of specialty tailor shops and also as a particular innovation related to the expanding ready-made clothing industry and the store itself (Breward 1999: 106–07). The acceptance of a fashionable dress that was ready-to-wear demanded the convenience of trying on the garment to assure a proper fit and to provide the opportunities for viewing and tailoring to ensure a final sale. Scant evidence on the nature of these almost invisible spaces, gleaned from retail promotional materials and trade and popular articles on the store, reflects their elusive and enigmatic nature. In the effusion of trade and popular literature on the department store at the turn of the century, as it was emerging as a business and cultural institution, only a few rare glimpses into the spaces of these interior rooms were provided. But when they do materialize, these behind-the-scenes views offer up a distinctly different version of the formation of woman of fashion as inanimate object and living body in the space of the department store.

If the scenes in shop windows were unfolding more and more like theatrical performances of an ideal fashionable life, those within the dressing rooms seem to be represented more pragmatically as business transactions. In her article, "Behind the Scenes in the Big Stores," *Munsey's Magazine* (1900), Anne O'Hagan celebrates the department store by showing the smooth functioning of all the hidden operations of this marvel of modern business efficiency. Focusing her attention on the activity in the workrooms, delivery rooms, and other backrooms beyond the selling floor, she ascribes the success of the gigantic retail organization to the individual efforts of the store employees. This "system which enables a buyer to costume herself for a festivity" is illustrated in a scene where two female clerks adeptly assist an elegant client trying on a fancy dress gown (Figure 10.4). The intimate confines of the dressing room, with its fabric-draped ceiling and angled mirrored walls to facilitate viewing, provide a protected and private enclosure, a kind of simulated boudoir for the customer to try on the well-fitted stylish gown and immerse herself in the resultant spectacle (Breward 1999: 107). Her transformation into sophisticated fashion model is made possible by the equally attractive team of sellers who busily work to perfect the fit and complete the transaction between the buyer and the object of her desire. Each player in the scene is intently engaged with their respective tasks, the salesclerks with the practicalities of the commercial exchange at hand and the customer dreamily absorbed with the multiple reflections of her own image. This reenactment of the ultimate consummation of the shopping ritual relies on the portrayal of these women as complete and active bodies and the interaction between the fixed gaze of the consumer and the actions of her energetic sellers (Iskin 242–43).

The dressing room can thus be seen as the intensely charged meeting place of clients and workers, a space that offered the potential of socialization across increasingly fluid lines of class demarcation but that also reflected the inherent problems of such transgressive behaviors (Porter-Benson 5–7). In a series of articles entitled "The Woman's Invasion," appearing in *Everybody's Magazine* between January and June of 1909, coauthors William Hard and Rheta Childe Dorr analyzed the rise of a female workforce in the retail industry acknowledging the numerous problems with working conditions and wages. Nevertheless, they

Figure 10.3 "The Vanishing Lady," *The Art of Decorating Dry Goods Windows and Interiors*, 1900.

concluded that the department store was a desirable option for working women, arguing that the sheer proximity to a better class can benefit the ambitious working woman. The photograph, entitled "You Can Fit Good Looking Women with Good-Looking Clothes," depicts a retail clerk poised to assist a potential client (or model) as seated customers look on (Figure 10.5). The confined enclosure of the dressing room provides an appropriate setting for the intimate exchange between clothing and the female body, and between the potential buyer and seller. Mirrored surfaces provide the illusion of openings, outweighed by the solid dark paneled walls of the low enclosure separated from the main selling floor. The female body in the transparent enclosure of the show window was shown to be dismembered in her exposed position as mass commodity and object of desire, perhaps to mitigate her growing power. But within these secluded rooms, the fashionable woman was more subtly constrained, allowing her to retain her wholeness and modesty. While appearing to be fully clothed, the woman at the center of attention is in the process of being wrapped or unwrapped, the frothy layers of her elegant dress held in the hands of her attendant, laid across the empty chair and even reflected in the mirrored wall. The body of this passive model is visually framed and supported by the alert but rigidly posed saleswoman who attends her and the row of mostly attentive spectators, one of whom however has dared to return the viewer's gaze. This crowded, even uncomfortable exchange portrays the woman of fashion in multiple guises, as the passive object/product of the consumptive process, as activated spectator/consumer and even as potentially mobilized worker; this fitting room/boudoir the site of multiple reflections and potential transformations of the female body (Iskin 251–52).

The interstitial spaces of the shop window and dressing room in the early department store provided the intimate settings for the meeting of commodity and individual that transformed shopping from business transaction into consumptive ritual. Within these enclosures that were seemingly opposed (public/private, transparent/solid), the ready-made clothing that was the department store's trademark product line was exhibited as goods for sale and as fashion icon. These spaces for the display and dressing of the female body provided fixed moments in which the infiniteness of the floor of modern selling contracted in order to refocus attention onto the individual items of clothing and the bodies of their intended wearers. Here we can trace the evolution of woman's fashion into a synthetic assemblage of raw materials and finished accessories and the formation of the female figure into a modern body, at once the object/product of mass production and the active spectator/agent in the rituals of consumption (Iskin 251–52). The figure of modernity represented in these varying stages of completeness in body and dress can be seen as embodying the essence of the department store as liminal space, in between public and private and as performative and yet protected terrain. Here, the fashionable woman

Figure 10.4 "The System Which Enables a Buyer to Costume Herself for a Festivity," "Behind the Scenes in the Big Stores," *Munseys Magazine.* January 1900.

performed a sanctioned striptease as she shifted guises between clothing fixture and lead actor, and between style-conscious shopper and aspiring retail clerk, hence, positioning feminine corporeality at the center of the complex network of commodity culture, consumer desire, and modern identity in early twentieth century America.

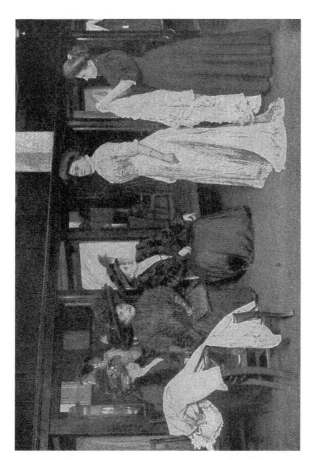

Figure 10.5 "You Can Fit Good-Looking Women with Good-Looking Clothes," "The Woman's Invasion," *Everybody's Magazine.* January 1909.

184   *Louisa Iarocci*

WORKS CITED

Baum, L. Frank *The Art of Decorating Dry Goods Windows and Interiors: A Complete Manual of Window Trimming.* Chicago: Show Window Publishing, 1900.

Breward, Christopher. *The Hidden Consumer: Masculinities, Fashion and City Life 1860–1914.* Manchester and New York: Manchester University Press, 1999.

———. *Fashion.* London: Oxford, 2003.

Carr, Frank L. Jr. *The Wide-Awake Window Dresser: A Treatise on the Art and Science of Show Window and Store Interior Construction, Economy and Decoration.* New York: The Dry Goods Economist, 1894.

Chaney, David. "The Department Store as Cultural Form." *Theory, Culture and Society,* 1, 3 (1983): 22–31.

Cole, George S. *A Complete Dictionary of Dry Goods and History of Silk, Cotton, Linen, Wool and other Fibrous Substances.* Chicago: W. B. Conkey, 1892.

Craik, Jennifer. *The Face of Fashion: Cultural Studies in Fashion.* London and New York: Routledge, 1994.

Culver, Stuart. "What Manikins Want: The Wonderful Wizard of Oz and the Art of Decorating Dry Goods Windows." *Representations* 21 (Winter 1988): 97–116.

Daves, Jessica. *The Ready-Made Miracle: The American Story of Fashion for the Millions.* New York: G.P. Putnam's Sons, 1967.

Entwistle, Joanne. *The Fashioned Body: Fashion, Dress and Modern Social Theory.* Malden, MA: Polity Press, 2000.

Fischer, Lucy. "The Lady Vanishes: Women, Magic and the Movies." In *Film Before Griffith,* edited by John L. Fell. Berkeley: University of California Press, 1983.

Green, Nancy. *Ready-to-Wear and Ready-to-Work: A Century of Industry and Immigrants.* Durham & London: Duke University Press, 1997.

Hard, William, and Rheta Childe Dorr. "The Woman's Invasion. III." *Everybody's Magazine* 20, 3 (January 1909): 73–85.

Iskin, Ruth E. "Selling, Seduction, and Soliciting the Eye: Manet's Bar at the Folies-Bergére." In *Reclaiming Female Agency: Feminist Art History after Postmodernism,* edited by Norma Broude and Mary D. Garrard. Berkeley: University of California Press, 2005: 235–57.

Leach, William. "Strategists of Display and the Production of Desire." In *Consuming Visions: Accumulation and Display of Goods in America 1880–1920,* edited by Simon J. Bronner. New York: Norton, 1989.

Leopold, Ellen. "The Manufacture of the Fashion System." In *Chic Thrills: A Fashion Reader,* edited by Juliet Ash and Elizabeth Wilson. Berkeley: University of California Press, 1992: 101–17.

Ley, Sandra. *Fashion for Everyone: The Story of Ready-to-Wear.* New York: Charles Scribners Sons, 1975.

Marcus, Leonard A. *The American Store Window.* New York and London: Architectural Press, 1978.

Marriott, J. H. Wilson. *Nearly Three Hundred Ways to Dress Show Windows: Also Suggestons and Ideas for Store Decoration.* Baltimore: Show Window Publishing Company, 1889.

McDonald, Gail. "The Mind a Department Store: Reconfiguring Space in the Gilded Age." *Modern Language Quarterly* 63: 2 (June 2002): 227–49.

O'Hagan, Annie. "Behind the Scenes in Big Stores." *Munsey's Magazine* 22, 4 (January 1900): 528–37.

Perrot, Phillippe. *Fashioning the Bourgeoisie: A History of Clothing in the Nineteenth Century*. Princeton, Princeton University Press: 1991.

Porter-Benson, Susan. *Counter Cultures: Saleswomen, Managers, and Customers in American Department Stores 1890–1940*. Urbana and Chicago: University of Illinois Press, 1986.

Raff, Daniel M. G. "The Wholesale and Retail Trade in the United States." Reginald H. Jones Center, Working Paper No. 07, Wharton School, University of Pennsylvania, 2003.

Schneider, Sara K. *Vital Mummies: Performance Design for the Show-Window Mannequin*. New Haven and London: Yale University Press, 1995.

Schorman, Rob. "Ready or Not: Custom-Made Ideals and Ready-Made Clothes in Late 19th-Century America," *The Journal of American Culture* 19, 4 (Winter 1996): 111–20.

Scranton, Phillip. "The Transition from Custom to Ready-To-Wear Clothing in Philadelphia, 1890–1930," In *The Textile Industries*, edited by Stanley D. Chapman. London: Tauris, 1997: 461–92.

Stubbs, Katherine. "Reading Material: Contextualizing Clothing in the Work of Anzia Yezierska." *Melus* (Summer 1998): 1–12.

Zakim, Michael. *Ready-Made Democracy: A History of Men's Dress in the American Republic, 1760–1860*. Chicago and London, University of Chicago Press, 1992.

11 The Logic of the Mannequin
Shop Windows and the Realist Novel

Vanessa Osborne

The popular leisure practice of window-shopping emerges in the United States during the late nineteenth-century as a marketing strategy designed to engage viewers' imaginations and consequently arouse their desires for the commodities displayed. Appealing to the voyeuristic inclinations of prospective consumers, these elaborate windows invite passers-by to glimpse mimetic representations of everyday life, entirely comprised of new, pleasingly displayed, saleable objects. These carefully rendered scenarios encourage viewers to compose narratives, linked to the displayed objects and clothed mannequins, which imbue the merchandise with characteristics such as class, taste, and respectability. Through these scenic depictions of idealized everyday life, populated by strategically arranged goods and elegantly clothed posed mannequins, shop windows induce the viewers to identify with the attributes of the displayed commodities in order to evoke desire.

In the reflections of everyday life approximated by shop windows, the human body as figured by the mannequin becomes indistinct and dispensable, a placeholder around which window dressers and, subsequently, consumers fashion narratives informed by the displayed clothing and other material objects. For example, *The Window Trimmer's Handbook* proposes that dressers craft a scene window depicting "theater boxes with occupants of figures in full evening dress" (International Correspondence School 275). This display features elegantly dressed and accessorized mannequins arranged and styled to emphasize attributes such as wealth, leisure, beauty, and prestige. The window invites the street-side observer to gaze upon the scene and invent a fantasy scenario to attach to its crafted conglomeration of objects and mannequins. The typical consumer idealizes the mannequins and desires the commodities displayed. But placed on or around nearly identical wax mannequins, the displayed items themselves, rather than a person who owns or wears them, become invested with the previously mentioned values. This effect, which I have named the *logic of the mannequin*, attends to the consequences of window displays' substitution of mannequins—interchangeable surrogate bodies made of wax and wood—for natural human bodies and their concomitant individual personalities. The logic of the mannequin proposes that shop windows contribute to a tendency to imbue material objects with a capacity to embody individual identity by creating scenarios that invest a wax mannequin with a narrative produced explicitly by its context by, the clothing it wears, and the products that surround it.

This marketing practice constructs a new body by prompting viewers to narrativize and subsequently desire or identify with the interchangeable and inanimate yet idealized bodies of mannequins surrounded by appealing commodities in the window's scenarios. An examination of the advice of veteran window dressers to those aspiring to jobs in this new profession elucidates how the strategies mobilized by these professionals embed narratives into the visual design of scenario windows, appropriate formal structures and dramatic techniques of the theatre and emphasize verisimilitude in the arrangement and styling of mannequins to approximate admirable stylish bodies. A turn to Theodore Dreiser's *Sister Carrie* (1900), a realist novel written soon after the widespread professionalization of window dressing, proposes that the logic of the mannequin is not confined exclusively to the realm of marketing and advertising strategies. It emerges in Dreiser's portrayal of Carrie, a woman characterized by her generic and indeterminate identity and her capacity for mimetic embodiment of the fashionable and stylish. Carrie's male suitors, men preoccupied with conspicuous consumption, exemplify how the dynamics of consumer desire prompted by shop windows materialize in instances of sexual desire in this urban society suffused with new opportunities for consumption and social class mobility.

THE MANNEQUIN ENTERS THE SHOP WINDOW

Technological developments, such as the adoption of the sewing machine and transformation of plate glass manufacturing processes, prepared the way for the emergence of window dressing as a specialized trade the in the United States in the late nineteenth century. Mass-produced clothing made by sewing machines and sold in department stores gradually replaced home-sewn clothing. Advances achieved in plate glass fabrication rendered the creation of large panes easier and quicker. These large-scale panes enabled merchants to remove problematic visual obstructions like sashes or mullions and allowed shops to construct comprehensive images of reality for the voyeuristic passer-by to narrativize. Furthermore, the widespread disbursement of electricity throughout cities in the 1880s improved the visual representational quality of the shop window through electric lighting. Moreover, in the late nineteenth century, mannequins began to replace the less human, headless dress forms in department store windows. In 1885, Gems Wax Models, a company that had originally created dress forms for the dressmakers of wealthy patrons, began exporting wax mannequins to the United States for use by merchants.[1]

Featuring a life-like mannequin placed in a beautifully decorated scenario, the *tableau* or scene window invited explicit theatricalization and anthropomorphization of the figures displayed. A realistically rendered mannequin functioned as a transitional figure by replacing the previous street-side marketing device, the salesperson with his verbal exhortations praising the product. Although advertisements in window dressers' manuals often referred to display cases and window displays as "silent salesmen," the true silent salespersons were the mannequins. Substituting for the street-side salesperson beckoning at the entrance, they congealed his persuasive verbal appeals into a visual incarnation, an artificial body with which the prospective consumer interacts.

During the first decade of the twentieth-century, shop window dressing expanded into a lucrative trade and a crucial strategy in the arsenal of retail marketers. Window dressing correspondence courses, professional journals, instructional handbooks, and trade groups proliferated during these years. Chicago advertising executive Alfred G. Bauer educated grocers in his 1902 *The Art of Window Dressing for Grocers* and proposed they consider window trimming as a "branch of business building . . . recognized as one of utmost importance [which is] being developed to a high point of perfection" (iii). To promote this new trade and encourage owners to hire window dressers to produce displays, window dressers' manuals described window dressing as both an integral marketing practice and an art. *The Art of Decorating* upbraids the recent past's inattention to aesthetically pleasing elaborate scenic windows by proposing that while managers believe that straightforward presentations of products in the window are "plain, business windows," they are really "fool windows" because they fail to garner attention or sales (Merchants Record Company 240).[2] Instead, window dressers recommended elaborate and appealing designs carefully crafted to captivate but not overwhelm or disturb the prospective consumer.

In his 1934 book *Window Display Above All,* business writer Herbert Casson offered an understanding of the psychology of prospective shoppers on urban streets that implies that the well-designed window establishes a relationship between the urban dweller and the mannequins and objects offered up to his or her gaze. He urged window dressers to scrutinize the behavior of the passers-by to recognize how the prospective consumer isolates himself from others on the street, each pedestrian avoiding eye contact with another. He reminded the reader that one must not "forget that the eyes of passers-by are dull to a certain extent because they are meeting other people on the street . . . [and] it is bad manners to stare" (66). What resonates most about this assertion is the condition of isolation surrounding the individual, and the window dresser's mandate to puncture that isolation so he might direct a prospective consumer's eyes to the window's exhibition. Instead of engaging in socially unacceptable behavior by meeting the eyes of approaching fellow pedestrians, the urban passer-by will rest his or her gaze on the displayed commodities or the surrogate human, the mannequin in the window. In contrast with the other person encountered on the street, the mannequin invites and even encourages the pedestrian to stare. It enables the pedestrian to avoid ill-mannered behavior and deflect his or her curious glance onto a captivating scenario featuring a life-like substitution for a fellow citizen.

The copious photographs and drawings of shop window designs in *The Art of Decorating* suggest that two basic types of windows predominate. The first type, the "stocky window," artistically arranged an abundance of the same or similar types of objects in an elaborate, attractive design or in a motion-producing mechanism. This window highlighted wealth, variety, and creativity in design.[3] Yet, as the profession developed further, the stocky window yielded to the *tableau* or scene window, a style that emphasized realistic renderings of everyday or slightly idealized life. *Tableau* windows created scenarios by constructing realistic environments where diverse groups of saleable objects and one or more mannequins wearing the shop's apparel were attractively displayed as though a spectator might be vicariously experiencing daily life.

In their descriptions of *tableau* window construction, window trimmers' manuals frequently advise dressers to create visual narratives and adopt formal structures analogous to those utilized by the theater. "Show windows," the early twentieth-century term for shop windows, resonates with the medium's close kinship to spectacle and the theater. *The Window Trimmer's Handbook* invokes the language of set decoration when it refers to the creation of the backgrounds for the display of commodities as "scene painting" (International Correspondence School 194). These settings, like theater backdrops, dramatize the space wherein the dresser places the products and mannequins. *The Art of Decorating* urged its readers to "[n]otice the stage settings in a theater" and attend to how the "handsome proscenium arch . . . forms a real frame for the scene" on stage (Merchants Record Company 16). It recommended that dressers imitate this framing device with elaborate constructions of fabric and plaster. According to these instructions, the best window displays aspire to imitate the theater by framing and illuminating the commodities and mannequins in a carefully arranged scenario in order to imbue them with the captivating qualities of the theater. Most of the city dwellers who pass the window display would have, at some point, attended a theatrical or vaudeville performance. Therefore, in response to the theatrical structures, the passer-by responds with the typical spectator's reaction to theatrical performance—captivation. *The Window Trimmer's Handbook* also recognized the window display's kinship with the theater, proposing that "the balcony scene from Romeo and Juliet may be used with marked success as an attraction in various displays" (International Correspondence School 274). In linking products and apparel with this familiar scene, the window dresser aspired to invest the displayed products and figures with the high culture status of Shakespearean theater and the heightened sense of romance and excitement linked to the early interactions of Romeo and Juliet.

Alongside their suggestions to appropriate the formal structures of theatrical set design, shop window manuals explicitly encouraged their readership to consider the dramatic content of window displays when they plan the season's windows. *The Art of Decorating*'s "Hint to Department Managers" proposed that shop managers articulate a narrative about the products they wish to display. In order to obtain the "best results" from the window, the manager should lay out all the goods for display, "call the window trimmer and let him look over them; *tell him the story*" (emphasis mine, Merchants Record Company 240). Together the manager and the trimmer were to compose a narrative that the goods communicated, and then craft a display that presented this story and brought the varied objects together for to the prospective shopper. Yet while the theatrical discourse invoked by these window trimmers emphasized how the spectacle of windows captivates, these practices cannot satisfactorily account for the identification between the viewer and the scenario evoked by the logic of the mannequin. Theatrical conventions mark the distance between the spectator and performance and thereby foreclose the interaction necessitated by the shop window to prompt sales.

In their attempts at verisimilitude, window dressers cast aside the conventions of the theater and employed the discourse of realism characteristic of literary narrative. They made the affinity between the spectator and the stylish, life-like mannequin as easy as possible for the prospective consumer by rendering their mannequins as realistic as possible. *The Art of Decorating* exhorted its pupils to master the art of posing figures by scrutinizing "the positions men and women assume when they are in repose" (Merchants Record Company 225). *The Window Trimmer's Handbook* emphasized the quotidian and the natural as opposed to the dramatic or theatrical when it proposed that dressers must "endeavor to reproduce faithfully some of the little things that are so natural for a person to do" (International Correspondence School 61). So that the mannequin portrayed the latest standards of attractiveness and fashionableness, the dresser could manipulate its environment, position, clothing, hair, and face. *The Art of Decorating* asserted that the mannequin's hair must be changed with regularity and "combed out well and dressed in the very latest style" (Merchants Record Company 221). Heavy wax and wood mannequins possessed detachable heads that could be easily removed and altered. Manuals offered detailed instructions explaining how to soften the wax of the faces in order to modify the look of the mannequins' features. Both books stipulated that the key to successful sales and artistically designed windows lay in the verisimilitude of the mannequins, that is, the realistic, natural, and skillful imitation of living people which the passer-by might identify with or admire.

Though most consumers did not truly conflate mannequins with fleshly bodies on display, several anecdotes imply that these figures occupied a liminal space—between fleshly and artificial, and between human and object. The "Gaba Girls," highly realistic mannequins produced in the 1930s by New York soap maker Lester Gaba, blurred the lines between human and

inanimate. Gaba composed narratives and characterizations for his mannequins—naming them, throwing parties in their honor in New York hotels
and dressing them in fine clothing and jewels. He developed a particular
preference for a mannequin named Cynthia and brought her with him to
various clubs, parties, and other social events (Marcus 30–31, 36–37). *The
Art of Decorating* includes an earlier example of this liminal status when it
recounts the debates surrounding the propriety of showing undergarments
on dress forms in window displays. While some merchants hardly considered these displays salacious, "several high-class stores . . . discontinued the
custom of displaying lingerie upon forms" because they claimed these sorts
of displays were "indelicate" (Merchants Record Company 138). This store
policy, which omitted the possibility of presenting more lifelike wax mannequins, suggests how exhibitions of dress forms clothed in women's undergarments might evoke feelings of sexual desire, embarrassment, or modesty
in observers.[4] To understand this store policy's rationale, we must assume
that the wood, fabric, and metal forms representing a woman's body elicits
titillation in a passer-by similar to that which the physical body of a woman
on display provokes.

THE MANNEQUIN ENTERS THE NOVEL

Shop windows share their claims to verisimilitude and their capacity for
narrative with the dominant novelistic tradition of the late nineteenth-century, literary realism. Theodore Dreiser, one of the most noted practitioners
of this style, set his 1900 novel *Sister Carrie* during the 1890s, the decades
when window dressing emerged as a professionalized marketing strategy.
Carrie's Chicago teems with office and factory workers who move briskly
down streets lined with office buildings, factories, and the plate glass window displays of department stores. The novel draws attention to the ubiq-
uity of large glass windows in Chicago, describing how the "huge plates of
window glass, now so common, were then rapidly coming into use" (16).
The novel, with its focus on the social transformations fostered by increasing
urbanization, new opportunities for leisure pursuits, and changing shopping
practices, exports the logic of the mannequin from the discourse of advertising and employs it in the characterization of Carrie. Carrie embodies the
logic of the mannequin. Like those fabricated bodies in carefully crafted
scenarios, Carrie becomes a placeholder around which the characters fashion narratives. Her viewers compose these narratives based on the material
objects she wears and possesses and, subsequently, feel the drag of desire, a
desire that conflates consumer and masculine sexual desires.

The novel structures its opening glimpse of Carrie akin to a description
of a *tableau* window. With Carrie sitting alongside the window on the train
to Chicago, this introduction renders her ripe for the imposition of a narrative based on her clothing and setting. The novel's beginning, with its vague

physical sketch of Carrie and its extraordinarily detailed inventory of her possessions, defines her by her exterior—where she is, what she wears and owns. This attention to material possessions is echoed by her attention to the inadequacy of her clothing and the recollection of "longings the displays in [clothier's shops] had cost her" (7). After this limited description, the text almost immediately renders her generic and indeterminate with its claim that "[w]hen a girl leaves her home at eighteen, she does one of two things. Either she falls into saving hands and becomes better, or she rapidly assumes the cosmopolitan standard of virtue and becomes worse" (3). With the invocation of this commonplace, Carrie becomes a type, a generic and passive placeholder thrust into a strange setting, who either will become transformed by the "saving hands" of a benevolent rescuer or reflect the debased values and standards of urban society.

Throughout the novel, her changes in status or circumstance reveal how the logic of the mannequin operates in Dreiser's characterization. Like the mannequin in the store window who elicits a new narrative for every clothing or scenario change wherein it appears, Carrie acquires a new identity based on each change in physical appearance and location. Her acceptance of Drouet's offer to live with him as his mistress and her desire to become an actress are prompted by the new clothing, accessories, and furnishings she knows accompany each change in station. As Carrie ascends in social rank, the novel clarifies that her predilection for fine clothing motivates her every decision. Putting aside the nagging concerns about the immorality of her living arrangement, she realizes that "she could possibly have conquered the fear of hunger and gone back . . . but spoil her appearance—be old-clothed and poor-appearing—never" (99). Carrie is literally captivated by new clothing. She allows its appeal to dominate her; the "shine and rustle of new things . . . [take] hold of her heart" (70).

This affinity for the latest stylish clothing fascinates Carrie to an extent that renders her passive and anthropomorphizes the appealingly displayed commodities. To her, fine clothing is a "vast persuasion" that actively pleads with her by speaking "tenderly and Jesuitically" (98). These "voices of the inanimate" sell themselves to the passive Carrie, echoing the verbal appeals a salesperson might make. A lace collar claims "I fit you beautifully" and a pair of shoes flatteringly asserts "how effectively I cover your little feet" (98). The painstakingly displayed items of clothing beckon Carrie to look at them and endeavor to evoke desire within her by inviting her to identify herself with them. The construction of these persuasions renders clothing the active party while Carrie remains the passive direct object of each sentence. They plead with her to imagine herself within their *tableau,* replacing the dress form or the mannequin with her own image clothed in these items.

The logic of the mannequin appears as more than a strategy of characterization; it materializes in the fashionable streets of New York, uniting consumer and sexual desire in a spectacle that resembles an animated *tableau* window:

> [Carrie] noticed of a sudden that Mrs. Vance's manner had rather stiffened under the gaze of handsome men and elegantly dressed ladies, whose glances were not modified by any rules of propriety. To stare seemed the proper and natural thing. Carrie found herself stared at and ogled. Men in flawless topcoats, high hats and silver-headed walking sticks elbowed near and looked too often into conscious eyes. Ladies rustled by in dresses of stiff cloth, shedding affected smiles and perfume. . . . With a start she awoke to find that she was in fashion's throng, on parade in a showplace—in such a showplace. Jewelers' windows gleamed along the path with remarkable frequency. Florist shops, furriers, haberdashers, confectioners, all followed in rapid procession. . . . Pompous doormen in immense coats with shiny brass belts and buttons waited in front of expensive salesrooms. Coachmen in tan boots, white tights and blue jackets waited obsequiously. . . . (Dreiser 323–24).

On this street lined with shop windows, the participants in this ostentatious processional transmute themselves into animated mannequins, favorably displaying the most flattering of fashions. This portrayal inventories the material objects of the scene, describing the clothing and accessories of each group of people present and ignoring individuals by reducing them to generic categories—men, women, doormen, or coachmen. Amongst the shops selling the most luxurious and least useful commodities—jewelry, flowers, fur, fashionable men's clothing, and candy, the promenading men and women fashion themselves into one more expensive commodity on display. This context metonymically implies that like the items in the shops, these men and women are also frivolous and luxurious commodities.

The dynamics of the gazes exchanged in this scene conflate both sexual and consumer desire as the participants seek to provoke admiration, covetousness, and even lust with their ostentatious displays. While ogling, with its sexual connotations, is deemed rude in conventional society, the Broadway spectacle preempts these formalities. The behavioral code on Broadway encourages staring as a "proper and natural thing" (323). The participants promenade for the express purpose of display of their apparel and possessions. Therefore, their bodies, like mannequins, must be gazed upon so that the viewer might recognize and desire the fashionable and ideal. When a gentleman gazes admiringly upon Mrs. Vance, she nearly metamorphoses into a mannequin. Carrie notices that "all of a sudden that Mrs. Vance's manner had rather *stiffened* under the gaze of handsome men and elegantly dressed ladies" (emphasis mine, 323). Mrs. Vance momentarily transmutes herself into an inanimate object, arresting her natural movement and posing to render her display more attractive and easier to view. Yet, she is not the only woman transforming herself into an attractive and fashionable display; women stroll down this street dispensing "affected smiles and perfume" with "rouged and powdered cheek and lips" (323). The text pointedly draws attention to the affectations these people manifest as they drape themselves in fashionable garments, pose in flattering positions, and artificially alter their faces and emotions to render themselves more sexually desirable and to display their expensive clothing in the most appealing manner.

But instead of representing the male viewers' desire as sexual, the novel invokes language of valuation, possession, and consumption when it describes Carrie's appeal. The text tacitly implies that Carrie's similarity to the mannequin, the artificial amalgam of female fashionableness designed to prompt acquisitive desires, renders her attractive. Like those artificial bodies made of wax, wood, and fabric, Carrie's body is not especially sexual or sensual. The novel confines its descriptions of Carrie to generic statements like, "Carrie had now developed an equally pleasing figure, and had grown in comeliness until she was a thoroughly attractive type of her color of beauty" (322). This vague portrait emphasizes Carrie's indeterminateness, the quality that encourages viewers and readers alike to invest her with an appealing narrative.

Sister Carrie depicts a society where the framing structures and visual dynamics evoked by shop windows render the enframed objects and individuals desirable. The image of Carrie rocking in her chair and gazing out the window is one of the most frequently appearing depictions of her. While references to Carrie framed by windows generously litter the novel, the scenes of her on the theater stage framed by a proscenium arch most compelling figure the desire for Carrie as analogous to the feelings evoked in the spectator by the mannequin in a shop window. These stages, sharing the window dressing techniques described in window dresser manuals, have been fabricated to emphasize the objects and individuals placed therein. During Carrie's first stage performance, Drouet and Hurstwood's desire exponentially intensifies when Carrie appears, framed on a stage. Like a commodity in a shop window, Carrie is presented, "framed almost in massy gold and shone upon by the appropriate lights of sentiment and personality" that heighten "her charm" (187). The lights, the set design, and the sentimentality of the scene endow Carrie with an increased attractiveness. Yet the feeling that this newly displayed appeal provokes in the viewer is not admiration or appreciation as such, but rather, a desire to possess. Hurstwood's response invokes the language of possession; he feels a "keen delight in realizing that she was his," but at the same time recognizes that she does not yet wholly belong to him because she is still Drouet's "prize" (185, 194). Her stage performance instills in him such an intense desire to possess Carrie that he confiscates her from Drouet's home and from Chicago, disregarding her objections. This moment on stage precipitates Hurstwood's objectification of Carrie by prompting him to perceive her as something to acquire without respect to her desires or autonomy.

Similarly, the novel depicts Drouet's response to Carrie framed on the stage as a surge of acquisitive desire. Drouet experiences a delight in "his possession" that prompts him to resolve to marry her because she is "worth it" (186, 192). This description of Carrie indicates that through her stage display Drouet recognizes her as an object of great value, worth overcoming his resistance to marriage and worth casting aside his pursuit of other women. It is no coincidence that the novel figures Drouet's response to Carrie's performance as a recognition of his ownership of something of supreme value. The novel aligns Drouet's pursuit of women with shopping, describing his habit of seeking new conquests "in the great department stores" where he would capture "the attention of some young woman while waiting for the cash boy to come back with his change" (6). Drouet imagines that he has finally acquired a prize of great value and therefore can discontinue his shopping for women in department stores.

Though Carrie's performance on the stage does mesmerize the audience, the novel does not specify what causes her to be so captivating. In fact, during the play's early scenes, the performance is overwhelmingly amateurish and dull. When Drouet senses Carrie's nervousness, he goes backstage to advise her how to improve her performance. For the most part, his advice consists of trite and repetitive encouragement; his only concrete recommendation cajoles her to "do that lively" and to "[p]ut life into it" (183). These recommendations foreground the artificiality of stage performance. This redundant exhortation to add life to life highlights Carrie's lack of animation; like the unsuccessful mannequin, her performance is inanimate and wooden. The fact that Carrie the woman is alive and present on the stage becomes secondary to the notion that she must successfully and realistically imitate life so that the audience may identify or empathize with her characterization. This emphasis placed on realistic mimicry of life aligns Carrie's performance with the operations of the successful mannequin. In order to captivate the audience, her performance should be as authentic as possible. This verisimilitude prompts the audience to imbue her with "life" and consequently to engage with the narrative her performance communicates. As mentioned earlier, the window dresser highlights authenticity; he must observe everyday people in repose so that he may pose and style his wax figures as realistically and stylishly as possible because the mannequin's capacity for engagement with the passer-by depends on its capacity for a natural looking embodiment of human characteristics.

Carrie's forays into professional theater further conflate her framed and performing body with the mannequin. When Carrie first looks for a stage job in Chicago, the scene emphasizes how women in the chorus function as animated, embodied costumes. After Carrie leaves the theater's office, the stage manager admits that she would "never make an actress"; she would be "just a pair of tights" (255). He judges she could only serve to attract the audience by revealing her objectified costumed legs as a chorus girl. In her first professional theatrical role, she performs as a chorus girl—one body in a line of identically costumed, repeating performing bodies. Each description in *Sister Carrie* of a chorus girl identifies her solely by her costumed body, depriving her of a name and personality. The narrative refers to Carrie's friend Lola first as a girl "arrayed in pink fleshings and an imitation golden helmet" and frequently as the "soldier" (396, 398–99). In these early references, Lola's costume becomes her identity; she and the other women in the chorus perform as placeholders, as animated bodies in costumes.

In a similar way to mannequins in shop windows, these costumed women provoke desire within the spectators by displaying their objectified costumed bodies. The provocative and revealing nature of their apparel implies that the chorus line entices the audience members visually. Carrie feels relieved that she will not be wearing just tights but has been chosen to be "part of a group of twelve . . . assigned pretty golden-hued skirts which came to a line about an inch above the knee" (393). This description not only refers to the sexually provocative nature of the tights, but also emphasizes the homology between sexual and economic desire. The chorus girls' costumes foreground their similarity to gold; these gold-clothed bodies function as interchangeable, indistinct objects of desire that perform on this stage and circulate through other Broadway theaters throughout New York City.

In her role as the "Frowning Quakeress" Carrie performs as nothing more than a living, frowning costume, yet her appearance evokes a surge of desire in the audience. The novel depicts this response as an intense desire to possess and to consume:

> The portly gentlemen in the front row began to feel that she was a delicious little morsel. It was the kind of frown they would have loved to force away with kisses. All the gentlemen yearned toward her. She was capital (447).

Carrie's performance as the Quakeress whets the appetites of these gluttonous consumers as the novel aligns sexual and gustatory appetites in order to accentuate how Carrie's motionless, frowning, costumed body elicits a desire to consume. The quotation further links Carrie's performing body with possession and consumption when it applies the slang term "capital" to her. This economic term analogizes Carrie to something of value characterized by its fundamental exchangeability. She is replaceable and generic. Her acting triumph stems not from any discernable talent, but rather from her capacity to stand motionlessly pouting in a costume and provoke fantasies of sexualized consumption in her admiring viewers.

In her stage role, Carrie and her chorus girl peers operate like mannequins in window displays, performing the costumed body. But Carrie's similarity to mannequins is not limited to her stage performances. Carrie's attractiveness stems from the qualities she shares with mannequins—her capacity to imitate and embody attributes, styles, or carriage that others conceive of as desirable. In contrast with the inanimate mannequin, Carrie possesses a degree of agency in her appropriation of different fashions, yet she ultimately adopts these styles by imitating what others, Drouet in particular, find attractive. She "instinctively" feels a "desire to imitate" whatever Drouet identifies as fashionable (99). This alignment of her imitative tendencies with "instinct" deprives her of her limited agency and asserts that her mimetic behavior is a wholly involuntary response to a stimulus. In a way, Drouet, like a window dresser, molds Carrie into pastiche of society's most stylish and well-regarded attributes.

Announcing her capacity for mannequin-like replication of the fashionable, the novel characterizes Carrie as a passive soul, a "mirror of the active world" who exhibits an "innate taste for imitation and no small ability" (157). She observes what others find admirable in appearance or carriage and transforms her body to approximate these attributes. This capacity for mimicry enables Carrie's social rise. She conforms to the standards of appearance that most appeal to the upper-class male consumers. These consumers—Drouet, Hurstwood, multiple male theater patrons—respond to her attractive display with a desire to acquire her through financial transactions. Drouet and Hurstwood, who both financially support Carrie, are model consumers. Drouet enjoys wearing expensive clothing, eating fine meals, and shopping for commodities and women in department stores. When Hurstwood's economic prospects decline, he laments that he no longer possesses the capacity for shopping that he once retained. He can no longer procure the "new fall patterns for suits displayed in a Broadway tailor's window" (311). Carrie's affection for Hurstwood wanes contemporaneously with his decline in fortune and capacity for consumption. The theater patrons proffer themselves in fan letters extolling their own financial statuses and infatuation. Furthermore, the male manager of a hotel offers her the remuneration of free rent in exchange for the privilege of asserting that she resides there. He wishes to use the mere suggestion that her body inhabits his hotel to induce others to pay for the privilege of living near and possibly seeing her.

Carrie's primary talent appears to be the ability to incite spending in male consumers through her precise visual embodiment of the qualities society deems desirable. This ability to conform to society's standards of attractiveness, to transform herself according to fashion's trends, and to elicit a financial response in her viewers, aligns Carrie with the operations of a mannequin. It is this similarity to the simulated woman, the mannequin that relies on the commodities that surround it and the narratives created by spectators to invest it with an identity, that renders Carrie exceedingly appealing. Ironically, the very attribute that makes this urban woman desirable is her capacity to transmute her living, fleshly body into what is essentially a dress form, reflecting the latest fashions to wealthy consumers.

Dreiser's novel highlights how the dynamics of desire prompted by shop windows transcend the discourse of marketing and emerge in a realist narrative's depiction of the transitional urban consumer spaces of the last few years of the nineteenth-century. The lifelike mannequin, draped in appealing fashionable clothing, steps out of the shop window and into the pages of the realist novel. Carrie incarnates the logic of the mannequin and trades in her various identities by acquiring new clothes and relocating to new domiciles paid for by admiring male patrons. These manifestations of the logic of the mannequin reveal how this embodiment of the human body is becoming an engine of culture, materializing in literature and in enterprise. In the urban public spaces of the United States, the widespread exhibition of the artificial fashionable body, depicted as an ideal to aspire to or desire, represents how commodified clothing participates in characterization. As the body becomes a placeholder identified and enlivened by the clothing on it and the other commodities around it, fashion contributes further to the identity formation of the modern consumer.

NOTES

1. From Fashion Institute of Design and Merchandising Online Exhibit "The Way We Were Posed": http://www.fidm.com/resources/museum+galleries/exhibits/adel-rootstein-mannequins/.
2. Zola's 1883 *Au Bonheur des Dames* compares the prospective consumers' reactions to traditional "business windows" and elaborate windows designed by a trained window trimmer (4–8).
3. Andrea Henderson's "Burney's *The Wanderer* and Early-Nineteenth-Century Commodity Fetishism" attends to the changing relationships among shopkeepers, shoppers, and commodities in eighteenth- and nineteenth-century Britain and proposes that product displays contribute to consumers' understanding of the commodity as autonomous.
4. Recent protests at Victoria's Secret stores directed at mannequins dressed in lingerie and posed in sexually suggestive positions suggest that lines between realistically rendered mannequins and women remain blurred. See "With a Pose Here, a Boa There" by Timothy Dwyer and Leef Smith in the 7 October 2005, *Washington Post*.

WORKS CITED

Bauer, Alfred G. *The Art of Window Dressing for Grocers*. Chicago: Sprague, Warner and Co., 1902.

Casson, Herbert N. *Window Display Above All*. London: The Efficiency Magazine, 1934.

Dreiser, Theodore. *Sister Carrie*. New York: Penguin Books, 1981.

Dwyer, Timothy, and Leef Smith. "With a Pose Here, a Boa There." *Washington Post* (7 October 2005): B1.

Henderson, Andrea. "Burney's *The Wanderer* and Early-Nineteenth-Century Commodity Fetishism." *Nineteenth Century Literature* 57 (2002): 1–30.

International Correspondence School. *The Window Trimmer's Handbook*. Scranton: International Textbook Company, 1912.

Marcus, L. S. *The American Store Window*. London: The Architectural Press, 1978.

Merchants Record Company. *The Art of Decorating: Show Windows and Interiors*. Edited by Charles A. Tracy. (4th ed.). Chicago: The Merchants' Record Company, 1909.

"The Way We Were Posed." *Fashion Institute of Design and Merchandise Online Exhibits*. 26 March 2005. FIDM. <http://www.fidm.com/resources/museum+galleries/exhibits/adel-rootstein-mannequins/>.

Zola, Emile. *The Ladies' Paradise*. Translated by Brian Nelson. New York: Oxford University Press, 1995.

12 Allure of the Silent Beauties
Mannequins and Display in America, 1935–70

Emily R. Klug

Resolute and imperial with undeniable grace and elegance, they can appear to be endlessly happy, unapproachable, and vacant, and sometimes hopelessly sad. They are often more than a little smug, bored with our endless ogling and constant fussing. From the humblest of stages to the most elaborate and dazzling sets, they are a united breed, the epitome of calculated beauty and meticulous perfection, inspiring the envious glances of women and admiring stares of men. While they are part of a long tradition constructed around concepts of ideal beauty, they were born with a specific purpose and retain their practical origins. Despite their seemingly effortless and immaculate appearance, mannequins work harder to sell clothes, elicit buyers, and encourage consumption than even the most expedient salespeople.

Today storefronts are ruled by long-limbed, doe-eyed beauties with endless legs, flawless skin, and wardrobes to kill for. The dominant twenty-first century perception of beauty may be most closely aligned with the taste for long, lean silhouettes from the 1920s, save the modern preference for significantly larger bustlines. This concept of elusive perfection is not definite or exclusive; gender, race, lifestyle, income, and geographical location all impact an individual's perception of an ideal, though one may argue that contemporary mass media's obsession with weight and beauty seeks to homogenize societal preferences. Accordingly, the tall, lithe creatures that rule modern store windows inspire the consumer and incite the desire to buy, while also inevitably isolating her, leaving her with feelings of inferiority.

The relationship between desire and consumption serves as an appropriate basis for evaluating the role of mannequins and display in the twentieth century. The spatial and psychological impact of store windows and interior store displays on the consumer are explored within the context of fashionability, ideals of feminine beauty, and consumerism. This chapter focuses on the use of mannequins in department store displays in the United States between 1935 and 1970, picking up where studies of 1920s Art Deco mannequins have left off. The evolution of both materials and forms in mannequin design directly influences the way mannequins are used in display. The significance of trends in fashionable dress, changing concepts of beauty and decorum, as well as the role of consumption are also shown to impact the space of the display window, and inevitably, the consumer. These windows function as liminal spaces, constructed environments that stand between the department store and the outside world, capable of invoking desire, fantasy, and curiosity just as they may incite feelings of inferiority, self-consciousness, or distaste by soliciting the senses. In this chapter, case studies of a diverse selection of display windows reveal the mannequin as the ultimately malleable vehicle of display, functioning both as the relatable star of endless cocktail parties, resort holidays, and afternoon teas and, paradoxically, as a nameless and at times faceless manifestation of feminine perfection. By including mannequins in their window designs, window dressers blur the line between fantasy and reality, and the spaces of display come alive, the lead actors endlessly poised for opening night.

In the late 1940s, artist and writer Russell Hoban made the facetious comment to a journalist friend: "people are looking different lately, the dummies must be changing" (Schneider 7). Although Hoban was by no means a fashion expert, his pointed observation was made in the same cultural moment when Christian Dior unveiled his first collection, which both revolutionized the postwar silhouette and scandalized the fashion world with what would be affectionately dubbed the "New Look" in February of 1947. Although likely spoken in passing, Hoban's incisive remark provides a candid perspective on fashionability and the relationship between consumer and display in the postwar period. Looking back on Dior's debut, fashion historian Francine du Plessix Gray wrote in the November 1996 issue of *The New Yorker:*

> Out stepped the models, walking very fast, whirling in the crowded room with provocative swinging movements, knocking over ashtrays with the huge flare of their skirts as the name of each outfit was announced—Amoureuse, Pompon, Caprice. The women attending Christian Dior's first New Look collection, who were wearing the frugal clothes imposed on them since the war years—short, narrow skirts and boxy jackets—started applauding early in the show and kept on applauding right through the final ovation. They were being treated to an opulent femininity that had not been seen in fashion for many years (Gray).

The overt suggestion that women deliberately fashioned themselves after mannequins in store windows and displays is particularly striking and aligns well with Gray's account of the overwhelmingly ardent reception of the nipped waists and full skirts paraded at Dior's premiere showing. While this moment in history can be seen as a particularly evocative example of the power of fashion, it is certainly not anomalous. Similarly, the relationship between the female consumer and the display mannequin has a complex history that extends back to the nineteenth century. Examining the mannequin as a primary component of visual display in relation to changing trends in fashion and women's roles illuminates the astuteness of Hoban's statement. It is worthwhile to suggest that the relationship between female consumer and mannequin is one of reciprocity, a partnership dependent not only on the fashion system and designers but also on the influences of film and the fantasy of Hollywood glamour, ethnicity, and consumer demand as well as the rise of both the mannequin designer and the window dresser as artists and arbiters of feminine beauty. The department store display window functions as a space of fantasy, a bridge between illusion and reality designed to elicit consumer desire and ultimately result in sales.

BIRTH OF A SOCIAL STAGE:
THE RISE OF THE DEPARTMENT STORE

While it quickly grew into a cross-cultural pastime, shopping as we know it today originated as a mid-nineteenth-century phenomenon with the rise of the department store in urban centers in the West. Although conspicuous consumption was certainly not an invention of the nineteenth century, the department store created an unusually undiscriminating environment of luxury, elegance, and social spectacle that people of all classes—especially women—could experience simultaneously. Wealthy and poor alike were drawn into the cavernous spaces which offered endless glittering wares along with the promise of an everchanging, often riotous social scene. Whether one came away from an afternoon of shopping with a carriage full of beautifully wrapped packages or a juicy bit of gossip, the department store allowed all consumers to see and touch the merchandise and fantasize about owning anything and everything under the store's grand roof. During the mid-nineteenth century, the display window became increasingly important as department stores in Paris, London, and New York established themselves as the arbiters of style, communicating trends in fashion and beauty through carefully designed displays. As sociologist Ken Parker observes, "it was in these early department stores that techniques of presenting goods taken from older institutions were refined and perfected" (Parker 354). Accordingly, what had originated as the tailor's blank canvas, the bust form began to take center stage in the nineteenth-century store window, emerging first as a simple display fixture, and quickly revolutionizing the presentation of merchandise in boutique and department store windows alike.

TROUPE OF DUMMIES: EARLY MANNEQUIN DESIGN

From Victorian-era wax "dummies" with hyperrealistic features and corseted silhouettes to the widely popular, stylized plaster models debuted by Siégel and Stockman at the 1925 *Paris Exposition internationale des arts décoratifs et industriels modernes,* Paris was the center of innovations in mannequin design in the first quarter of the twentieth century. After separating from Stockman in the late 1920s, Siégel continued as the leading manufacturer of plaster mannequins until the early 1940s. In a 1939 jewelry spread for Paris *Vogue,* one of Siégel's mannequins was featured in conjunction with a female model, both covered in netting, bodies wrapped in silk, adorned with jewels from Boucheron and Van Cleef & Arpel. Images of both mannequin and model are cut off below the shoulder and laid out opposite one another, almost like a mirror image. The model is placed lower on the left page of the spread, eyes closed, giving the impression that she is dreaming of the mannequin featured at the upper right, whose wide glass eyes shine with vacant repose. The model is presented as a human version of the mannequin (rather than the other way around) and represents an unrealistic beauty and unobtainable lifestyle while simultaneously eliciting desire. Both images represent ideals of feminine beauty, and by pairing them they become one and the same, a blank canvas whose sole purpose is to display sparkling baubles, the "jewels of dreams."

Despite these elitist connotations, the Siégel mannequin featured in *Vogue* does represent a return to a more feminine ideal, markedly less severe in appearance than the featureless, bald-headed mannequins exhibited at the 1925 Paris Exposition. While the head of the 1939 mannequin remains perfectly oval, its neck is not nearly so attenuated. The eyes remain wide-set, but are more dramatically shaped and are articulated with more detail, particularly with a heavy fringe of dark eyelashes. The nose is long, straight, and slim, but the lips are fuller, much closer in resemblance to natural female physiognomy. The stylized Art Deco mannequin which abstracted the female face altogether has been transformed into the embodiment of the glamorous Hollywood starlet, complete with voluptuous, womanly features.

WARTIME INNOVATIONS: AMERICAN MANNEQUIN MANUFACTURE

Given the physical and material devastation of France in the aftermath of World War II, it is not surprising that American designers excelled in mannequin design and display during the early 1940s (Veillon 32). As French couturiers found it more and more difficult to purchase quantities of quality fabrics, not to mention thread, buttons, and other trimmings, salons that had seen the height of success only several years earlier began to shut their doors, and Parisian department stores experienced severe decreases in sales (Veillon 59). Extreme rationing in France brought the fashion capital of the world to a virtual halt by 1943, leaving room for American fashion designers, mannequin manufacturers, and window dressers who had survived the depression era to make their own mark on the world of fashion.

In the mid-1920s, American window dresser Cora Scovil won fame for her "patch-poster" window displays consisting of flat paper figures dressed with garments cut and pinned against their fronts and placed in whimsical settings (Schneider 115). By the late 1930s, Scovil was one of the first mannequin designers to take inspiration from Hollywood, fashioning mannequin heads with features meant to emulate those of famous actresses, attaching them to stuffed cloth torsos with moveable plaster limbs. The designer was also particularly fond of felt, constructing dramatically long eyelashes and sensuous pouty lips from the material and creating striking, fantastical figures that moved beyond the homogeneous manufactured look of plaster models (Schneider 115). Scovil opened her own mannequin manufactory, Vajah Inc., in New York in the 1930s, and in addition to plaster and rubber, began working with less costly materials including paper and foam which were particularly popular during the war years (Hale). At the 1939 New York World's Fair Vajah Inc. unveiled its "Women of the World of Tomorrow" mannequins, which featured jointed arms, legs, waists, and hands that would allow a window dresser to pose the forms in more realistic active and engaged positions. This trend paralleled the increasing popularity of sportswear clothing lines produced by American designers like Claire McCardell who acknowledged that women could be both active and elegant and needed wardrobes to match (Steele 6).

While most mannequin manufacturers were not as free-spirited or innovative in their design as Scovil, the trend in American mannequin design was towards dramatic, striking facial features and womanly, curved bodies. In 1940, Dana O'Clare (active 1938–50s) designed a boudoir scene entitled "Pageantry in Privacy" for Lord & Taylor in New York using plaster mannequins that epitomized these strong features (Schneider 81). The high cheekbones and broad shoulders of the display's two mannequins bore a strong resemblance to Joan Crafword's physiognomy. One mannequin was posed at the right, her long and lean, yet powerful stance balancing a reclining figure in bed, whose face was dramatically turned away and eyes downcast. A large screen in the background acted as a headboard, but also defined the space, lending a theatrical quality that suggested one had stumbled upon a scene rehearsal for a Broadway play or a Hollywood movie. In keeping with Hollywood-inspired mannequins, poses, props, and lighting were all reminiscent of what one might see in a contemporary film. The space of the display window became a cinema-inspired set for a visual narrative in which everything was for sale, from the Baroque-carved bed frame to the frothy dressing gowns and silver-embroidered slippers.

As much as O'Clare was in demand for his unconventional use of interior space, mannequins, and props, he was also known as a particularly demanding window dresser, calling for a staff of "experts only" for his Lord & Taylor designs (Schneider 16). Such attitudes were typical among window dressers working for high-end department stores in large cities for, as self-proclaimed masters like O'Clare insisted, they were artists. The most respected window dressers surrounded themselves with the most capable teams, leaving much of the grunt work of display preparation to their workers. O'Clare, however, was also renowned for being particularly involved with his projects. In one case, he pushed the limits of the glass storefront and appealed to the olfactory as well as visual sense, rigging up a machine to dispense bursts of the perfume featured in his display (Schneider 17). Such innovations bridged the department store with the street, blurring the boundaries between the product, display, and the space of everyday life. By appealing to senses beyond sight, O'Clare enticed the consumer in a new way by featuring the perfume as part of a complete lifestyle that could be purchased.

THE PLACE OF ETHNICITY: CONSUMER-SPECIFIC DISPLAY

This chapter largely focuses on the inclusion of mannequins in window displays of high-end department stores, although innovations in mannequin design and display were not exclusive to the grand retailers. In 1935, a Detroit newspaper ran a full-page advertisement introducing "the world's premier showing of the first all-colored mannequin" which was featured as the centerpiece of a modest neighborhood department store window (Schneider 78). Acknowledgment of ethnic diversity was not entirely new; past attempts at conveying ethnicity in mannequin design included the darkening of skin tone with powdered pigments or paint to achieve olive or bronzed complexions. The 1935 example, however, marks one of the first mannequin designs that took into account ethnic features. Rather than simply darkening the complexions of figures with characteristically Caucasian features, the designer based the mannequin's facial features on a female model of color. The pride with which the "colored" mannequin was introduced suggests that the store was likely located in one of Detroit's predominantly black neighborhoods where such a display would have been most well received.

By 1940, there were over two million African-Americans living within the city limits of Detroit, four times the number forty years earlier. Such a significant increase in population suggests an impact on consumer-driven displays, which would become more prevalent in the 1950s (Swanbrow). The example of the Detroit store window supports the claim that geographical location and specific economic, social, and racial commonalities of a given community increasingly influenced the design of store displays in many cities. For fashion to become more accessible, for products to be transformed into objects of desire, the spaces of display needed to be relatable and relevant to the consumers' lifestyle in some specific way. Invented spaces, fictional occasions, carefully styled mannequins, and creative vision must come together in the store window and speak to the consumer on some level in order to create a successful stage on which to close the sale.

In the 1930s and 1940s, retailers, attempting to broaden and/or cater more directly to their client bases, began to recognize the relationship between customer identification with the product and sales figures. If the space of the display window was to illicit desire, to present an elegant evening dress, a new spring hat, or extravagant necklace as an attainable luxury, then the key to triggering that desire required a combination of visual appeal, easy identification, and an acknowledgment of the human fascination with beauty. By creating spaces concurrent with a certain lifestyle, window dressers and ultimately retailers were able to capitalize on existing consumer demand while simultaneously shaping demand through visual narratives that cleverly communicated trends. Despite the acknowledgement of minority markets, ethnic mannequins were rarely featured in high-end department store displays prior to the 1980s, although smaller manufacturers began producing black and hispanic mannequins as early as the 1950s.

A discussion of ethnicity situates mannequins as models of ideal feminine beauty that were used by retailers as marketing tools. The appeal of the product in terms of fashion, beauty, and lifestyle is linked to race as defined by skin color and a selection of stereotypical physical features. While the intentions of the manufacturer and the retailer in Detroit were clearly positive, the display does invite the question of what defines ethnicity beyond the physical. Ann duCille skillfully addresses this issue in her examination of ethnic Barbie dolls in her book *Skin Trade* (1996). duCille suggests that in reducing the African-American race to a more rounded buttock and darkened skin tone, companies like "Mattel may be taking us back to the eugenics and scientific racism of earlier centuries" (duCille 12). Does the Detroit store window symbolize an early movement towards racial equality or does it simply commodify ethnicity? Even with the addition of ethnic features, the mannequin still represents an ideal of feminine beauty, and as with the plastic Barbie doll, beauty remains largely unattainable.

POSTWAR ABUNDANCE: FASHIONING AN IDEAL

Virtually overnight, strict rationing of the war years and declining sales for French couture houses and department stores were transformed with the 1947 debut of Dior's "New Look." Although some women were dazzled by Dior's extravagant use of fabrics and the luxuriousness of his cuts, what began as an era reaffirming the importance of fashion grew into a period when the line between real and ideal became blurred. Such trends in fashion and beauty increasingly encouraged women to model themselves after mannequins rather than the other way around. In the 1950s, the manner in which women dressed themselves, applied their makeup, and styled their hair became critical reflections of their worth as spouses, mothers, and respectable members of communities. In mannequin design, the consistent removal of identifying physical features of the female sex, including nipples and genitalia, reduced the defining elements of the ideal woman to her bust, waist, and hip measurements.

In 1950, prolific window dresser Gene Moore revealed the technology that went into producing a plaster mannequin in his eight-window series for Saks Fifth Avenue, "The Making of a Mannequin," while simultaneously constructing his own version of the "ideal woman" (Schneider 75). In one window, Moore placed fragments of a plaster cast and mold next to a plaster mannequin model still in the mold and a fully dressed mannequin, illustrating the three basic steps of production. The fully finished mannequin was positioned with hand on hip, chin held high, and eyes downcast at the plaster fragments, giving the figure a strong, lifelike quality as if the mannequin was no longer plaster at all, but the perfect woman, carefully constructed and refined, looking down imperiously at her humble origins. Moore's series suggested to both male and female viewers that an impeccably groomed and mannered woman could be styled and manufactured just as the mannequin was produced in a factory. This focus on the process of mannequin production elevated it to an art, as it had been understood by manufacturers like Siégel and Stockman at the 1925 Paris Exposition. In "The Making of a Mannequin," Moore positioned plaster figure production as a skilled craft that was as complex and important as women's own personal refinement. As Moore remarked, he "wanted his ladies ladylike," and it seems he thought of his mannequins in much the same way (Schneider 76). Once again, the space of the department store window functions as a bridge between the sidewalk and the store, between reality and fantasy, between real women and the ideals embodied in mannequins.

In a 1950s publicity still taken for Moore's mannequin manufacturing company Greneker, the designer was pictured in a tuxedo, "dancing" with one of his creations. Convincing as the smooth, gentlemanly dance partner, Moore's date appears as the perfectly demure and graceful lady. While Moore did understand mannequin production as an act of artistic expression, he did not separate mannequins from their role in window display and the presentation of fashion. He once commented:

> I longed for nipples, but I'm not responsible for them. Someone else came up with nipples on the breasts of mannequins. The bellybutton is mine though. I was up in the Bronx at the Greneker factory one day and just poked my index finger into one of the clay figures to show where I wanted it. This was nothing lascivious—the addition of a properly placed navel helped me to center garments on the mannequins (Moore 34).

Moore's statement supports his self-perception as a window dresser rather than an artist, concerned with a mannequin's anatomy for the purpose of more convenient dressing rather than anatomical realism. Moore was fully engaged with this role, designing window displays with the sole purpose of highlighting and selling products, albeit with an exceptionally creative flair. Although he had been hired by the New York-based mannequin manufactory Greneker to oversee design and production beginning in 1950, Moore continued to pursue window display, producing designs for the New York department store Bonwit Teller for over sixteen years, as well as Saks Fifth Avenue and Tiffany & Co. Moore had been an innovator of window displays since the 1930s when he was inspired by Cora Scovil's mannequins, which he found to be "the most realistic" (Moore 34). He first used one of Scovil's figures in a 1938 window for Delman in which he surrounded the mannequin with encroaching mountains of shoe boxes, pulled out at different intervals serving as shelves for the display of numerous pairs of shoes modeled on plaster foot forms. Even at this early date, Moore's insistence on showcasing the shoes with actual "feet" in them exhibits his interest in closing the gap between constructed fantasy and reality in display, revealing his perception of the mannequin as an indispensable tool of the trade.

THE QUESTION OF CHOICE: DISPLAY AND ABSTRACTION

Moore's interest in fragmented mannequins grew throughout the 1950s, culminating most memorably in a series for Tiffany & Co. he produced in 1957 through 1958. "I was very fond of suspended hands at the time," Moore recalled of his "Cat's Cradle," "Broken Egg," and "Love Letter" windows (Moore 89). For the first of these, Moore suspended plaster hands and laced the fingers with yarn and a diamond flower sprig brooch fastened at the center. A ball of yarn below was affixed with a larger version of the brooch above. For Easter 1957, Moore laid a shallow planter of grass at the base of a window and positioned a Hibachi grill at the center. "Floating" hands held the halves of a broken eggshell with a diamond necklace yoke dripping elegantly into the pan. When asked about the finished product, Moore wittily commented: "Cook yourself an omelet, honey, or fry yourself an egg, so long as you get a diamond out of it!" (Moore 82). For "Love Letter," Moore arranged one bejeweled hand with a piece of stationery and the other with a pen. A glass jar of ink also suspended in midair completed the scene, along with a scattering of discarded note cards artfully arranged on ethereal tulle and fairy lights below. Moore's affection for pairing glamorous jewels and housewares with fragmented hands was highly effective, achieving a very current artistic and modern feel while also encouraging the viewer to insert herself into each scene, take on each role, don each jewel. The shop window began to dissolve, and each display became the viewer's own backyard, her own writing desk, her own private space. At the same time, every space became an appropriate place for fashion, elegance, and beauty, an occasion worthy of the ideal. The oddity of such windows effectively drew attention to the cleverly displayed baubles rather than the props. Moore was aware that using more traditional bust mannequins would not have resulted in the same striking, product-focused displays.

Another accomplished New York window dresser, Henry Callahan worked exclusively for Saks Fifth Avenue in the 1950s and 1960s, producing window displays that reflected a new abstraction of the mannequin form (Schneider 100). Callahan never designed mannequins, so he worked with them from a different perspective than perhaps Scovil or Moore, focusing more on the product/prop relationship rather than understanding the mannequin as an art form. Although some of his displays maintained more traditional "situational" designs, as in his nightclub window for Saks Fifth Avenue (1958), which featured two elegantly dressed female mannequins flanking a tuxedoed male mannequin seated on a plush zebra-striped banquet, all three gazing out to the dance floor (and inevitably, the street) (Schneider 101). A fourth mannequin was placed to the side of the group, the solemn expression on her perfectly painted face suggesting that perhaps she was abandoned by her dance partner. The mood of the scene was convincing, a chic nightclub interior brought to life. In contrast with the presumably bustling crowds filing up and down Fifth Avenue, Callahan's scene offered a glamorous sanctuary from the mundane, a night of fantasy and the perfect party dress waiting behind the glass.

Many of Callahan's other window designs commented on material abundance and bodily fragmentation. One such window, also from 1958, placed a mannequin in a mock-boutique or closet space with gloved mannequin hands extending from the walls, each offering a different handbag to the contemplative figure. While the mannequin was already outfitted with a handbag of her own, Callahan provided her with eleven other options, gloved arm and all, suggesting that the mannequin herself had the ability to choose a different purse, needing only to remove her arm and replace it with another. The simplicity of the fabric-covered walls in Callahan's display is modern and minimalist, but more importantly, brings the space behind the glass into every woman's dressing room. The store window is a place where choices abound, where having twelve different handbags moves from fantasy to reality and luxury is presented as a choice rather than a wish. The fragmentation of the hands emphasizes the changeability of fashion and trends, suggesting that beauty and perhaps even self-worth are increasingly based on the goods one owns. In an earlier window for B. Altman of New York City from 1952, "The Woman who Couldn't Make up her Mind," Callahan placed a female mannequin within a mock shoe department complete with an attending male salesclerk, both surrounded by dozens of shoe boxes and shoes of every imaginable color and style (Schneider 105). As with Moore's window for Delman, Callahan's display commented on material abundance and consumer demand, encouraging the female buyer to take her shopping seriously, to evaluate her choices. Not so subtly, both displays also imply that the woman need not choose, but instead purchase multiple options for her pleasure and convenience.

Building on Moore's fondness for fragmented mannequin forms, in 1959 Callahan installed a surrealist-inspired window at Saks Fifth Avenue that was in keeping with his handbag display from the previous year. In this display, Callahan removed the mannequin altogether, instead fitting an afternoon dress and gloves over a simple dress form traditionally used by tailors and seamstresses. Gloved "arms" pinned to the sides of the torso were lightly stuffed, appearing deliberately unrealistic in shape, and the neck of the dress form was topped with a giant, precarious bouquet of daisies and roses flanked with antler-like tree branches. This playful take on the traditional mannequin distanced the association of mannequin with the female form, although a closed-eyed mannequin head positioned on a nearby chair gave the eerie suggestion that fitting the dress form with the head would bring the figure to life. Choices of shoes, stockings, and handbags laid out as possible accessories for the ensemble were presented with the fragmentary status of a doll's accoutrements and gave the display an unfinished feeling as though the putative viewer was meant to assemble her perfect outfit in an adult game of paper dolls. She was no longer limited to the role of consumer, but was instead invited to become her own stylist. Gene Moore commented that "before being dressed, they just stand around in the big dark store and wait their turn" (Moore 34). Callahan's display has captured these moments before the mannequin is dressed and brought to life.

The female viewer/consumer of Callahan's window was invited to put together the pieces of the puzzle, encouraged to create the ensemble that would magically inject the nameless and faceless female figure with personality, style, and decorum. But if one were to put all of Callahan's pieces together, would the finished product really represent an ideal? It seems more that the window dresser deliberately draws attention to fragmented concepts of beauty and fashionability through this and the previously discussed window displays. The main ideal that is being sold through Callahan's assemblage of objects is that of choice, as with the B. Altman display. Four hats, two pairs of shoes, two handbags, and multiple pieces of jewelry seem to be only some of many possible selections from this fictitious dressing room. The mannequin represents every woman in her dream closet, filled with only the finest garments and accessories.

Callahan took the abstraction of the mannequin to a new level in 1964, with his "invisible mannequin" window for Saks Fifth Avenue. A sparkling knee-length evening gown was suspended and fitted around a molded and cut plastic form that invisibly filled out the dress in all of the necessary places. To complete the effect, gloved arms held an ethereal tulle wrap around the gown and a luxurious, sparkling hair ornament was suspended high above, suggesting an exaggeratedly long neck. The entire display was surrounded by a giant oval starburst frame that floated as lightly as the delicate gown. The window card below proclaimed in feathery script: "For a season of gala events" (Schneider 101).

By removing the traditional mannequin from the window design and any trace of personality not essential to the display of the gown, Callahan invited the viewer to enter the store and allowed her to envision herself in the dress and wrap, the picture of elegance and style. Callahan's "invisible mannequin" window did not mark the end of using figures in display. The focus on selling and making a profit, on molding the ideal consumer through spaces that convincingly blurred the line between fantasy and reality, is something that became more and more evident throughout the twentieth century as designers like Moore and Callahan enjoyed continued success in their careers. As this survey illuminates, the mannequin was and is the central tool of clothing display and sale, the star of innumerable scenes that make consumers believe they not only want, but need to possess a certain product. From the smallest specialty shop to the greatest department stores in the world, retailers have cultivated identities for themselves based on their ever-changing window displays, which more often than not, are populated by a troupe of leggy mannequins.

One cannot help but wonder how Russell Hoban might have reacted to contemporary fashions, to the manifested forms that style takes on the streets of culturally, socially, and economically diverse cities like New York, Paris, and Tokyo. Who reigns supreme at the moment? Have the mannequins taken control, or have the Hollywood starlets, young fashion designers, or the window dressers of Barneys and Bergdorf Goodman? Or has the display window become every woman's virtual closet, the space where fashion is presented, chosen, styled, and made her own?

In her discussion of trends in 1920s display, Tag Gronberg observes that "sales devices such as the mannequin [were seen as] the means of arousing a female desire, desire for the 'ever-new' constituted by women's fashion." She goes on to clarify that "the crucial thing about the shop window mannequin was that it was identified as a vital component of the modern city street" (Gronberg 377). What was true of 1925 Paris and New York still resonates today. Shop windows function as liminal spaces, bridging the world of the street with the many departments inside. Windows recreating the closet, dressing room, or shoe department entice buyers to enter, to take part in the fantasy and spaces behind the glass. By featuring private spaces in which women choose their clothes, get dressed in the morning, try on a new look, the display window functions as a site of transformation, a place that can be interpreted differently by each viewer and draw her into the public spaces of consumption. In this context, the display window mannequins are simulacra of the ideal consumer, stand-ins for the viewer at any and every occasion, enlivened in the recreated spaces of the everyday. As the shop window joins the street to the department store, the display and, more specifically, the mannequin acts as an intermediary between the consumer pre- and postshopping trip and presumably pre- and postbeautification. This proposed "beautification" occurs with each visit to the lingerie department, every trip to the sportswear floor. Beauty and fashion are commodities to be bought and sold, and the shop window is the space where that initial desire is sparked, where the possibility of the ideal is posed, draped, pinned, and lit to perfection.

While the widespread use of mannequin displays are not striking to the modern viewer, consumers continue to observe and react to these displays, sometimes even changing the methods by which they are encouraged to choose their clothing and gather their knowledge of style and fashion trends. Although women are undoubtedly impacted by representations of a physical ideal, they do not always fall prey to the mandates of fashion and beauty industries. In 2004, an article appearing in the *New York Times* discussed Ralph Pucci's new collection of "fuller-bottomed" mannequins displayed in Macy's department store (Navarro). "Goddess" mannequins were described as "hot and sexy . . . certainly no waifs," touted as revolutionary because of an extra two-and-a-half inches of curve added around the hips.[1] While Pucci's "goddess" may not have entirely answered consumer demands to see clothes displayed on more realistic female bodies, the more curvaceous figures are symbolic of the evolution of design and a shift in who dictates contours of beauty.

Even more recently, Pucci has produced the "Shapes" collection, which features full-figured mannequins in sizes 18 through 22 that the company describes as having "big rear-ends [but] still sexy" (Navarro). Decter has unveiled both "Seduction" and "Courage" models since 2004, attempting to evoke the named characteristics through the mannequins' facial expressions and poses. Such progressions in mannequin design may be understood as a reversal of Hoban's original observation. People are looking different lately, taking style and concepts of beauty into their own hands, and mannequins, manifestations of what constitutes the ideal, just may be changing.

What began with the rise of the department store in France and the United States in the mid-nineteenth century has become an international way of life. Shopping is a social experience, a comfort, both fun and maddening, inspiring and superficial. Visual display continues to play with the variant emotions of the consumer, encouraging and discouraging certain trends and ideals, molding style and reacting to culture. Just as we rely on retailers, fashion designers, and window dressers to inform us of trends, these companies and creative minds rely on the consumer for acceptance and fiscal success. Similarly, the relationship between mannequin and consumer is reciprocal, based on acceptance and demand, perceptions of ideal beauty, and real, live beauty, something that cannot be captured in plastic, paper, or plaster.

WORKS CITED:

duCille, Ann. "Toy Theory: Black Barbie and the Deep Play of Difference." In *Skin Trade*. Cambridge, MA and London, England: Harvard University Press, 1996: 8–59.

Gray, Francine du Plessix. "Prophets of Seduction." *The New Yorker* (8 November 1996) www.newyorker.com

Gronberg, Tag. "Beware Beautiful Women: The 1920s Shop Window Mannequin and a Physiognomy of Effacement." *Art History* 20.3 (1997): 375–96.

Hale, Marsha Bentley. "Mannequins: Fascinating Fantasy Figures." Fashion Windows. URL: http://www.fashionwindows.com/mannequin_history.default. asp (15 March 2006).

Moore, Gene and Jay Hyams. *My Time at Tiffany's*. New York: St. Martin's Press, 1990.

Navarro, Mireya. "Store Mannequins Can Now Breath Out." *The New York Times* (14 November 2004): 9.1.4.

Parker, Ken. "Sign Consumption in the 19th Century Department Store: An Examination of Visual Merchandising in the Grand Emporiums (1846–1900)." *Journal of Sociology* 39.4 (2003): 353–71.

Schneider, Sara K. *Vital Mummies: Performance Design for the Show-Window Mannequin*. New Haven: Yale University Press, 1995.

Steele, Valerie. *Fifty Years of Fashion: New Look to Now*. New Haven: Yale University Press, 1997.

Swanbrow, Diane. "The University of Michigan study of African American Health." The University of Michigan. URL: http://www.sph.umich.edu/cbph/ programs/simhim/African-amer/African-manual.pd (3 January 2006).

Veillon, Dominique. *Fashion Under the Occupation*. New York: Oxford, 2002.

Vogue Paris. Paris: Editions Condé Nast, February 1939.

13 "A House That Is Made of Hats"
The Lilly Daché Building, 1937–68

Rebecca Jumper Matheson

On 13 September 1937, milliner Lilly Daché opened a building that she would later characterize as "a house that is made of hats" (Daché 1946: 5). Located at 78 East 56th Street in New York City, the building housed her retail and wholesale businesses, workrooms for millinery manufacturing and perfume bottling, rental space for a hairdresser, a furrier, and Daché's own home occupying the duplex penthouse (Daché 1946: 179). Daché wrote that "this building of chromium and pink satin and mirrors, of leopard-skins and gold, is a sort of showcase for myself as well as for my hats" (1946: 9). The interiors of the building served multiple purposes: they elevated the purchase of millinery into an experience of fantasy, they were a repository for works of art that inspired Daché designs and, most of all, they promoted the image of the designer herself.

Lilly Daché's life story appealed to the American public as an ideal immigration narrative. She was born in France around 1893 and moved to the United States as a young working woman (Daché 1946: 26–27, 50–51; Milbank 90). Daché worked her way from millinery apprentice in Paris, to hat saleswoman at Macy's in New York, to custom hat designer for and owner of Lilly Daché Inc. (Daché 1946: 64, 110–11, 113; Milbank 90). She later wrote that "[o]ut of a hat have come a worldwide business, a skyscraper building, and a certain fame" (1946: 13).

In Daché's 1946 memoirs, *Talking Through My Hats,* she recalled how during her childhood in France she dreamed of moving to the United States, a landscape she pictured as dotted with tall buildings (20). Whether this was truly her memory or simply good wartime marketing, she did not encounter this glamorous urban skyline in her first days across the Atlantic. When she arrived in the United States on 13 September 1924, she found herself in Hoboken, New Jersey, followed by Burlington, New Jersey, then Philadelphia (Daché 1946: 26–27, 44–45, 144). None of these places lived up to her childhood imagination of an "America" of skyscrapers. Daché finally made the trip to New York City and was delighted to find the "America" she had imagined: "[h]ere, then, were the skyscrapers! At last! Great stores. Tall office buildings. . . . So I stood at the corner of 34th Street and Broadway, in the city of New York, and discovered America" (1946: 50, 51).

Daché's success in New York is all the more impressive given the state of the millinery industry in the years 1925 and 1926 when she first began working independently, buying out her employer and then her partner in one of Broadway's "little milliner" establishments (Daché 1946: 58, 90, 110–11, 113). In 1925, the United States millinery business "had its own miniature industrial revolution," as technology was developed to mechanize the hat-making process ("$2,000,000 Worth of Flats" 50). This mechanization, along with the pressures of style pirating, pushed many small milliners out of business just as Daché was starting (ibid. 52). A 1935 *Fortune* article states: "In 1929 sales were down to $300,000,000 from the 1925 figure of $350,000,000, and millinery workers had dropped from 60,000 to 35,000. The depression, with still more bitter price wars, increased the damage. Last year, with sales of $200,000,000, workers had dropped to not much more that 30,000." Small businesses, often run by women, were being pushed out of the market by the mass-manufacturing firms, primarily controlled by men. Yet during these years, Daché transformed herself from a small custom milliner to America's top selling designer of expensive hats ($20.50 and up) (ibid. 52, 54). Daché was one of a few charismatic and creative women of the early-to-mid-twentieth century who was able to manage both the corporate and the design aspects of her own business, and refused to accept societal norms which subjugated women's careers in favor of the traditional roles of wife and mother. Lilly Daché describes how her original business partner in the "little milliner" shop longed to get married and stop working, according to prevailing norms (Daché 1946: 110). Daché, however, insisted on continuing her design career after her 1931 marriage to Jean Despres, telling her husband: "I had put too much of myself, my dreams, my hopes into this business to throw it away as if it were nothing" (Daché 1946: 144–45). Instead, she continued to expand Lilly Daché Inc., which would eventually include ready-to-wear, coats, stockings, shoes, costume jewelry, and perfume, housed in a building that would market Daché's signature style (Milbank 187; Pope).

For thousands of years, architecture has been used as a form of monument making. The Lilly Daché building, both in the exterior and interior spaces, was also a monument to Daché's product image and to her success as a woman entrepreneur. Daché admitted: "I live in a kind of stage setting most of the time, but underneath I am not like that. The setting—that is good business. . . . My advisors have told me that I must live up to my legend" (Daché 1946: 9). In an interior that incorporated both business and domestic space, Daché literally lived up to the public persona of glamour she had created.

Neighborhoods, like clothing styles, go in and out of fashion. Daché had previously moved her stores based on the changing locations of the fashionable shopping districts. In 1929, she consolidated her business from separate locations in Midtown and on the Upper West Side, to a single location in Midtown, where she occupied the fourth floor of the Columbia Broadcasting System Building ("Business Leases" 50; Daché 1946: 122). For her new building, Daché desired a location that would be "smart, but near to the center of things. Exclusive, but not hidden away" (Daché 1946: 173). She chose the site as carefully as she selected materials for the design of a new hat; her final selection was "just off Park Avenue and far enough uptown to be smart, near enough to be handy" (Daché 1946: 5).

On 8 November 1936, Daché announced that she had purchased the property in 78 and 80 East 56th Street, adjoining the southwest corner of Park Avenue. The headlines read: "Modiste to Erect Midtown Building; Lilly Daché Buys Property in East 56th Street for Modern Structure." The site's preexisting buildings would be torn down to make way for what the *New York Times* anticipated as a "modernistic structure [ready] for occupancy about 1 June 1937" ("Modiste to Erect Midtown Building" 37).

In a move typical of Daché's business acumen, a corporation separate from the millinery business was formed to own the building. Daché was president of the new 78 East Fifty-Sixth Street Realty Corporation, which in March 1937 "gave to the John Hancock Mutual Life Insurance Co. a mortgage for $200,000, due in ten years at 5 percent" ("Manhattan Mortgages" 37). Daché's husband was concerned about going into debt during a depression to fund the building, but Daché was determined (Daché 1956: 20). Daché wrote:

> So at last we signed the papers for the property, and then we started planning the building which was to be a monument to hats, and to beauty, and to the things that seem frivolous and silly sometimes, but which really are so important in the life of every woman. (1946: 175)

To make her building come to fruition, Daché needed just the right architect. The architectural firm of Shreve, Lamb and Harmon was selected, in conjunction with the French architect Georges Letelié ("Modiste to Erect Midtown Building" 37). Daché called Letelié "a brilliant young architect of France, who had won the Prix de Rome for some of his work." Daché believed firmly that, "(i)f Georges could come, I was sure, my building would be the picture of my dreams" (1946: 176). Daché was related to Letelié by marriage, as he also happened to be the husband of Jean Despres' sister, Marguerite.

In her memoirs, however, Daché does not mention Shreve, Lamb and Harmon. Instead, her entire focus centers on the contribution of Letelié, with whom she seems to have had a great rapport: "Georges said that my building should be a little gem among business buildings—as perfect as one of my own hats. It must have great distinction and elegance, he said, as well as being practical and functional" (1946: 176). Here, Daché herself draws the parallel between the image of her hats and that of her building. The French architect was favored by the French designer as the person whom she could most trust to translate the art of her millinery into an inhabitable space.

Daché wrote: "When at last the workmen broke ground for the building, I watched with as much pride and wonder as a mother who sees her first-born for the first time, and I said a little prayer of thankfulness. . . ." (1946: 176). The builders for the project were the Hegemon-Harris Company ("New Edifices Win"). Daché described watching the building's construction "brick by brick" (1946: 5). The exterior of the building was finished in Indiana limestone on the first two floors, with brick and hollow tile back-up, with the upper floors finished in stucco ("New York: Miliner Builds" 53). However, the building's framework was of structural steel, which is an interesting parallel to Daché's earliest hat designs, which had a metal wire base, like other hats of the period (*Architectural Record* March 1938: 53; Daché 1946: 19).

At 11:30 a.m. on 15 April 1937, Daché held a ceremony for the laying of the cornerstone, inviting dignitaries such as Charles Ferry de Fontnouvelle, French Consul General in New York. The *New York Times* heralded the planned building for its plan of incorporating glass bricks into the façade ("To Lay Corner Today and New Edifices Win"; Ibid. 53; Daché 1939). The cornerstone represented the first "interior" space in the building, and Lilly Daché forged a very physical connection between fashion and the interior spaces of her building from this first moment; there, fashion was buried within the architecture. Daché filled the cornerstone with the first hat she had created as an independent milliner, a live horned toad, a newspaper article with her first praise in the United States, a poem by Maud Moody (millinery editor of *Women's Wear Daily*), a parchment scroll signed by the dignitaries present, and "sentimental mementos from France" (Daché 1946: 177). Daché held a luncheon at the nearby Drake Hotel after the ceremony (Daché Building started).

The publicity surrounding the cornerstone ceremony was also indicative of Daché's ability to use the building to promote her designs (Daché 1946: 178). The "lucky" horned toad was a gift from Daché's friend Alice Hughes, a journalist, who had heard about a horned toad unearthed, live, from a cornerstone. Hughes then wrote a newspaper article on the cornerstone dedication ceremony, manufacturing a publicity scandal by also reporting the toad-in-foundation to the American Society for the Prevention of Cruelty to Animals (ASPCA). The controversy forced Daché to have the work stopped, the foundations torn down again, and the toad removed before continuing construction (Daché 1946: 178). While Daché's memoirs describe the event as slowing down the construction process, in reality the horned toad was only in the cornerstone for one day, so it is doubtful whether much building had yet occurred, or whether the construction was even *intended* to resume until after the publicity stunt. The next day's headlines read: "'Good-Luck' Plan Fails Mme. Lilly Daché; Toad Wins Release From Cornerstone; A.S.P.C.A. Orders Removal of Good Luck

Symbol From New Building of Milliner; Penthouse Home Instead; Agent Insists on Sunshine for Once-Doomed Pet, So Owner Provides a Roof Garden" (*New York Times* 17 April 1939). The toad came to live in a terrarium in the penthouse, becoming something of a mascot for Daché.

Daché took a very personal, hands-on approach to the fitting of her custom hats and was very involved with her building during the construction process ("$2,000,000 Worth of Hats January 1935" 82). She would later write:

> So that is my house of hats. All the time it was being built I was underfoot all the time, getting in the way of the workmen, interrupting the contractors and the architects, being, I am sure, most bothersome. But this was something into which I had put my heart, and I intended to know every stone and every beam of it. Through it all, Georges was most sympathetic, and did not mind when I wanted to help the plasterers mix plaster or assist the painters in mixing paint (1946: 180).

Daché started selling hats out of the new building before it was actually completed, and urged the workers to have the building ready by her lucky day, 13 September.

The opening day of the Lilly Daché building began at 9 a.m., 13 September 1937, with interviews with the architectural press. Daché recalled how "[t]here were toasts to the new building and to me and to my hats, and to Georges, who had helped to turn this dream house of mine into bricks and stone" (1946: 181).

The exterior of the nine-story Lilly Daché building began with a base that extended up two stories; the base contained the lobby and retail spaces (Figure 13.1). The first story had a smooth, rectangular recessed entrance area, with circular columns on either side of the front entrance. The second story had a symmetrical arrangement of a horizontal panel of individually framed glass bricks, flanked on either side by a small circular window, reminiscent of those used in many townhouses of the period, which linked the building with the still-residential character of Park Avenue. Daché wrote: "My name is written big and bold, in my husband's handwriting, on the mat in front of the big glass doors of my building. . . . When I look at my name in front of the door I know that this is mine—a house that is made of hats" (1946: 5). Her name was also placed on either side of the first-floor entrance, in small letters.

The shaft of the building encompassed floors three through seven, home to wholesale, manufacturing, and rental spaces.

The crown of the building had a thin cornice and featured ribbon windows on the eighth floor. The ninth floor was slightly recessed, with a roof garden terrace for Daché's potted geraniums (Daché 1956: 199). Daché's penthouse home was inside this "hat" of the building (Daché 1946: 5). By 1958, the building also had the word "DACHÉ" written on the western

Figure 13.1 Exterior of the Lilly Daché Building. Photograph by Fay S. Lincoln, 1937. Fay S. Lincoln Photograph Collections. Courtesy of Historical Collections and Labor Archives, Special Collections, The Pennsylvania State University.

side of the building, extending down from the eighth to the sixth floor, visually linking Daché's personal and work life.

The interiors of the building were designed by T. H. Robsjohn-Gibbings, with elements by Lester Gaba, and also incorporated some features that were to Daché's own specifications, such as circular rooms (Daché 1946: 5, 180; "Shifts in Shops" 68). Robert A. M. Stern, Gregory Gilmartin, and Thomas Mellins describe the interiors as a mixture of styles: "Here Daché's offices, shop and private apartment combined the opulent minimalism of Ely Jacques Kahn's work for Yardley with the surrealism of the Helena Rubenstein salon" (327).

FIRST FLOOR: RECEPTION ROOM
AND GRAND STAIRCASE

The lobby of a building functions as an introductory space, often designed to impress the viewer, and assists the transition between street and interior spaces. Daché described her first floor as an "entrance hall, behind thick glass doors, with a few showcases about, showing jeweled fripperies and perfume, mostly for atmosphere" (Daché 1946: 179).

The reception room had large horsehide rugs laid over floors of Montana travertine. The walls were beige with a wax finish. A settee, desk, and chair were made of birch, upholstered in black buffalo hide. A Ming dynasty carved wooden statue stood guard by the grand staircase, which was carpeted with beige broadloom (New York: Miliner Builds 54). Her lobby introduced themes that would be further developed upstairs: modernist furniture with simple, undecorated lines; exotic collections of Asian statuary, animal skins, and an overall impression of Hollywood-styled glamour.

Daché's love of the exotic is most notably expressed in her signature turban designs, which were a staple of her millinery collections for many years. Daché also collected and decorated with exotic, non-Western pieces, evoking the combination of the foreign and familiar in her own designs. Exoticism can be a problematic source of design inspiration, as one must confront issues ranging from imperialism and racism to trivialization or commercialization of other cultures. However, the exoticism in Daché's fashion spaces ultimately seems to be more about seeking inspiration for fantasy and less about intentionally perpetuating negative stereotypes. As Richard Martin and Harold Koda note: "Orientalism is not a picture of the East. . . . It represents longing, option, and faraway perfection" (13). Furthermore, as Peter Wollen posits, a designer's "facination with scenarios of the Orient can correspond, to a significant degree, to the desire of women to re-shape, or re-signify, their own bodies" (30). Daché's exoticism allowed her, by means of aesthetic control over her building's interiors, to link in her customer's minds the purchase of millinery with an expression of desire.

SECOND FLOOR: GRAND SALON AND VIP SALONS

Daché's retail custom millinery salon was located on the second floor (Figure 13.2). The centerpiece of this level was a circular room with mirrored walls, echoing the shape of a hat or hatbox (Daché 1946: 179). Building her own space allowed Daché to control the interior layouts, something not afforded by a tenant. Working as both producer and patron, Daché is a perfect exemplar of female agency in the mid-twentieth century, countering what Norma Broude and Mary D. Garrard see as repressive "gender expectations conflict[ing] with a desire for cultural achievement or a public voice" (3). In considering the interior of her building, Daché insisted that "it must be beautiful and luxurious. It must have a room all round and made of mirrors, and another padded in satin, and it must have leopard-skin furniture and many windows to let in the light" (1946: 173). While Daché was certainly not alone in embracing the design—for example, in 1928 interior designer Eleanor McMillen Brown transformed the square dining room of her Sutton Place duplex into a circular room—in choosing this shape for her salon Daché reinforced her position as a designer of unique and modern hats (Stoddard 70). This shape was also very evocative of a certain genre of exaggerated Art Deco film sets used in Hollywood musicals: one could almost visualize Ginger Rogers and Fred Astaire dancing up the grand staircase and twirling in the circular salon.

Vogue reported that the circular shape was carried through to the ceiling: "T. H. Robsjohn-Gibbings designed the interiors, with a grand staircase sweeping up to the Salon, where there are circular mirrored walls framed in white flogged hide, torchères of frosted crystal, and a great domed ceiling" ("Shifts in Shops" 1937). T. H. Robsjohn-Gibbings first considered a career in architecture, but instead became an interior designer, furniture designer, and commentator on American interiors. Robsjohn-Gibbings felt strongly that American design should not be a wholesale appropriation of an idealized European past; he wrote that "(t)he antique furniture cancer is a deeply rooted evil" (Robsjohn-Gibbings, 1944). He embraced neither the historical and overtly decorative style of interior designers such as Elsie de Wolfe and Dorothy Draper nor the "machine for living" sterility of Le Corbusier (Robsjohn-Gibbings, 1944: 25, 50; 1954: 82). Robsjohn-Gibbings brought to the Daché interiors a perspective that was committed to the modernity and to the individuality of the client, firmly grounded in its moment in the twentieth century and perfectly suited to the expression of up-to-date fashion millinery.

The second floor salon had floors of polished cork with rugs of horse-hide. There were curtains of black metallic gauze. Daché invoked exoticism with chairs covered in handwoven Balinese fabric and a settee covered in a striped Indian cotton fabric (*Architectural Record* March 1938: 55). Daché wrote that the atmosphere was completed by "[t]hick carpets on the floor, soft lights, sleek saleswomen—it all spells Elegance with a capital E"

Figure 13.2 Daché's main salon on the second floor. Photograph by Fay S. Lincoln, 1937. Fay S. Lincoln Photograph Collections. Courtesy of Historical Collections and Labor Archives, Special Collections, The Pennsylvania State University.

(1946: 179). That Daché writes about her saleswomen as though they were part of the décor tells much about the roles of women in the business of selling fashion. These women had to be as streamlined and modern as the interiors where they worked.

Blonde celebrities visiting the salon were fitted in a gold dressing room, while brunette celebrities were shown into a dressing room of silver (Daché 1946: 6, 173). The gold dressing room was accessed by parting a curtain of "rough spun fabric with gold metallic thread" ("New York: Miliner Builds" 55). The appropriate metallic was intended to flatter the client's complexion, just as the custom Daché-designed hat would. From the moment a client entered the Lilly Daché building, she stepped into a world where bodies and spaces had to conform to the aesthetic of the designer. Film stars such as Carole Lombard, Marlene Dietrich, Carmen Miranda, Betty Grable, and Olivia de Haviland all wore Daché creations, and in the custom salon they could be fitted in a space luxurious enough for their public relations photographs (Daché 1946: 157–66).

THIRD FLOOR: "BUREAU DE LILLY" AND WHOLESALE SALON

The jungle-themed third floor contained the wholesale salon, spaces for three assistant designers, a stockroom, workspaces for milliners, including an area for blocking hats, and finally Daché's office—the "Bureau de Lilly" (Figure 13.3). The Bureau de Lilly had walls of glass brick and beige plaster, bronze-green broadloom carpet, and doors of stretched hide, dyed bronze-green. A starkly modern dressing table was paired with exotic chairs upholstered in Tibetan wolf ("New York: Miliner Builds" 54).

Daché's wholesale customers had the privilege of entering a small circular fitting room with padded walls of tufted pink satin and a leopard-skin divan (Figure 13.4). Daché described this room as a "beautiful padded cell," and added that "[i]t is a great comfort, that pink satin padded room." Daché joked that this room allowed her to "bump [her]head in comfort" (1946: 6).

There is a direct connection between Daché's fashion and her interiors through the leopard-skin pattern. Daché sometimes dressed to match the building, wearing leopard-skin slippers of the same material used both in her bedroom and in the upholstery of the wholesale salons (1946: 8).

The choice of leopard skin as a signature fabric marks Daché's expression of power as a successful female designer and business owner. Shannon Bell-Price, in the catalogue to the Costume Institute's exhibition *Wild: Fashion Untamed,* posits that in the image of the Amazon woman, "[p]ower, savagery, barbarism, and otherness are often signified . . . by the wearing of animal skins, in particular the leopard, as the female of the species was known to be a superior fighter" (Bolton 36). Daché represented a type of woman who translated her artistic sense into economic power, certainly a shift away from roles women primarily performed as either unpaid or low-waged.

In addition to the leopard-skin upholstery, there was a jungle scene painted on the wall by Lester Gaba, who also painted French mottoes on

Figure 13.3 The "Bureau de Lilly": Daché's third floor office space. Photograph by Fay S. Lincoln, 1937. Fay S. Lincoln Photograph Collections. Courtesy of Historical Collections and Labor Archives, Special Collections, The Pennsylvania State University.

Daché's kitchen walls, and "china cats with pink roses" in a bathroom (Daché 1946: 179, 185). Gaba was a multitalented individual who worked as a commercial artist, "display man" (visual merchandiser), producer of fashion shows, and writer. Some of Gaba's earliest commercial projects were soap sculptures used in venues as diverse as advertisements and Christmas cards (Gaba 1935: 82–86).

Figure 13.4 The third floor wholesale salon had walls of tufted pink satin. Photograph by Fay S. Lincoln, 1937. Fay S. Lincoln Photograph Collections. Courtesy of Historical Collections and Labor Archives, Special Collections, The Pennsylvania State University.

Gaba's sculptural contribution to the publicity for the Daché Building's opening was a life-size store window mannequin named Cynthia. Cynthia was originally part of a group of mannequins that Gaba had designed, but he was so taken with the finished product that he had one made for his own apartment. Lilly Daché "met" Cynthia in Gaba's home and, with Daché's special knack for publicity, invited Cynthia to the opening of the new building (with hats and wardrobe styled by Daché) (Gaba 1952: 11).

Gaba described Cynthia's debut: "Smartly dressed, and seated in front of an enormous mirror in the Daché salon, Cynthia was the center of attraction. Everyone wanted to meet her and discover the identity of the beautiful mystery woman who sat in disdainful silence, refusing to talk to anyone" (1952: 11). Dorothy Shaver of Lord and Taylor followed suit by inviting Cynthia to a party at her store. From there, Gaba's creation went from being another odd publicity stunt for the Daché Building to gaining a certain celebrity status in her own right. Gaba, accompanied by Cynthia, was known to frequent "21" and the Stork Club,[1] to attend events sponsored by Elizabeth Arden and Howard Greer, and to wear borrowed diamonds from Cartier, Tiffany, and Harry Winston (Gaba 1952: 11).

FOURTH THROUGH SEVENTH FLOORS: MANUFACTURING AND RENTAL SPACES

When the Lilly Daché Building opened, the fourth floor was completely occupied by millinery workrooms (Daché 1946: 179). The fifth through seventh floors were originally designed as loft spaces to be rented to commercial or service industry tenants (New York: "Miliner Builds" 52). In 1937, *Vogue* reported that the fifth floor would contain retail space in which "Jonai, newly affiliated with Daché, will open a shop of day and evening clothes" (15 April 1937). In April 1938, Jonai ran an advertisement in *Harper's Bazaar* featuring a sketch of the Daché building (38). By 1946, the fifth floor was used for bottling and packaging Daché's perfume. During this period, levels six and seven were rented to a furrier and a hairdresser (Daché 1946: 179).

EIGHTH AND NINTH FLOORS: RESIDENTIAL PENTHOUSE

Lilly Daché wrote of her building: "On top of it I had the builders put a penthouse, so that I could live with my hats. And so I do" (Daché 1946: 5). The eighth and ninth floors formed a duplex apartment for Daché, her husband Jean Despres, and later their daughter Suzanne.

In the hall of the apartment, Daché literally did live with her hats—not hats of her design, but sources of inspiration: a collection of African headdresses, mounted and displayed along a hall wall as pieces of sculpture.

Years later, T. H. Robsjohn-Gibbings would characterize this style of decoration as a trend of the 1930s: "Aboriginal modern" (1954: 49). Daché would later donate these headdresses to the Costume Institute at the Metropolitan Museum of Art in 1974.

According to a feature article in *Life* magazine on the day Daché's building was inaugurated, Daché purchased the collection of hats made in the Belgian Congo for $2,500 in July 1937 ("Africa's Belgian Congo" 53). The African hats had previously been exhibited at the Charles Ratton Galleries in Paris, and were also featured in *Harper's Bazaar* (Eluard 106). The *Life* article illustrated both "Congo originals" and "Lilly Daché's African Adaptations," as well as photographs of Daché at work, adapting the hats.

The original 1937 decor of Daché's living room included a brown and beige pebble-tufted carpet, beige walls, draperies of "white rough spun fabric with gold thread," and glass curtains of "white metallic gauze." Chairs were of acacia or rosewood, and upholstered in Chinese chintz or "orchid green rough silk" (New York: Miliner Builds 56). Over the years, the living room would continue to house her everexpanding collection of Asian and modern art.

By 1960, her living room contained a carousel dragon, a Salvador Dalí painting, and a black and white abstract painting, in addition to "unhung paintings on a bench and on the floor, the Nepalese altar piece over the fireplace, the television set and behind it the Oriental sculptures the size of small children." There was also "a low, square table" piled with books. The living room contained bookshelves at one end of the room, in an alcove (Nordell). In 1964, *Women's Wear Daily* reported that "[t]he spacious, uncluttered, living room of her apartment is filled with art . . . contemporary and Oriental. An intricately worked Nepalese altar surrounded by Siamese and Indian buddhas [sic] dominates one wall of the room, while paintings by Dalí, the French painter Napp, who is also art director of *Elle*, and Larry Rivers hang on another. The tables in the room are covered with an impressive collection of jade" ("Hats are Back" 11).

The penthouse living room was still an extension of her public face. She often granted interviews in the living area. Sometimes even official business events were held in her "private" space. As early as 1933, Daché was a proponent of the theory that all elements of a woman's appearance should be planned together as a whole ("Wrap of Anna Blue" 7). By 1954, her penthouse apartment was the venue for fashion shows displaying her designs which by then had included hats, ready-to-wear, hair, makeup, stockings, and shoes (Pope). Daché's building and interiors gave her the opportunity to sell not just a head-to-toe look, but also a lifestyle concept, the application of her principles of glamorous design to every aspect of life at home.

The master bedroom had separate bath-dressing rooms for Daché and Despres. Daché's dressing area had marble floors with a monkey fur rug. Her dressing room had green curtains, while the bedroom had rose-beige

window treatments. Surfaces in the bedroom were luxuriously tactile, ranging from a green plush chair to the rose pink tufted velvet bedspread to a
chaise lounge covered in fox fur ("New York: Miliner Builds" 56).

According to Daché, her husband sometimes complained about living
over her business, saying that she "would be completely happy if I had a
brass pole, like a fireman, and could slide down to my workrooms in the
middle of the night . . . Maybe I shall do that sometime" (1946: 179–80).
There is a working-class association with living over one's place of business. Perhaps this was part of Despres' objection, as well as the issues of
privacy and the difficulty of escaping work. Even their bedroom functioned
as a public space as well as a private one, as in the 1930s and 1940s Daché
made it her rule to begin her day's work from bed. Daché wrote:

> My day always begins with this "bedline," and there is a parade
> through my bedroom all morning of my secretaries, my milliners, my
> masseuse, my manager, even sometimes buyers. I try to do as much
> work as possible in bed, as this is the only way I can conserve my ener-
> gies. Most of my hats are designed in bed, my letters are dictated there,
> and often I buy materials from my bed, as manufacturers bring in their
> wares (1946: 8).

A *Life* article from 1945 shows Daché working this way, while her staff
hovers around dressing her hair, fitting her slacks, and adjusting the trimmings on her hat ("Packing for Paris" 128–29).

Though Daché may have indeed preferred to work this way, what she
terms the "bedline" was most likely part of her public image. This private
yet public ritual use of bedroom space evoked a lifestyle of luxury. It is
reminiscent of the dressing rituals of the kings and queens of France in the
eighteenth century (Ribeiro 181–83). The concept of working from bed
may also have been fashionable and appealing during the Great Depression, when so many women labored to simply survive. A *Vogue* editorial section from January 1938 "For a Life of Ease" begins: "As so many
ladies of leisure do, she plans her day in bed—with an assortment of little
path-smoothers that keep the household running quietly as a well-tended
machine" (87). The facing photograph displays a woman in a bed of satin
and mirrored surfaces, planning for the lifestyle of a socialite. Daché, who
projected an image of leisure even while designing for and running her
own company, wrote of her bedroom: "It is a madhouse, really. But it is
the most quiet spot in this building of mine which is a monument to hats"
(Daché 1946: 5).

The critical reception of the building appears to have been positive. On
5 February 1939, the Fifth Avenue Association announced that the Lilly
Daché building had won its award for "best individual building" in the
Fifth Avenue area for the period 1 January 1932 through 1 October 1938.[2]
Architects Shreve, Lamb & Harmon, along with associate Georges Leteliè,

would receive certificates ("New Edifices Win; Rockefeller Gets Award"). The April 1938 issue of *Harper's Bazaar* featured an article on Robsjohn-Gibbings' new interiors for the Paul Flato shop in Los Angeles (153). A room very similar to the interiors of the Daché building boasted an Asian statue, animal skin rug, and minimalist furniture. The room was described as a "magnificent success." This praise suggests that the Daché interiors were also a success, and further reinforces the connection between the style of the interior decoration and Hollywood glamour and appeal.

The Lilly Daché Building's interior design and uses did not remain static. As the focus of Daché's expanding business changed, so too did the building that housed it. Daché wrote in 1956:

> Now only one floor of the nine is devoted to hats—my workrooms are elsewhere. The top two floors are still for living, the place where Jean and I can live our private lives. The street floor is my boutique, where we sell dresses and costumes, fashions and their fripperies—the blouses, handbags, jewelry and knickknacks that form the frosting on the cake. But the other five floors are now a vast laboratory of glamour. I now have a real businesslike office, instead of doing my designing in bed as I have always done . . . (24).

By this point, Daché was focusing more on her cosmetics, hair-care and fragrance businesses than on her millinery (Daché 1956: 23–24). Around the summer of 1955, Kenneth Battelle took "charge of Miss Daché's elegant pink and gray rotunda-shaped salon" (McCarty 20). In December 1960, Daché opened a hair salon for girls, ages eight to sixteen, in a nook on one side of the women's salon. In a departure from the building's usual elegant mood, the girls' salon was decorated with pink and white gingham walls and curtains ("Girls Now Have Their Own Nook" 30).

Lilly Daché continued to live and work in her building until 1967, when she moved out and ended her manufacturing (Morris FS16). Although the Lilly Daché building would have been at the forefront of fashionable architecture when first constructed, by the late 1960s a nine-story building at Park Avenue and Fifty-sixth Street was an anachronism in a landscape dominated by the very tall office skyscrapers of the post-War period. In a similar way, a milliner was an anachronism in a period when hats had become less important. Daché herself admitted that she seldom wore a hat, other than to weddings and churches, and recognized that her building occupied "a valuable space, and it [was] idiotic to manufacture in it" (Morris FS16). In December 1968, the Lilly Daché building was finally sold to the investment group R. & N. Associates; the Park Avenue Tower at 65 East 55th Street has occupied the former Daché building site since 1987 ("News of Realty" 39).

The Lilly Daché building was a monument to Daché's art and her business, a three-dimensional representation of female agency. Daché wrote in her memoirs: "I do know that I have followed my own recipe for happiness—To do what you love, with the people you love, in the place that you love" (1946: 265). For almost thirty years Daché was able to do the millinery work that she loved, in the building that she loved.

NOTES

1. The 21 Club and the Stork Club were fashionable New York nightlife venues, which began as speakeasies covertly selling alcohol during the 1920s Prohibition Era. The Stork Club continued as a supper club, offering dining and live entertainment, and closed in 1965. The 21 Club still lives on as a restaurant.
2. The Fifth Avenue Association was founded in 1907 to promote upscale development of the Fifth Avenue Area and to discourage factories from building there.

WORKS CITED

"Africa's Belgian Congo Sets the Style in Hats for American Women." *Life* (13 September 1937): 53–54.

Bolton, Andrew, Shannon Bell-Price, and Elyssa Da Cruz. *Wild: Fashion Untamed*. New York: Metropolitan Museum of Art and New Haven: Yale University Press, 2004.

Broude, Norma and Mary D. Garrard. "Introduction." *Reclaiming Female Agency: Feminist Art History after Postmodernism*. Berkeley: University of California Press, 2005.

"Business Leases." *New York Times* (24 April 1929): 50.

"Daché Building Started; Variety of Objects Put into the Cornerstone of Millinery House." *New York Times* (16 April 1937): 25.

Daché, Lilly. *Talking Through My Hats*. New York: Coward-McCann, 1946.

———. *Lilly Daché's Glamour Book*. Philadelphia: JB Lippincott, 1956.

Eluard, Paul. "The Bushongo of Africa." *Harper's Bazaar* (November 1937): 106.

"For a Life of Ease." *Vogue* (15 January 1938): 86–87.

Gaba, Lester. *On Soap Sculpture*. New York: Henry Holt, 1935.

———. *The Art of Window Display*. New York and London: The Studio Publications, 1952.

"Girls Now Have Their Own Nook in Beauty Salon." *New York Times* (28 December 1960): 30.

Goldberger, Paul. "Architecture View; Crowding Can Vitiate Design—Good and Bad." *New York Times* (8 February 1987).

"'Good-Luck' Plan Fails Mme. Lilly Daché; Toad Wins Release From Cornerstone." *New York Times* (17 April 1937): 19.

Harper's Bazaar (April 1938): 153.

"Hats Are back!" *Women's Wear Daily* (19 March 1964): 11.

Jonai. Advertisement. *Harper's Bazaar* (April 1938): 38.

"Manhattan Mortgages." *New York Times* (22 March 1937): 37.

Martin, Richard and Harold Koda. *Orientalism: Visions of the East in Western Dress*. New York: The Metropolitan Museum of Art, 1994.

McCarty, Agnes. "Hair Stylist Finds His Job Allows Him to Be Creative." *New York Times* (17 July 1956): 20.

Milbank, Caroline Rennolds. *New York Fashion: The Evolution of American Style.* New York: Abrams, 1989.

"Modiste to Erect Midtown Building; Lilly Daché Buys Property in East 56th Street for Modern Structure." *New York Times* (9 November 1936): 37.

Morris, Bernadine. "The Everlasting Lilly Daché." *New York Times* (14 October 1967): FS16.

"New Edifices Win Fifth Ave. Awards." *New York Times* (5 February 1939): RE1.

"New York: Milliner Builds Multi-Story Establishment." *Architectural Record* (March 1938): 52–56.

"News of Realty." *New York Times* (24 December 1968): 39.

Nordell, Rod. "'When I Read Rilke I Feel Sublime.'" *Christian Science Monitor* (14 April 1960).

"Packing for Paris." *Life* (10 September 1945): 127–31.

Pope, Virginia. "Lilly Daché Puts New Theory on Dressing Into Her Exhibit." *New York Times* (23 September 1954): 41.

Ribeiro, Aileen. *Dress In Eighteenth-Century Europe 1715–1789.* New Haven: Yale University Press, 2002.

Robsjohn-Gibbings, T[erence] H[arold]. *Good-bye, Mr. Chippendale.* New York: Alfred A. Knopf, 1944.

———. *Homes of the Brave.* New York: Alfred A. Knopf, 1954.

"Rockefeller Gets Award for Center." *New York Times* (8 February 1939): 29.

"Shifts in Shops." *Vogue* 15 September 1937, 68.

Stern, Robert A.M., Gregory Gilmartin, and Thomas Mellins. *New York 1930: Architecture and Urbanism Between the Two World Wars.* New York: Rizzoli, 2000.

Stoddard, Alexandra. *The Decoration of Houses.* New York: William Morrow, 1997.

"To Lay Corner Today: Lilly Daché Will Erect 9-Story Glass Building in 56th Street." *New York Times* (15 April 1937): 43.

"$200,000,000 Worth of Hats." *Fortune* (January 1935): 50+.

"Wrap of 'Anna Blue' for Mrs. Roosevelt." *New York Times* (25 February 1933): 7.

Wollen, Peter. *Raiding the Icebox: Reflections on Twentieth Century Culture.* Bloomington: Indiana University Press, 1993.

14 From "Paradise" to Cyberspace

The Revival of the Bourgeois Marketplace

Elyssa Dimant

First came the wonderful power of the piling up of the goods, all accumulated at one point, sustaining and pushing each other, never any stand-still, the article of the season always on hand; and from counter to counter the customer found herself seized, buying here the material, further on the cotton, elsewhere the mantle, everything necessary to complete her dress in fact, then falling into unforeseen purchases, yielding to her longing for the useless and the pretty.

—Emile Zola, *Au Bonheur des Dames* (1882)

Through the lens of nineteenth-century industrialism and emerging globalism, Emile Zola's *Au Bonheur des Dames* (*The Ladies' Paradise*) presents the department store as the mechanism for a compulsive, conspicuous consumption of fashion. Zola completed the novel in 1882 after exhaustive research at the Parisian department stores Le Printemps, the Louvre, and especially the Bon Marché. *Au Bonheur des Dames* is an amalgam of these formidable institutions, a model that delineates the practical developments and modes of expansion common to many department stores of the Second Empire (1852–70). Fueled by their own profits, bolstered by complex structures of organization and entrepreneurial strategy and accessible to a wide range of socioeconomic classes, the department stores served as focal points of late nineteenth-century popular culture as well, with a determined cultivation of sociability and community participation on the part of the proprietor. Perhaps most notably, the early department store was championed as the vehicle for all societal advancement—industrial, artistic, and technological—that was deemed "modern."

In the twenty-first century, the department store, with the exception of the grand houses of Bergdorf Goodman and Barney's in New York, has become an obsolete venue for bourgeois consumption, suffocated by a bloated global marketplace and a modern emphasis on individuality through channels of exclusivity or elitism. The department store no longer seems qualified to house the self-propelling machine, with all of its tools and gears intact, that Zola delineated in his *Au Bonheur des Dames*. In its place, present-day society has adapted by providing more accessible and appealing purchasing outlets. In *Counter Cultures: Saleswomen, Managers, and Customers in American Department Stores, 1890–1940,* historian Susan Porter Benson explains that "[t]he department store no longer holds an unchallenged place at the pinnacle of American retailing; pressures from discount stores on one side and from exclusive boutiques on the other have put it into a defensive posture" (293). The discount store, now characterized by multinational conglomerates such as Walmart, Target, or Kmart, offers a vast range of affordable clothing lines, while urban boutique culture promotes a seemingly endless number of higher end fashion market niches. Yet it is the Internet marketplace that provides all of the convenience and accessibility of the former and the avant-gardism and exclusivity of the latter, but moreover has revived the traditional role of the nineteenth-century department store as the mainstay of enterprising innovation and "modern" progress.

As the center of fashion is no longer dictated by one city, but is, in fact, a global panorama configured from the personalities of satellites like Milan, London, New York, Paris, Tokyo, and Hong Kong, primarily, and to a lesser extent Sao Paulo, Antwerp, Berlin, and Madrid, it seems logical that the venue from which fashionable objects, silhouettes, and trends are dispersed must be portable and accessible. As the anatomies of the Internet boutique, fashion news website, and online fashion auction are each derived from components of the traditional department store, this chapter addresses fixtures established by nineteenth- and early twentieth-century entrepreneurs that have been transplanted and adapted to the Internet in order to configure a successful bourgeois marketplace. As a vehicle for global consumption, the Internet continues to inform and transform the pillars of convenience, versatility, and promotion that existed as the primary goals and functions of the nineteenth-century department store venture.

LE GRAND MAGASIN: THE RISE OF THE DEPARTMENT STORE

The configuration of the department store, or *le grand magasin,* can be traced back to just after the French Revolution, and can be defined primarily as an emporium of various products arranged into distinct departments with skilled salesmen and managers working together in a determined hierarchy.[1] The guild system that was formerly in place to regulate trade and craftsmanship was initially overrun by *les magasins de nouveauté:* predecessors of the department stores that specialized in dry goods and trimmings and often housed several departments. These *magasins* were quite common in the first half of the nineteenth century in Europe, as well as abroad in the eastern seaboard cities of North America (Wilson 146). They offered clients product versatility that was previously lacking in the specialized boutique, and were able to fix prices instead of perpetuating the elaborate bargaining process between proprietor and customer that had previously dictated fashion consumption.[2] Though fashion theorist and historian Elizabeth Wilson, in her seminal textbook *Adorned in Dreams,* insists that the department store model familiar to the modern era emerged from England (146), Paris's Bon Marché is unofficially credited as the first true department store venture, whose founders cultivated shrewd sales and display strategies which have remained part of the prototypical enterprise through to the present day.

The Bon Marché was purchased as a small left bank Parisian haunt with only 450,000 francs yearly sales volume in 1852. However, proprietor Aristide Boucicault developed it to become perhaps the largest retail enterprise in the world by the time of his death in 1877 (Miller 40). In the early 1880s, most stores had only fifteen departments, amongst them jewelry, toys, stationary, equestrian articles, shoes, and perfume—a department that Boucicault is said to have been the first to add in 1875—alongside the fabric, or dry goods area, and the ready-to-wear undergarments, dresses, and cloaks (Leach 50). By 1910, some stores offered as many as 125 separate departments (Leach 51). In organizing these departments, strategies necessarily emerged to move both customers and goods more effectively through display, as well as purchasing and delivery subdivisions. Entrepreneurs like Boucicault in Paris, and A.T. Stewart, Roland Macy, and John Wanamaker in the United States were amongst the most proactive in establishing benchmarks in customer service, technologically advanced interiors, and visual and promotional lures intended to draw in and please patrons. These elements fused to conceive a new urban shopping experience, which promoted pleasure as well as efficiency. Benson observes: "The message was that they [department stores] were the exemplars of rising urban standards of beauty and convenience" (19).

HOW CAN WE HELP YOU? CUSTOMER PLEASERS

Aristide Boucicault aggressively trained his employees to emulate the aristocrat's servant, in this way duplicating the upper-class consumer experience. He decreed that salespersons were to be courteous, well spoken, honest, and tidy in both appearance and presentation. Employees were also encouraged to become specialty tradesmen—masters of persuasion and outlets of infinite expertise in relation to stockings, or dry goods, or millinery—and were marketed as such for the benefit of the fickle consumer. Boucicault even went so far as to offer language lessons to his regular salesclerks, but only in those tongues (like Spanish or English) that would assist in communication with the customers; "it is scarcely difficult to understand . . . why he did not choose to provide instruction in Latin or Greek" (Miller 108). These practices set a new standard for the broader experience of buying: in effect, to reverse the traditional negotiations between salesclerk and customer so that it was now the employee who would bend over backwards to satiate the customer, and not the latter who was formerly required to go to great lengths to acquire desired goods.

The prodding and encouragement of a polite clerk expressly increased sales within the department stores, but proprietors also invested in the physical structures of the emporiums in order to facilitate the flow of traffic and quantity of consumption in more subtle ways. A. T. Stewart's was founded in 1848 and was aptly named the Marble Palace, as it sat exalted along a full block in downtown Manhattan, "majestic on its white Corinthian columns and illuminated by gaslight and hundreds of windows" into which the passersby could longingly stare (Leach 21). John Wanamaker introduced electric lights in his stores by the 1870s, and was the first in the world to feature the pneumatic tube system, which expedited the flow of cash from one department to another, in 1880 (Benson 19). For the convenience of the shopper, Wanamaker had "moving stairways," or escalators, in both of his big emporiums by 1912 (Leach 73). Advances in iron and glass were perhaps the most impacting in terms of the evolution of the stores' interior layouts. Historian Michael B. Miller explains that "[t]he role of iron was to provide for open, spacious bays in which large quantities of goods could readily be displayed. . . . The skylights . . . were to permit a maximum influx of natural light, which was deemed necessary for display purposes" (42). Aristide Boucicault chose L. A. Boileau as his architect and engineer Gustave Eiffel to erect the renovated 1869 home of the Bon Marché, "two men who were pioneers in the functional architectural uses that could be made of iron and glass" (Miller 42). Mirrored glass was used extensively in many of the large stores to activate an illusion that served to "increase the apparent floor space" and suggest "depth" in the showcases (*Dry Goods Economist* 24 September 1898), both of which contributed to the presentation of the showroom as a grand house of alluring wares, vast and magical in what it might offer the consumer. Electricity, continuous-process machines, new energy resources, and the expansion of railroads and streets all operated as tools for evolution of the department store as well, and for what Emily Fogg Mead pronounced at the turn of the century as "a never-ending scale of expansion" (165).

THE INSTITUTION OF DESIRE

In 1902, Louis Comfort Tiffany designed an iridescent glass mosaic dome for Marshall Field that was inspired by Blakean mysticism. Configured from green and blue glass, the dome's symbology implied an "infinity of needs" and promoted a dialogue of "longing and desire" (Leach 77). It was the perfect crown for the Chicago-based department store, itself a church of modern consumption. Wilson observes that "[l]ife in the nineteenth century was more sharply than before divided between working hours, repaid in wages, and 'leisure' during which wages could be spent" (Wilson 144). The designation of leisure time was bolstered by a known repertoire of certain activities: visiting a museum, going for a picnic, or going *shopping*, a term that had emerged in the mid-nineteenth century and implied a superfluous consumption regime intrinsically associated with one's pleasure and, ultimately, responsible for one's happiness.

The department store, with its fully dressed settings of interiors, accessories, and up-to-date fashions, engineered a generation of consumers ready to find a new ensemble, a new living room, a new *life* behind the cast iron and glass gates of the large emporium.[3] The procurement of the vast commodities of the department store, the sculpted corsets, and impeccable trimmings, the lush dress fabrics, and the fine linens—all on sale—reiterated the ideals of the respectable bourgeois: self-restraint, modesty, and propriety. In his sociological discourse on the impact of the Bon Marché on Parisian shoppers, Miller elaborates:

> The Bon Marché . . . became a bourgeois instrument of social homogenization, a means for disseminating the values and life style of the Parisian upper middle-class to French middle class society as a whole. It did this by so lowering prices that the former's possessions became mass-consumer items. But it also did this by becoming a kind of cultural primer. The Bon Marché showed people how they should dress, how they should furnish their home, and how they should spend their leisure time. It defined the ideals and goals for French society (183).

Whereas the French department store offered the bourgeois woman an aesthetic model after which to mold her own home and person, and additionally provided a venue where working-class women and men could come to acquire a lifestyle more esteemed than their own, the American department store was championed as an intrinsic part of the "free" market, and therefore a benchmark for democracy. Economist John Bates Clark noted that despite a "vast and ever-growing inequality" of wealth and power in America (Ross 1991: 121), a ballooning supply of goods and services were being made available to the public, and at the forefront of this availability was the implication that citizens of every economic class had an equal right to desire the luxuries offered by the department store (Leach 6). Customers' financial anxieties were quieted by comprehensive sales on goods, displayed and advertised boldly in store windows and passed notices. In-store sales offered lower prices than those found in surrounding businesses, and therefore erected the department store as an early discount warehouse, a more cost-effective couturier. Yet, while it trumpeted the bourgeois, or democratic, model as an easily obtainable ideal, the department store simultaneously catered to the insecurities of its customers by juxtaposing merchandise that was affordable with that which was overpriced and ostentatiously *luxe*. This served to inspire feelings of inadequacy and promote impulse buying.

In *La Societé de Consommation*, cultural theorist Jean Baudrillard affirms, "Everyone has to be up-to-date and recycle himself annually, monthly, seasonally in his clothes, his things. . . . If he doesn't, then he is not a true citizen of consumer society" (149). Department stores began to promote the styles mandated seasonally by fashion magazines, advertisements, and catalogues that required the fashionable customer to constantly update her wardrobe to coincide with everchanging trends. Benson recounts how "[i]n 1915, for example, Macy's sent each of its buyers a subscription to *Vogue* and instructed them in detail about how to apply the magazine's information to their departments" (59). During these first decades of the twentieth century, stylists, marketed as "taste professionals," were harnessed for their ability to persuade a customer to purchase products that would concurrently emphasize flattering traits and pander to the dictates of fashion's retail and media outlets.

Amongst the most divisive strategies employed by the department store proprietor were those intended, admittedly, to confuse or disillusion the customer into reckless purchasing. Boucicault was notorious for rotating his goods from the stockrooms to the displays several times daily, which allowed the appearance of a limited quantity of what were ultimately mass-produced and readily accessible goods. In *Les Inventeurs du Commerce Moderne* (1966), Etienne Thil quotes the proprietor:

> What's necessary. . . . is that they walk around for hours, that they get lost. First of all, they [the shoppers] will seem more numerous. Secondly . . . the store will seem larger to them. And lastly, it would really be too much if, as they wander around in this organized disorder, lost, driven crazy, they don't set foot in some departments where they had no intention of going, and if they don't succumb at the sight of things which grab them on the way (34).

These tactics rendered the consumer powerless amidst lavish displays of goods, but they also offered an alternate reality via an endless array of exotic, colorful commodities, many of which were arranged thematically. In *Just Looking: Consumer Culture in Dreiser, Gissing, and Zola*, cultural theorist Rachel Bowlby discusses the importance of configuring the spectacle in and around the department store; for the aimless browser, ready to purchase, "the image is all" (6).

FROM NEAR AND FAR: ADVERTISING THE FASHIONABLE COMMODITY

> The greatest source of the empire's prosperity lay not in bringing its subjects to the center, but rather in bringing the center to them (Miller 61).

In the late nineteenth century, railroads were developed and a surge in the volume and speed of dry goods facilitated a more grandiose system

of business and trade. Just years later, expanding upon the urban planning strategies of John Nash in London and Baron Haussman in Paris,
early twentieth-century mass transportation systems began to connect
cityscapes, extending through the provinces or suburbs and allowing a
larger clientele for *les grand magasins*. Though the potential pool of consumers was vaster, the proprietor could not rely on the impressiveness of
his building's façade, with all of its modern edifices intact, nor the irre-
sistible appeal of an exhaustive volume of goods on display to draw in
those out-of-town crowds. In *Couture Culture,* Nancy J. Troy asserts that
"[t]o be recognizable as a movement, and therefore marketable as a style
. . . fashion required not only adherents, but audiences and avenues of
dissemination" (60). The advertisement, in all of its various mutations,
became paramount to the success of the twentieth-century department
store once mass transport systems took hold. In New York, Roland Macy
reformed existing layout and typography in newspaper advertisements
that had previously read dryly as classified notices, while John Wanamaker
came out with a full page advertisement as early as 1879 (Benson 17–18).
Wanamaker emphasized the momentum of continuous advertising for the
department store with the famous dictate: "The time to advertise is all the
time" (*The Advertising World 22, 179*). While advertising cards, passed
out promotionally within the stores as well as on the streets, dominated
department store marketing in the 1880s and 1890s, by the time larger
retail and discount stores like Sears, Roebuck and Company and Mont-
gomery Ward's emerged in the early twentieth century, the mail-order catalogue, complete with images, claimed the majority of advertisers' budgets
(Leach 44). Three innovations in advertising formed the bridge between
the antiquated print notice and the contemporary promotion. The first,
the electrical image, offered a progressive vehicle for department stores
to confirm their relevance and modernity. After 1900, the electrical sign
became the premiere mode for outdoor advertising and commanded an
almost compulsory attention from the viewer. The second innovation was
that of color in printed images and typography alike. Derived in part from
the painted posters of nineteenth-century artists Jules Cheret and Eugene
Grasset, the color image featured a more realistic representation of the
product, and was therefore more effective in luring customers to see the
genuine article. Color was used regularly in American advertising by 1895,
and acquired such pioneering proponents as Artemas Ward, the editor of
Fame, who championed "the grain, the texture, the juiciness, the savori-
ness" of the commodity in the color image. As "the priceless ingredient . . .
[color] creates desire for the goods displayed." The color print "speaks the
universal picture language" (Ward 18–21).

Finally, an invention of the late 1890s, the shop window, took the broad
appeal of the color image to the next level: a full color panorama where the
objects featured, though still behind glass, were well within reach. Early
twentieth century trimmer Walter F. Allert conceived windows with dramatic

compositions, but always made sure to display the object properly and at the foreground of the configuration. His vision was of a "City inspired by the word DISPLAY, built up . . . on the principle of Display" (*Dry Goods Economist* 22 April 1916). Simon Doonan, notorious for his late twentieth-century concoctions within the display windows of Barney's New York, mused that "Window dressers specifically deal with the creation of the desire to shop. They dramatize, and emotionalize props, mannequins, and merchandise into inviting and compelling tableaux morts" (8).

These consecutive innovations emphasized the importance of visual culture in the persistent application of consumerism to a global population. "The stores . . . spread the idea that art through clothing was possible for everyone" (Green 25).

COGNESCENTI: THE DISPERSAL OF
FASHION AND CULTURE

By the early twentieth century, art exhibitions, concerts, cafés, lectures, and other worldly indulgences had become well-established components of the department store. This luxurious environment was cultivated for the express purpose of allowing clients the notion that they were participating in the most refined arenas of consumption. Therefore, it was not surprising that the American department store took its cue from the New York specialty shop and began staging renditions of the exclusive Parisian fashion shows as promotional events.[4]

The fashion show, which developed out of late nineteenth-century dramaturgy in France and Britain, had evolved by the second decade of the twentieth century to comprise universal features such as living mannequins, a staging area adjacent to a spotlighted ramp, and even an engineered soundtrack, which allowed the show a "dramatic effect, as in the theater" (Evans 128; Leach 101–02). In the department store, these shows were intended to evoke or, in some cases even, imitate the couture shows that were staged seasonally in Paris.

Parisian couturier Paul Poiret, known for his elaborate presentations, frequently used the lush gardens of his couture house as a backdrop for uniquely orchestrated exhibitions (Bolton 149). With an undeniable purchasing power present in the American marketplace, Poiret, who had (alongside most couturiers) previously reserved his designs for "elite sites of fashionability," began to stage his dress parades in the public spaces of the department store. "These fashion shows allowed a vast middle-class clientele to see and purchase his designs" (Bolton 149). In a larger attempt to bridge the gap between the astronomically priced couture garment and the mass-produced or ready-made article that had gained popularity by the mid-nineteenth century, Poiret created his own line of ready-made clothing in spring 1917, and described the models as "genuine reproductions" (Troy

302). Troy notes that "[a]s a hybrid devised to reconcile the contradiction between art and industry, the genuine reproduction preserved the modernist fictions of originality and authorial prerogative; at the same time it acknowledged the modern realities of industrial production and consumer demand" (302).

The genuine Parisian reproduction, which ultimately morphed into the designer ready-to-wear label, and the fashion show, which was often arranged thematically according to Persian, Russian, Mexican, Arabian aesthetics (Leach 102) allowed department store customers an impression of the styles and luxuries of the "other," with commodities that lead them halfway around the globe or gave them a glimpse into the trousseaux of the upper crust. Department store proprietors, even in Zola's fictional portrayal, frequently transformed their showrooms into dens of otherworldly treasures. Zola describes Mouret's display: "This sumptuous pacha's tent was furnished with divans and arm-chairs, made with camel sacks, some ornamented with many-coloured lozenges, others with primitive roses. Turkey, Arabia, and the Indies were all there. They had emptied the palaces, plundered the mosques and bazaars . . ." (78). Exoticism within the department store coincided with a general imperial adventurism in Western society, but it also emerged to fulfill yet another longing of the western consumer: to experience something different and new—something that could not be extrapolated from Parisian, London, or urban American society at any socioeconomic level. Via the shiek's tent or the Nepalese pagoda, the Ottoman carpet or the Chinese robe, the department store paved the way for the configuration of a single world marketplace. In the contemporary era, this marketplace has been appropriated and transformed by the investors and proprietors of the online fashion system, where each visitor can glimpse the ornaments of another culture, whether it be past or future, close by or far away.

THE "DECENTERED" CITY

The chain department stores and discount super-ventures that emerged in North America and Europe between the two world wars catalyzed a fashion experience based on familiarity and convenience: wherever one was in the western world, he or she could shop at similar venues to those found at home. While these developments have made fashion more accessible to provincials by providing rural outlets at which seasonal silhouettes, fabrics, or even designer lines can be sold, they have also served to offset the impact of the localized shopping esplanade. In effect, the modern chain store epidemic desaturates the fragmented personalities of regional fashion, fusing them into a single, affordable market that dictates a universal selection of fashionable commodities every three to six months. Wilson acknowledges "a new kind of consumerist dream world for the new 'decentred' concept of a city, a shopping nirvana, a complete world or city of its own" (153). The key to this "decentred city" is the modem or the wireless port, available in nearly every country around the world; millions can plug in and patronize larger conglomerates and privatized boutiques alike in a "shopping nirvana" built to exploit the consumer potential of the global marketplace and celebrate the local flavor of the traditional boutique.

Fashion historian Christopher Breward asserts that "[t]he twentieth century can so far boast of no other virtues than those of utility, comfort, and convenience" (253). As such, it is no wonder that the invention of computerized searching, browsing, and eventually shopping has utilized the efficiencies of technology to champion these virtues and apply them broadly to fashion consumption. The Internet marketplace, as the progressive vehicle for these functions, owes its structures, whether site-based or strategic, to the department store. Like the nineteenth-century store, the Internet site is motivated by guiding the pedestrian through a premeditated and manipulative layout, whether directionally from one purchasing department to another, or recklessly to encourage one's disillusion and loss of critical judgment. Whereas Boucicault created monstrous displays to pull the customer this way and that, the Internet exploits this distraction principle with a system of links that moves shoppers from one purchase to the next. These links and their overdesigned icons occupy every inch of the screen, allowing the browser any number of journeys through the online "store" without ever having to leave his or her chair.

The traditional department store, with its reliance on tangible attractions and the interactive relationships between salespeople, customers, and goods-on-hand, could not maximize upon early twentieth century advancements in cinematography and film for fear of pushing its corporeal body into obsolescence. If consumers only required appealing imagery in order to proceed with a purchase, the structures of display and interdepartmental flow that had taken decades to resurrect would become outdated. However, as a construct inherently limited to image-based advertisements, displays, and even shopping carts, the Internet has endlessly exploited the lure of the moving picture. AfterEffects©, perhaps the most successful two-dimensional animation software, allows web fashion designers to collage and animate objects and graphics into cinematic advertisements, fast-paced promotional flashes to accommodate our shrinking attention span. In 1901, Fogg Mead observed that "[t]he successful advertisement is obtrusive. . . . Everyone reads it involuntarily. It is a subtle, persistent, unavoidable presence that creeps into the reader's inner consciousness" (165). Nowhere is this assault more evident than in the barrage of pop-up advertisements engineered for each fashion site. Whether as full page glossies or page-appropriate segment advertisements that might surround a basic Google search for handbags, coats, or other such items, the Internet advertisement has realized the shared vision of early fashion merchandisers as a theatrical

strategy par excellence, peddling desire, anxiety, and the promise of fulfill-
ment via material gratification.

While the façade treatment of the fashion web page may provide lim-
itless comparisons to the store window, the organization of the content
pages of each site mirrors the stock layout of the department store as well.
Sites like www.shopbop.com and www.revolveclothing.com take cues
from the versatility of *le grand magasin* by offering a variety of products;
some feature a "Shop by Brand" (Designers), "Shop by Trend" (i.e. "Reflect
Yourself," which includes all that glitters), or "Shop by Category" option,
the latter being the most derivative of the typical department store divide,
with dresses, shoes, scarves, handbags, and other such items each finding
their own web page (www.shopbop.com). Such sites have also adapted the
department store's free delivery system, which emerged between 1880 and
1915 (Leach 123), to offer free shipping, and have expanded to include overnight or anywhere-in-the-world options as well. Charge accounts, though
preexistent in local shops, were heavily promoted by the nineteenth-century department store, and are now standard components of many Internet
shopping sites. Ebay.com, the largest online fashion auction site, conve-
niently offers the PayPal option for expedited purchasing (www.eBay.com).
Customer service links, care instructions, sizing charts, and description of
materials are virtually mandatory components of shopping or auction websites, providing the same support and expertise that a specialty salesclerk
might in Zola's era. Inasmuch as the traditional department store was the
discount alternative to the specialty shop, the Internet offers consumers
cheaper alternatives to many boutique products. Despite the recent growth
of boutique culture in urban centers like New York and Paris, the shopper
no longer must traipse around the city searching for discounts; he or she
simply initiates an Internet search to find online shops that offer sales up to
70% off retail price (www.shopbop.com).

High-end fashion companies like Prada, Jean Paul Gaultier, and Chanel have commissioned cutting-edge sites, valuable for their awe-inspiring
design and alluring brand identification, but also for their ease of maneu-
verability. In "A Model Store Front," a columnist for the *Dry Goods Economist* regarded the strategies undertaken by the grand department stores
to stimulate easier inward movement: "A step at the entrance is a mistake.
No hindrance should be offered to people who may drift into the store" ("A
Model Store Front" 5 February 1898: 9). Likewise, most fashion company
sites utilize software like Flash® to ensure that their pages are accessible to
the average search engine. Video and image compression software affords
the sites the ability to tout the footage of the exclusive fashion shows, now
weeklong events in New York, London, Paris, and Milan. Christian Dior
Couture featured the entirety of its two-hour-plus spring/summer 2007
haute couture presentation on its house website (www.dior.com), even
though most consumers wealthy enough to afford the genuine article were
likely sitting in Dior's front rows. Similarly to the presentations initiated by

the department store, these online shows serve to showcase the lavishness of the high-end product, therefore lending more cachet to the subsidiary lines affordable to the average Internet browser. While a designer website might feature a single fashion show from the most recent season, powerhouse sites like Elle.com and Firstview.com archive fashion presentations for up to fifteen years, providing an invaluable archive for researchers, but additionally serving, in much the same way as the department store's taste professionals, as visible, accessible authorities, bolstering the impact and success of the fashion system as a whole. While Style.com's "Style File" and cult website Dailycandy.com clue consumers in to the hottest trends of the moment through fashion icons like Candy Pratts Price, independent (yet growing) blogs like "The Sartorialist" (www.thesartorialist.com) promote themselves as stylists for the fashion insider.

With the realization of the department store as the first democratic marketplace in the 1880s and 1890s, two types of consumers were born that have been identified by cultural theorist Rosalind Williams as "elitist" or "democratic" (110). While the elitist consumer, embodied by the nineteenth-century dandy, often revolted at the thought of patronizing the department store, as his or her style was defined by exquisite anomaly, the democratic consumer embraced the socialist spirit of *les grands magasins* and their intents to bring artistic clothing and dry goods to every level of the economy. The formation of the Internet marketplace satiates both consumer groups. With a nearly infinite number of online vendors and stylists (especially in the blogger domain) based worldwide, the elitist consumer is fulfilled by the wishful notion that he or she is wearing items yet undiscovered by local peers, and additionally has a more vast trading city in which to pursue the obscure trend or designer. Alternately, the vast systems of production and distribution that the Internet perpetuates allow the dispersal of a seemingly endless supply of fashionable goods to a global clientele that comprises a multitude of socioeconomic subgroups, thereby effectuating the mandate of the democratic consumer.

The Internet marketplace has secured alternate consumer demographics as well. In conceiving sites like Mensstyle.com, which showcases fashion shows and new trends for male consumers, the online fashion marketplace has facilitated the growth of a populace of male shoppers that were absent from the queues at traditional store registers.[5] And while the department store forecasted the importance of the youth demographic from the 1870s, and attempted to cater to younger customers with free favors, on-site playgrounds and, by the mid-twentieth century with internal "boutiques" like Macy's Little Shop or Bergdorf Goodman's Miss Bergdorf department (Wilson 152), the format of the Internet store facilitates a nearly effortless relationship with new generations of customers. More enthusiastic about utilizing technology to fulfill their needs and desires, younger shoppers are inherently more at ease with the Internet as a site for consumption. Teen-targeted websites like www.ellegirl.com and www.cosmogirl.com only serve to bolster this relationship by providing interactive questionnaires on personal style and featuring links to online products (www.ellegirl.com); in effect, these sites are breeding a new generation of consumer—one reliant on the Internet for her sense of sartorial and aesthetic expression. In A.T. Stewart's obituary, written by Gail Hamilton in 1876 for *Harper's Bazaar,* the popular columnist hailed the proprietor for encouraging Americans to pursue wealth and to revel in materialism (Hamilton). Stewart's legacy was a country of eager shoppers, consumed by the necessity of acquisition in order to define their role in society, and of being seen as a participant in the vast consumer cycle that motivated the department store's earnings and success. By the time of Stewart's death, the department store had become a sodality for the community shoppers, and fraternization amidst the piled goods and dressed mannequins was "as typical of modern mass consumption as the sociability of the salon was typical of pre-Revolutionary upper-class consumption" (Williams 67). In the early twenty-first century, through a haze of blogs, chat rooms, boutiques, and news websites that allow one to "email a friend" an image or product (MacDonnell www.style.com), the Internet marketplace has emerged as the contemporary site for fashionable discourse. The frantic cycle of fashion consumption birthed by nineteenth-century development has reached its frenzy through digital incarnations of the specialty clerk, color and moving image advertisements, the promotional sale, and the enlivened display.

As relevant as "The Painter of Modern Life" (1863) was in assessing mid-nineteenth-century modernity, Baudelaire's impressions of "the ephemeral, the fugitive, the contingent" so too embody the zeitgeist of the current era (12). The Internet, as a consumer agent neither tangible nor consistent, has nonetheless transformed the pioneering strategies of the traditional department store to accommodate an evolved consumerism, informed by the whims and yearnings of the contemporary shopper. As the crux of the global fashion system, the World Wide Web vivifies Zola's mesmerizing words in regarding his *Au Bonheur des Dames* and renders them prescient, "beneath the rain—it shone out like a lighthouse, and seemed to be of itself the light and life of the city" (28).

NOTES

1. Michael B. Miller. *The Bon Marché: Bourgeois Culture and the Department Store, 1869–1920.* Princeton, New Jersey: Princeton University Press, 1981. "Extreme division of labor, a corps of middle and top managers, and an inexorable impulse towards seeking the most efficient means of carrying out operations were the components that made the department store work" (71).
2. Ibid. Miller informs us that the Coin de Rue, the Petit Saint-Thomas, and the Deux Magots, amongst others, could all "trace their origins as far back as the Restoration." He elaborates his description of this precursor to the modern department store, "The Ville de Paris, by far the largest magasin

de nouveautés in the 1840s (it claimed a workforce of 150 employees and a yearly sales volume of 10–12 million francs in 1844), was . . . selling at low prices for high turnover" (25).

3. William Leach. *Land of Desire: Merchants, Power, and the Rise of a New American Culture.* New York: Vintage Books, 1993. "In 1908, John Wanamaker's in New York opened the 'House Palatial,' the largest permanent exhibition of furniture and accessories yet seen, a 'real' two-story, twenty-four room dwelling right in the heart of the store's rotunda and extending from the sixth to the eighth floors. . . . 'Authentic in almost every way,' it could have been lifted right off a Belasco or Mackaye stage" (80).

4. Ibid."In New York City, Ehrich Brothers, founded by Rebecca Ehrich in 1857 as a fancy specialty house that catered to upper-middle-class women, probably put on the first show, in 1903, although the precise beginnings of such trends are almost impossible to nail down" (101–02).

5. Thomas Richards. *The Commodity Culture of Victorian England: Advertising and Spectacle 1851–1914.* London: Verso, 1991. "Advertising managed to establish a female model for consumption, without ceding the activity entirely to women. Advertisers defined consumption as an extension of the sexual division of labor enshrined in the Victorian household. . . . [s]o consumption became something that women undertook on behalf of men" (206).

WORKS CITED

The Advertising World 22 (November 1917).

Baudelaire, Charles. "The Painter of Modern Life." *The Painter of Modern Life and Other Essays.* Translated by J. Mayne. London: Phaidon Press, 1964 [1854].

Baudrillard, Jean. *La Societé de Consommation.* Paris: S.G.P.P., 1970.

Benson, Susan Porter. *Counter Cultures: Saleswomen, Managers, and Customers in American Department Stores, 1890–1940.* Chicago: University of Illinois Press, 1986.

Bolton, Andrew. "Response." In *Fashion and Modernity,* edited by Christopher Breward and Caroline Evans. London: Berg, 2005: 145–50.

Bowlby, Rachel. *Just Looking: Consumer Culture in Dreiser, Gissing, and Zola.* New York: Methuen, 1985.

Beward, Christopher. *The Hidden Consumer: Masculinities, Fashion, and City Life, 1860–1914.* New York and Manchester: Manchester University Press, 1999.

Doonan, Simon. *Confessions of a Window Dresser.* New York: Viking Studio, 2001.

Dry Goods Economist 24 September 1898.

———. (22 April 1916).

Evans, Caroline. "Multiple, Movement, Model, Mode: The Manequin Parade, 1900–1929." In *Fashion and Modernity,* edited by Christopher Breward and Caroline Evans. London: Berg, 2005: 125–45.

Green, Nancy L. *Ready-To-Wear, Ready-To-Work, A Century of Industry and Immigrants in Paris and New York.* Durham, NC: Duke University Press, 1997.

Hamilton, Gail. "The Blameworthiness of Wealth." *Harper's Bazaar* (10 June 1876).

Leach, William. *Land of Desire: Merchants, Power, and the Rise of a New American Culture.* New York: Vintage Books, 1993.

Macdonell, Nancy (ed.). "Style File" (26 February 2007) <http://www.style.com/trends/blogs/style_file>.

Mead, Emily Fogg. "The Place of Advertising in Modern Business." *Fame* 10 (1901): 165.

Miller, Michael B. *The Bon Marche: Bourgeois Culture and the Department Store, 1869–1920*. Princeton, NJ: Princeton University Press, 1981.

"A Model Store Front." *Dry Goods Economist* (5 February 1898): 9.

Richards, Thomas. *The Commodity Culture of Victorian England: Advertising and Spectacle 1851–1914*. London: Verso, 1991.

Ross, Dorothy. *The Origins of American Social Science*. Cambridge, MA: Cambridge University Press, 1991.

Thil, Etienne. *Les Inventeurs de Commerce Moderne*. Paris: Arthaud, 1966.

Troy, Nancy J. *Couture Culture: A Study in Modern Art and Fashion*. Cambridge, MA: The MIT Press, 2003.

Ward, Artemas. "A Pictorial Presentation of Interborough Medium." New York: 1925.

Williams, Rosalind H. *Dream Worlds: Mass Consumption in Late Nineteenth Century France*. Oxford: University of California Press, 1982.

Wilson, Elizabeth. *Adorned in Dreams: Fashion and Modernity*. Berkeley and Los Angeles: University of California, 1985.

Zola, Emile. *Au Bonheur des Dames*. Paris: 1883.

3 February 2007 <http://us.ebayobjects.com/2c;9739597;9123118;z?https://www.paypal.com/ ebay>.

26 February 2007 <http://www.ellegirl.com/>.

16 March 2007 <http://www.shopbop.com/shop/product_browse.jsp?FOLDER%3C%3Efolder_id=2534374302029887>.

15 Armani/Architecture
The Timelessness and Textures of Space

John Potvin

To borrow Pierre Bourdieu's notion of "symbolic magic," a fashion designer's label possesses the auratic potency to conjure the mystique of distinction, authenticity, and exclusivity which in turn engenders a fervent dedication (verging on the religious) on the part of faithful costumers. The aura surrounding the name of the designer transforms objects of no real value to objects of luxury, preciousness, and desire. However, the label itself is not enough; it requires to be housed in a space equally endowed with the potential to elicit reverence and pleasure, a coveted destination. Boutiques offer up affective spatial attenuation of the auratic nature of the designer's label through the preferred pathways of engagement with the space and merchandise. In his discussion of retail design Otto Riewoldt contends that "[w]ith the same care and professionalism as in the theatre, the sequence of events [of shopping] must be worked out in detail, including everything from props to stage directions, in order to transform the sale of merchandise into an experience-intensive act—one in which the potential customers are actors rather than passive spectators" (Riewoldt 9). To best achieve this, a designer must create spaces which communicate his brand, as distinct from all other designer and public spaces. As a designer attempts to make his mark, therefore, so too must he employ an architect whose own unmistakable material signature will assist in the proposition and perpetuation of an authentic designer material and visual identity. The boutique itself must be equally as visually effective and materially auratic as the discreet label sewn into an Armani garment. Through space, the brand must not only articulate a "distinctive message" but also an "emotional identity" (Reitwoldt 10). Robert Triefus, executive vice-president of worldwide communications for Giorgio Armani in Milan, makes a similar claim when he states that "[s]tores are the face of a brand. . . . It is the entire image as we want it to be seen. Architecture is a very important part of brand communication. When you arrive [at a store] it should conform to your expectations of the brand" (Triefus in Turngate 77).

Perhaps it might be instructive to elucidate how Armani sews together the aura of both his name and space in the actual label used for every *prêt-a-porter* high-end garment. The black label reads "Giorgio Armani A Milano—Borgonuovo 21." The label says it all: the designer's name, the city of his humble origins and meteoric success, and finally the address of both his home and design headquarters. Unlike with most designers, for Armani location and identity are endemic to each other. The mystique surrounding Armani is made palpable in the rarefied minimalist spaces of his boutiques around the world. His auratic presence made tangible through absences of objects, a subtle reminder of control and power over his imperial domain.

In order for Armani to successfully achieve a potent impact on the cultural landscape of fashion and design, he must make his presence felt in key outposts around the world by way of consistent spaces. Developed in the designer's Milan headquarters and created by way of his flagship boutique in Sant' Andrea, global image (through repetition) is tantamount not simply to the identity of the designer but also, and perhaps more significantly, for the consumer. For his new Beijing boutique, located in the Palace Hotel, which opened its doors in October 1998, the designer wanted to create "something that will last, not too retro, not too avant-garde, not too classic and not too futuristic" (Armani in *WWD* 9/10/1998). Originally designed by Italian architect Giancarlo Ortelli, the boutique featured black granite floors, rice-colored walls, and fitting rooms with red doors with each area divided into different categories of merchandise. For Armani, the boutique achieved an important balance.

A few short years later, the boutique was refitted no longer to reflect a putative indigenous design, but rather to mirror more exactly the "authentic" Armani aesthetic showcased in the original Milan boutique. Clearly the Chinese customer desired something unique and typically Armani, rather than a quotidian aesthetic endemic to their cultural milieu effectively staging the designer's boutique as separate and removed from the everyday. Perhaps a helpful way to think through the significance of the aura of a boutique's space is through Michel Foucault's notion of the heterotopia. While Foucault outlined numerous definitions for the term, most useful is how a heterotopia marks out a space of difference, and through the rituals associated with that space occupies a position "outside of all [other ordinary] places" (Foucault 24). Boutiques are viewed at once as "mythic and real, imbued with elements of fictional space and material space. . . . Heterotopias do not exist in isolation, but become visible through their differences with other sites as they upset spatial relations or provide alternative representations of them" (Quinn 28). As a space of luxury and by default exclusivity, Armani's boutiques operate as an aesthetic destination of calm and beauty while also serving as countersites to what Armani has argued as the aggression of most design in the world at large. In this light, the aura of the boutique and hence the label itself is maintained by way of its separateness. The footprint of the boutique and its marked difference from the streets' culture outside force complete immersion, imagination, and transformation. Through the rituals of consumption and hence belonging performed within what is staged as a temple-like space, what occurs is a sort of transubstantiation whereby the visual image of fashion object (seen through the spectacle of advertising and runway presentations) is mythically and materially transformed into reality through the embodied fashioned subject. The final touch which adds to the auratic is how through absences and presences the boutique accommodates and spatially translates "the magical timeless quality of an Armani collection with the equally time-less quality of a distinguished . . . building" ("Alluring Armani" 25). The sim-plicity and unadorned "timeless" architecture Armani always commissions acts as antidote to and defiant critique of the fashion system and its endless, fast-paced cycles.

Armani opened his first Giorgio Armani flagship boutique in 1981 in Milan, less than one year before the designer was featured on the cover of *Time* mag-azine. Both events made clear Armani himself had arrived on both the cul-tural and fashion maps. Over the past thirty years, the Milan-based designer has collaborated with no less than ten design firms, which have included the late Naomi Leff, Giancarlo Ortelli, London restaurateur Michael Chow, S. Russell Groves, Thomas O'Brien, Peter Marino, Massimiliano and Doriana Fuksas, Thane Roberts, Tadao Ando, and more recently Claudio Silvestrin to design some of the most beautiful and sophisticated retail environments in the world. Given his association with Hollywood and his pervasive influence in the worlds of cinema, design, and fashion, Giorgio Armani flagship stores have also featured prominently in a number of films as backdrops, usually as sites for personal, social, financial, and, of course, sartorial transformation. However, the idea that Armani boutiques are sites of transformation is not strictly confined to the cinema. In real life, we constantly witness the trans-formation of people like 50 Cent, rappers who shed their urban street clothes for dark, slick, and sophisticated Armani suits to designate they too have "arrived." Armani's most recent collaboration with London-based architect Claudio Silvestrin has seen the total redesign and rebuilding of most of his *prêt-a-porter* Borgonuovo (commonly referred to as Black Label) boutiques and in-shop outlets in department stores around the world. Seen through the metaphor of transformation, this chapter examines the Giorgio Armani bou-tiques in New York redesigned by Peter Marino, the global renovation scheme designed by Silvestrin, and the most recent permutations and adaptations of Silvestrin's blueprint which have incorporated fabric walls to expose the ways in which Armani has gradually adapted the vocabulary of minimalism and the semantics of architecture itself to evolve a boutique culture wherein the dematerialization of architecture is made possible and echoes the current ascendancy of fashion within the cultural landscape.

THE PHYSIOGNOMY OF MODERNISM

In 1996, Armani commissioned architect and interior designer Peter Marino to design a new and significantly larger boutique at 760 Madison Avenue, a few blocks south of where the original store stood since 1984 (Figure 15.1). Marino has gained a reputation as a retail architect who has acquired an impressive roster of clients within and beyond the fashion industry. Marino was also responsible for the 1988 renovation of the designer's Milan seventeenth-century palazzo in Via Borgonuovo; the designer's choice is significant, not only because Marino's spare aesthetic is in keeping with Armani's own minimalist rigor, but also because the designer wanted the boutique to hold "a familiar atmosphere similar to that of a friend's home" (translation mine, "Boutiques de Luxe et de Mode" 107). However, despite Armani's best efforts to conjure a homely space, the reception of the boutique was less than friendly.

The proposed building designs were presented to Manhattan's Community Board 8 for approval which in turn voted fourteen to twelve to send the proposal back for changes. The Board members who voted against the project felt it was ill-suited for its Upper East Side historical surrounding. However, Shelley S. Friedman, a lawyer for Armani, stated that the "minimalist building reflects the artistic values of Giorgio Armani" ("Neighbourhood Report" 19 March 1995: 136). Although minor adjustments were suggested and concessions were made, the final plan kept within Marino's and Armani's minimalist vision. In the end, Marino deferred to the strict codes established by the New York City Landmarks Preservation Commission by keeping the boutique's height at 61 feet, flush with those of its neighboring brownstones. To add some architectural detail or slight decorative flourish, the architect also incorporated a recessed bay and centrally placed terrace on the third of the four floors.

Ned Cramer claimed that Marino attempted to "echo the Italian designer's sophisticated clothes through a minimalist wrapper for his new store. But other than adhering to Adolf Loos's axiom that ornament is crime, his rectilinear architecture turns its back on Modernism's basic tenents." He continues: "To mask the building's awkwardness, and to relieve his clear discomfort

Figure 15.1 Giorgio Armani New York boutique in Madison Avenue. Author's own.

with unadorned surfaces, Marino employs an extravagant material palette on the interior" (Cramer 45). Although Cramer spares barely enough ink to criticize the boutique's interior as well as its furnishings, like many detractors he saves his hostility for the outside, that is, the façade. Critics such as Cramer suffer from a sort of superficial physiognomic reading of architecture, ignoring the spatial dimension within and beyond the space created by the designer and what it might suggest about the development of minimalist architecture and its relationship to consumption and display. As a method of ascertaining meaning through surfaces, a physiognomic reading, I wish to suggest, is not dissimilar to the minimalist *geist* itself.

Minimalist space and architecture allow for the brand's identity to be clearly articulated, ensuring the consumer-viewer is neither distracted nor dissuaded from the goal, that is, the purchase of a lifestyle. In the New York boutique, boundaries are created—both perceived and material. The solidity of the cream-colored repetitive panels of French limestone used for the facade is counterposed with the purported transparency of the glass panels featured in the central portion of the building. Yet, the glass panels, including those on the ground floor, forbid the viewer's visual access to the boutique's interior spaces. Thick scrims divide the outside from the inside, allowing some light to pour in, while obstructing the view. The only visibility given to the pedestrian is through the central glass doors. While the scrims function as curtains, they remain uncompromising backdrops to the mannequins and simple displays featured in windows on the ground level (Figure 15.2). By way of the seemingly intrusive minimalist architecture as well as the scrims, the Armani boutique clearly sets itself apart from the neighborhood and outside world and is beholden only to its own rules, rituals, and regulations. Shop minimalism, with its spare display of objects, is not unlike the minimalism of a modern art gallery; it stands to represent importance through the creation of an aura of originality and exclusivity. Within a minimalist landscape, as a sort of immediate experience, the embodied subject enters the rarefied realm of fashion and is impelled to create its own narrative, its own sensorial perceptions of the spaces of fashion. The minimalist "aesthetic of emptiness initially attracts the gaze of passers-by and, as the naked walls offer no further distraction, attracts them magnetically to the strategically placed goods" (Ruby 21–22). Armani himself wrote of the importance of the space of the boutique and how it should communicate to the customer:

> Furnishings must reflect the soul of the product, the brand, as well as create what I call a thousand and one complicities—the subtle temptations which lure a consumer into the store for a quick look. If he or she is then captivated by a friendly space, by easy-to-look-at displays and pleasant lighting, the store will be successful. It will be even more successful if the second element of atmosphere is there. I'm talking about the salespeople (Armani 9).

Figure 15.2 Giorgio Armani New York boutique in Madison Avenue. Author's own.

Once inside the boutique, luxury, while restrained, is subtly perceived in the ebonized French wood floors which are partially covered with thick and soft custom-made gray or espresso woven linen carpets that help to mark out unique spaces of consumption, each suggesting its own narrative. The individual sales rooms, which flank either side of each floor's central sales areas, have walls of either French limestone, bleached cerused curly hickory, or bleached anigre against whose surfaces pegs feature complete outfits, hung equidistant from each other. Not unlike the manner in which the critics viewed the design of the building, Armani invites his visitors to participate in a form of surface readings by way of the garments' textiles.

TIMELESSNESS AND THE LUXURY OF MINIMALISM

In 1999, Armani commissioned London-based architect Claudio Silvestrin to create a new design concept for the renovation of his boutiques around the world. The first to be refitted was not his Milan flagship, but the Paris boutique, the purported capital of high fashion. Over the course of six years, Silvestrin would renovate over twenty Giorgio Armani boutiques around the world in cities like Tokyo, Dusseldorf, Atlanta, Sao Paulo, and Costa Mesa (see Figures 15.3–15.5). These many boutiques share in common an absolute and uncompromisingly similar use of materials, design, space, and textures.

Figure 15.3 Giorgio Armani Costa Mesa boutique. Photography by Michael Weschler. Courtesy of Michael Weschler Photography.

Figure 15.4 Giorgio Armani Atlanta boutique. Photography by Michael Weschler. Courtesy of Michael Weschler Photography.

Figure 15.5 Giorgio Armani Atlanta boutique. Photography by Michael Weschler. Courtesy of Michael Weschler Photography.

Originally inaugurated in 1987, with the Paris boutique in Place Vendôme Armani purposefully removed it from the fashion sector and commercial areas and opted for a location traditionally known for its exclusive jewelers. Place Vendôme, according to Armani, defied the logic of the fashion system. Referring to the streets made famous for their high-end designer boutiques, Armani claimed that "[t]hose areas are like fashion. They're always changing. Place Vendôme will always be Place Vendôme." By locating his boutique in this time-honored square not only implies a spatial removal from the quotidian or typical, once again, but also and perhaps more suggestively a desire on the part of the designer to deploy the historically rich and architecturally significant neighborhood to make his own claims for longevity, a classic style at once outside of and removed from the relentless system of fashion itself. For this boutique, Armani wanted something "elegant, luxurious that work[ed] with the surrounding environment" and yet at the same time something that was undeniably his style once again marking his undeniable presence (*WWD* 1/26/1987). Originally designed by Giancarlo Ortelli, the boutique, in keeping with Armani's fascination with the 1920s and 1930s, offered customers segmented intimate salons for the womenswear on the first floor. The second floor, which housed the menswear, displayed the garments along the circumference and featured at the center the staircase which connected the two floors allowing for a perfect, unabashed panoptic purview of the comings and goings of the first floor.

While Silvestrin's redesign of the Place Vendôme boutique in 1999 places greater emphasis on the luxury of space, he also controls the manner in which the visitor immerses him or herself into the boutique, contriving a gradual and segmented approach to the inner sanctum. According to Silvestrin, "the entrance becomes a poetic pause between the exterior and the display area for Armani's collections" (Serrats 112). Once inside the entrance, a limestone wall obstructs a complete gaze into the interior space. "One then enters a second space of transition defined by a sculptural vase of the same stone as the walls and floors. This creates the effect of continuity and sobriety that so characterises the work of Armani" (Mostadi 92). While water is not a feature of the vase, it nonetheless conjures the baptismal fonts displayed prominently in the entrance of Roman Catholic churches. Mirrors not only operate in a typical way, extending and expanding the sensation of space, but also mark transitional points as the customer moves through the boutique. The lighting also helps to articulate and define the space. As has always been the tradition in a Giorgio Armani boutique, special, soft lighting hidden in the ceiling and embedded in the walls add a calming and luxurious tone, focusing solely on the garments displayed at exact intervals, a lighting and spatial effect which mimics the runway in his Milan studio in via Borgonuovo. Referring specifically to the new prototype created by Silvestrin, Armani states: "I'm always looking to create an environment where the store architecture supports the presentation of the collections in a way that is modern and accessible for our customers" (Armani

Press Release 22 September 2000). Although Paris might have served as the initial prototype for the global retail face of Armani, and while each store might feature a special distinctive and often soothing element such as a water fountain (London) or even a glass water fall (Milan), the materials and spaces conjured are consistent with a clearly defined global image so that no matter where the modern customer may find him or herself, there is comfort in knowing what can be expected in a Giorgio Armani retail space. The exquisitely rare and precious St. Maximin, a soft compact cream-colored stone, is prominently featured throughout the boutiques both for the walls and flooring and is contrasted with the deep Macassar ebony and oxidized brass selected for the furniture and the fixtures designed by Silvestrin. The exclusive and limited use of one type of stone and one type of wood removes any complications or distractions; here architecture is stripped bare of itself, only to reveal the essential of Armani, his textiles hanging on the walls or folded on the display cabinets.

Modern, pure, timeless, and sleek are adjectives used to describe this new boutique design which is more often than not likened to a temple. Referring to Silvestrin's redesign of the boutique, Arian Mostadi claims that "[o]ne could say that time stood still at the precise moment when Place Vendôme was created" (92). The Paris boutique forms a natural continuity with its outside environment as it extends the stone facades of Place Vendôme and the solemnity of the square, which once housed a monastery. Silvestrin has interpreted Armani's classical and modern ethos to create a minimalist space without a hard edge. According to the architect, minimalism should be at once "[s]trong but not intimidating," "[e]legant but not ostentatious" (Bertoni 226), and he speaks of architecture in terms of the "thickness of space and depth of the world" (Bertoni 204). "Mediterranean Minimal" has been used to describe Silvestrin's own subcategory of minimalist architecture, as it evokes warmth, sun-baked stone, and perhaps maybe even Italy itself.

In a world of increasing fast-fashion, where customers are called upon more and more to serve themselves (and do all the work, such as rehang garments), minimalist designer boutiques stand out more as spaces of exclusivity marked by reverential service rituals. These spaces are antidotes to the rapidity by which we conceive of the world changing around us. Speaking of the sense of the sacred with which Silvestrin imbues his spaces, Massimo Vignelli states that

> [m]inimalism is not a style, it is an attitude. It is a fundamental reaction against noise, visual noise, disorder, vulgarity. Minimalism is the pursuit of the essence, not the appearance. It is the persistent search for purity, as an expression of unconditional being, the search for serenity, for silence as a presence, for the thickness of spaces, for space as immensity. Minimalism is beyond time—it is timeless, it is noble and

simple materials, it is the stillness of perfection, it has to be the being itself, uncovered by useless crusts, not naked by completely defined by itself, by its being (Bertoni 226).

In actuality, things move relatively slowly, and these Silvestrin walls remind us of the solidity of time and Armani's own earnest desire "to provide a modern, timeless, but at the same time accessible environment" (Armani Press Release 22 September 2000). Minimalism, according to James Meyer, "removes any trace of emotion or intuitive decision-making. . . . Minimal does not allude to anything beyond its literal presence, or its existence in the physical world" (Meyer 15). While it never alludes to a past moment, a historical point of reference is never enabled, the boutique appears as though it has always occupied the location and, like the monastery before it, the rituals of the space seemingly appear as though the vagaries and impact of time have no place here. It is the silhouettes and textiles, however, which define the sequence of time as seen through the cycles of fashion.

DISAPPEARING WALLS/DISAPPEARING ARCHITECTS

After five successful years of collaboration with Silvestrin, Armani, for whom the architect renovated and rebuilt no less than twenty-four boutiques around the globe, collaborated once again with the architect to refashion and renew his retail space concept with the inauguration of his Shanghai boutique in April 2004. Located in the Bund immediately adjoining his cheekier and younger Emporio Armani label, the Borgonuovo boutique incorporated small spaces for his fledging Armani/Fiori (flowers) and Armani/Dolci (sweets) enterprises and a total of 560 square meters for his women's, men's, and accessories collections. Both the location and updated style of the boutique at once reveal the designer's affinity for a city's historically rich building sites, while at the same time imposing his distinct modern vision on the landscape of public architecture. According to an Armani press release, the boutique deployed "[u]nique designs that reflect and respect the intrinsic materials used in the building's architecture, while providing pure and simple backdrops for the products on display" (Armani Press Release 17 April 2004). Rather than locating his boutique in the much busier retail districts of Pudong or Nanking Road, the designer opted to "focus on the value of urban history and architectural heritage" and was the first designer to open shop on the strip (Vercelloni 36). Boasting some of the city's grandest and most sophisticated architecture and located along the Huangpu River, the Bund is the heart of the historic foreign presence in Shanghai; specifically its coordinates mark out the British Concession which began in 1846. Built in the 1920s, the building perfectly reflects Armani's continued aesthetic interest in the interwar period.

For the Shanghai boutique, the now "traditional" Armani trademark St. Maximin stone has been replaced with a natural cotton canvas, horizontally pleated over panels which span the five meter high walls of the space. The natural, soft, and textured effect this has is juxtaposed with the verticality of the stainless steel plated columns which double as mirrors. Along with the Macassar ebony wood storage and display cabinets (17 meters in length), these columns are the only architectural features which attempt any division of what is functionally one large expansive room. The mirrored columns at once block a complete purview of the space, while at the same time, through its reflective surface, prolong and expand parts of the space; in this way, at any given time, certain fashions' presence is repeated while others are occluded. Simple black steel clothing racks are used to display the clothing and are located either along the walls or between the columns. Like the display boxes used to showcase accessories affixed to the walls with horizontal and vertical black steel rods, the garment racks reiterate the vertical and horizontal axes while also emphasizing the constant play between spaces of void and the places of objects: between each garment spaced evenly; between each garment rack; between each mirrored column; and between each display case resting along the floor. The places of fashion and the spaces in between continue the playful choreography marking out absences and presences. Without succumbing to a modernist structural grid, the boutique precariously balances verticality with horizontality, natural materials with futuristic effects, dark hues with reflective surfaces.

Much has been made of designers hiring celebrated—or celebrity—architects to design or reinvigorate their retail spaces. In turn, architects themselves have recognized the power, potential, and potency of fashion in society and within their own praxis in particular. After all, the architecture of today, produced for the fashion and clothing industry, is an architecture of display and consumption and not that of production. However, within this ongoing and renewed dialogue, one thing stands out as a definitive cultural turn: the supremacy of fashion within the arena of high culture, even to the point of looming larger than architecture itself. No longer are fashion designers the feeble little sisters to international bankers, Internet barons and industrial giants, but global powerhouses in their own right with sales, staff, and influence no longer easy to measure in strictly monetary terms. I suggest that, with the opening of the Shanghai boutique, a new chapter was penned in the story of Armani retail and architecture, which at the same time neatly folds into the larger global cultural trend alluded to above. The material culture of the fabric walls is a result of Armani's introduction one year earlier of his now staple handbag, the plisse, despite the bag's original vertical folds. The bag, introduced as emblematic of summer itself, was initially made with *plongée* plisse nappa leather and featured a round tubular handle. The tacit influence of a (female) accessory (the quintessential emblem of the fast-past fashion system) and the move toward textiled walls serve as a metaphor for the dematerialization of architecture in favor of the softness of textiles and the ephemerality of fashion. With boutiques like this, I posit that what we are witnessing is the ascendancy of fashion or in the very least a more clearly articulated symbiosis.

The metamorphosis from architectural space to fashioned space iterated in the move from architectural object to clothed subject and the interplay between surface and depth returns us to the nineteenth century, to the influential writings of Gottfried Semper. According to Semper, "[i]n all Germanic languages the word *Wand* [wall], which has the same root and basic meaning as *Gewand* [garment], directly alludes to the ancient origin and type of the *visible* spatial enclosure" (Semper 248). By exploring the etymological origins and overlaps of wall and garment, Semper makes a claim for the body and space as synonymous ways to engender spatial division. Walls clothe and give shape to space as much as garments clothe and define the contours of the body. This clothing, this shelter, also visibly marks out space itself within and around the body and the space within the frame of architecture. As Semper himself clearly states: "[t]he wall is the architectural element that formally represents and makes visible *enclosed space as such*" (Semper 247). In this way, then, the fabric walls of the Shanghai boutique give shape and meaning to the now layered body. Armani wants to ensure that the body of his customer is not simply clothed, but is clothed in the fabric of space. Both clothing and architecture mark out spatial, territorial, and conceptual boundaries, while at the same time providing shelter, safety, and comfort for the body. Space is literally, figuratively, and materially fashioned. In his reading of Semper, architectural historian Mark Wigley asserts that, as part of the construction of space, textiles are the "mask that dissimulates rather than represents the structure. . . . As its origin in dissimulation, its essence is no longer construction but the masking of construction. . . . Buildings are worn rather than simply occupied" (Wigley 12). Armani's new retail ethos is one predicated on fashion's new cultural agency.

Despite being labeled as "unsuccessful" by Silvestrin's public relations representative in a brief interview I had with him in May 2006, Armani has elected to continue his use of textiled walls for his Paris (2007) boutique. Moving his store from Place Vendôme, the new Paris boutique is located in the prestigious Avenue Montaigne, a street known for housing the fashion capital's haute couture salons (Figure 15.6). With the inauguration of his own haute couture atelier, Armani Privé (2005), whose showroom is located at 2 Avenue Montaigne and by moving his boutique from Place Vendôme to a few feet away from his atelier, Armani definitively makes his claim to the highest order of fashion (haute couture) and makes his presence felt on the cultural map of fashion's elite global clientele who descend on Paris twice a year for the collections' runway presentations. Covering slightly more than 400 square meters on three floors, "[t]he new concept," according to a press release, was "especially conceived for this Paris boutique [and] was designed by Giorgio Armani himself in collaboration with a team of in-house architects and the Silvestrin studio" (Armani Press Release 19 December 2006).

Figure 15.6 Giorgio Armani Paris boutique in Avenue Montaigne. Author's own.

Recognizing the ebb and flow of a city's fashionable places of consumption and display, the designer opted to open on the street because, according to him,

> Avenue Montaigne has reassumed its place among the world's most prestigious high fashion retail destinations. The street also represents a great symbol of historic European architecture which creates an atmosphere of classic sophistication and elegance. In the design solution for my new boutique I therefore wanted to provide a modern rendition of what is now a by-gone era with the sense of a personal and intimate space where the collections are presented in wardrobes and trunks. The result is intimate and luxurious, a truly personalised experience that perfectly matches the history and grandure of this world renowned avenue (Armani Press Release 19 December 2006).

Armani opted to furnish this boutique with pieces from his Armani/Casa collection of homewares. With a slight Oriental flair, while retaining the classic minimalist Armani aesthetic, the furniture replaces Silvestrin's specially designed chairs and display cabinets made in Macassar wood. The newly unveiled translucent resin mannequins force the eye to focus on the clothing. Like in Shangahi, in his Paris boutique Armani literally dresses the architecture, softens it, making it a space of texture and textiles. The space is at once atmospheric, dark, and intimate in an attempt to carve out personal space within the very public realm of consumption. Wardrobes and trunks showcase the collections. For the walls, two luxurious and distinctive materials play off each other and mark out the gendered use of space to create similar yet subtly distinct environments. Devoted to menswear, on the first level, the walls are covered by gray horizontally pleated brushed silk, picked up in the tops of the black lacquered display tables, which creates a sensually smooth yet variegated feel and look. On the second floor, devoted to Armani's womenswear and ever-expanding accessories collections, the sense of luxury displayed on the first floor is matched by onyx. Clearly marked as the inner sanctum of the boutique, the room furthest away from the main door and street level showcases women's evening wear. Seen all over the world at red carpet events, the glamorous evening wear is presented in a dark and intimate salon. Here the walls are once again pleated brushed silk, but in black, lending a distinctly night time atmosphere to the room ideally suited for ball gowns and cocktail dresses. Continuity between the two levels of retail space is achieved through the onyx flooring and the furniture. Typical of all Armani retail spaces, luminescent backlights and recessed lamps help to softly spotlight each individual garment and displayed object, but in this instance adds warmth to the onyx flooring and brings life to the resin mannequins.

As Riewoldt points out: "[o]nly through real-life experiences, through an unmediated encounter with the tangible attractions of beautiful things, can it [retail space] hope to win through against the convenience and efficiency of e-commerce" (9). Ultimately, I believe Riewoldt is advocating a defense of the phenomenology of shopping which extends visual pleasure into a broader sensory realm. Armani's use of Silvestrin as his architect of choice for the past seven years is significant and speaks to the phenomenological investments Armani places in both his fashion and spatial designs. The writings of the French phenomenologist Maurice Merleau-Ponty have resonated strongly with Silvestrin in the way the philosopher "attributed more importance to perception" (in Bertoni 174–75). "Space," "orientation," and "depth" vital to his architectural praxis were quickly redeveloped to think about meaning through perception (Bertoni 174–75). For Silvestrin, working through Merleau-Ponty and influenced by Italian minimalist architects like A. G. Fronzoni, perception through feeling supercedes thinking which is ideally suited to the experience of consumption.

Recently it appears that designer boutiques have more to do with the business of museums, while museums are redefining themselves as shops. Yet, unlike museums which privilege sight and condemn touch, the ethos of Armani textiles and spatial programs compel, force even, the customer to touch and enjoy the haptic experience of being in space. Armani, I posit, reinvigorates modernist space by attracting the visitor-consumer by controlling the sensory experience: sound: quiet or specially selected music;

scent: the smell of Acqua di Gio from the menswear cologne collection; taste: any beverage is brought to the consumer during the process of selection and fitting; touch: one stone, one wood, myriad fabrics; and finally sight: the displayed garments and objects and the bodies of the sales staff and other costumers.

"The rejection of decoration in favor of the cultivated eye is explicitly understood as a form of purification" (Wigley 3). As Wigley points out rather convincingly, modern architecture, seen through the aesthetic lens of whitewashed walls and espoused by architectural giants like Adolf Loos and Le Corbusier, was not so much a renouncing of clothing and its system, but rather very much a part of it; the erratic logic of clothing is projected onto these white walls and the architecture which props fashion up. Patina, as Riewoldt discloses, "is a vital ingredient of timelessness" (22). As the term suggests, a patina is characterized as a build up over time, the sediments of longevity, the thickness of the haptic. Armani reinvests the sensuality lost in the modernist white wall interiors, by using a stone whose surfaces are porous, soft, sensual, and textured. Minimalism in the context of an Armani boutique marks out a space in which textiles come alive, provides meaning through haptic discernment, and elicits desire. As I have outlined elsewhere, an Armani boutique is ideally suited for those who wish to recreate their own Armani-inspired garments at home (see Potvin). In a series of articles published in *Threads* magazine, devoted to "home sewers," Anne Hyde, one of the articles' author, argues for the necessity of a visit to an Armani boutique, for it provides "the best way to experience Armani's exquisite fabric judgement" (Hyde 27). Hyde's suggestion to visit the boutique is simply to "feel the fabrics." The simple, yet revealing, act of touching provides the truth to material sought after by modernists like Armani, but, perhaps more importantly, the truth of space itself.

WORKS CITED

"Alluring Armani." *Interior Design* (May 1989): 25
Armani, Giorgio. "Foreword." In *Shops and Boutique*, by Grant Camden Kirkpatrick. New York: Rizzoli International Publications, 1994.
Bertoni, Franco. *Claudio Silvestrin*. Basel; Boston; Berlin: Birhhauser, 1999.
"Boutiques de Luxe et de Mode." *Architecture Interieure Crée* No. 275 (1997): 106–07.
Cramer, Ned. "Fashion Victim." *Architecture* (February 1997): 45.
Foucault, Michel. "Of Other Places." In *Visual Culture Reader,* edited by Nicholas Mirzoeff. London and New York: Routledge, 1998: 238–44.
Hyde, Ann. "Inside an Armani Jacket: Exploring the Secrets of the Master of Milan." *Threads* (August/Sept. 1990): 24–27.
Meyer, James (ed.). *Minimalism*. London: Phaidon, 2000.
Mostadi, Arian. *Hotshops*. Barcelona: Carlos Broto and Josep M. Minguet, 2003.
"Neighbourhood Report: Upper East Side: New Armani Facade Draws a Frown." *New York Times* (19 March 1995): 136.

Potvin, John. "Lost in Translation? Giorgio Armani and the Textualities of Touch." In *Neocraft: Modernity and the Crafts*, edited by Sandra Alfoldi. Halifax: Nova Scotia College of Art and Design University Press, 2007: 83–98.

Quinn, Bradley. *The Fashion of Architecture*. Oxford and New York: Berg, 2003.

Riewoldt, Otto. *Retail Design*. London: Laurence King Publishing, 2000.

Ruby, Ilka and Andreas. "Essential, Meta-, Trans-, The Chimeras of Minimalist Architecture." In *Minimal Architecture*. Munich, New York, Berlin and London: Prestel, 2003: 16–26.

Semper, Gotfried. *Style in the Technical and Tectonic Arts, or, Practical Aesthetics*. Los Angeles: Getty Research Institute, 2004.

Serrats, Marta. *New Shops and Boutiques*. New York: Harper Design, 2004.

Turngate, Mark. *Fashion Brands: Branding Style From Armani to Zara*. London: Kogan Page, 2004.

Vercelloni, Matteo. "Sul Bund Di Shanghai." *Interni* No. 544 (September 2004): 34–39.

Wigley, Mark. *White Walls, Designer Dresses: The Fashioning of Modern Architecture*. Cambrige, MA; London: The MIT Press, 1995.

Contributors

Anne Anderson is Research Fellow at Exeter University. Trained as an art historian and archaeologist at Leicester University, she was elected a Fellow of the Society of Antiquaries, London, in 1996 and was Senior Lecturer in History of Art and Design at Southampton Solent University from 1993 until 2007. She has published widely in leading commercial and academic journals, including the *Antique Dealer and Collector's Guide, The Victorian, Journal of the History of Education, Women's History Review, The Wildea: Journal of the Oscar Wilde Society,* and *Journal of Design History.* She is the author of *Interpreting Pottery* (Batsford, 1984) and *The Cube Teapot* (Richard Dennis Publications, 1999).

Christopher Bedford is an Assistant Curator at the Los Angeles County Museum of Art, and is a PhD candidate in Art History at the Courtauld Institute of Art, where he is writing his dissertation on Chris Burden's early performance work with Dr. Mignon Nixon. He has published essays, book reviews, editorials, and exhibition reviews in *The Burlington Magazine, Artforum, Artforum.com, Art in America, Tema Celeste,* the *Sculpture Journal, The Art Book, Afterall, October,* and *caa.reviews.* He is currently working on edited volumes for Duke University Press and the *Sculpture Journal.* He is on the editorial board of the Los Angeles-based journal, *X-TRA.*

Heidi Brevik-Zender is Visiting Assistant Professor of French at Scripps College in Claremont, California, and received her PhD in French Studies from Brown University in 2006. Her research interests include fashion, gender studies, theories of consumption, and cultural history, with a particular emphasis on Paris in the nineteenth century. Her current research focuses on the intersection of fashion theory, gender studies, and literary and cultural criticism. Heidi's dissertation, "From Fashion Writing to Writing Fashion: Modernity, Gender, and *La Mode* in the Literature of Fin-de-siècle France," treated works by the late-nineteenth-century Paris-based authors Stéphane Mallarmé, Rachilde, Émile Zola, and Octave Uzanne.

Deirdre Clemente is a doctoral candidate in History at Carnegie Mellon University where she studies the interface between clothing and cultural change. Clemente has published her work in *Journal of Labor Studies*, *The Journal of American Culture*, and *Journal of Social History*. Her dissertation, entitled "The Collegiate Style: Campus Culture and the Transformation of the American Wardrobe, 1900–1960," explores the role college students played in influencing causal clothing trends.

Margaret Denny is a doctoral candidate in Art History at the University of Illinois at Chicago with a focus on the history of photography and women's studies. She is also Adjunct Instructor at Columbia College and at the University of Illinois at Chicago. Recent publications include entries in the *Encyclopedia of Twentieth-Century Photography*, Lynne Warren, editor (Routledge, 2006) and *Home Front Heroes: A Biographical Dictionary of Americans During Wartime* (Greenwood Publishing Group, 2006). She has held research positions in the Department of Photography at The Art Institute of Chicago and the Jane Addams Hull-House Museum.

Elyssa Dimant holds an MA from the Fashion Institute of Technology and is currently a Curatorial Research Associate at The Metropolitan Museum of Art's Costume Institute. She is an adjunct graduate professor at The New School/Parson's School of Design, where her courses cover modern textiles and contemporary fashion. Elyssa is the coauthor of the exhibition catalogue for *WILD: Fashion Untamed* (Yale University Press, 2004), as well as *Fashioning Fabrics: Contemporary Textiles in Fashion* (Black Dog Publishing, 2006). She has also contributed articles to *The Encyclopedia of Clothing and Fashion, Zink, Selvedge, DecArts,* and *Elle Canada,* and is the featured fashion columnist for *CITY Magazine.*

Mila Ganeva is Associate Professor in German Studies at Miami University in Ohio. Her research interests include visual arts and mass media in early twentieth century, film history, urban studies, and contemporary German film and literature. She has published numerous articles on fashion journalism, fashion photography, and mannequins in the Weimar Republic, early German film comedies, Berlin in film, and German literature, and culture of the 1990s. Her book, *Women in Weimar Fashion: Discourses and Displays in German Culture, 1918–1933,* is forthcoming with Camden House in 2008.

Louisa Iarocci is Assistant Professor in the Department of Architecture at the University of Washington in Seattle where she teaches architectural history, theory, and design. She has taught at Western Washington University, University of British Columbia, and Boston University, where she received her PhD in 2003. She is currently working on a book manuscript based on her dissertation, which examines the rise of the department store at the turn of the century around issues of consumerism, representation, and spatial theory.

Emily R. Klug is an Assistant Registrar at PaceWildenstein LLC in New York City, where she works with some of the most important art and artists of the twentieth and twenty-first centuries. She graduated Magna Cum Laude from Union College in Schenectady, New York, in 2003 with a Bachelor of Arts in Art History and a minor in English. In the spring of 2006, Emily graduated with a Masters of Arts from the Bard Graduate Center of Decorative Arts, Design, and Culture in New York, New York, where she concentrated on the history of eighteenth through nineteenth century interiors and twentieth century fashion history.

Rebecca Jumper Matheson is a fashion historian and former Research Assistant at the Costume Institute, the Metropolitan Museum of Art. She holds a BA in English from Rice University, a JD from the University of Texas at Austin, and is a licensed attorney. In 2005, she received an MA in Fashion and Textile Studies: History Theory and Museum Practice from the Fashion Institute of Technology in New York City. She cocurated the Museum at FIT graduate student exhibition, *Designing the It Girl: Lucile and Her Style,* the first exhibition to focus on the life and career of the designer Lucile, in addition to coauthoring the accompanying catalogue.

Alison Matthews David is a historian of dress and textiles specializing in the nineteenth and early twentieth centuries. She obtained her doctorate in Art History from Stanford University in 2002 and is currently Assistant Professor in the Department of Fashion Design and Communication, Ryerson University, Canada. Her publications include articles on tailoring, military uniforms and footwear, synthetic dyes and the aesthetic movement, and the origins of *Vogue* magazine. She is currently writing a book for Berg Press entitled *Fashion Victims: Death by Clothing,* about the potentially lethal consequences of fashionable dress.

Peter McNeil works across critical theories and histories of design. He conducts research in the fields of fashion studies, design history, and art history, with an emphasis upon fashion and social identity, fashion and representation, and fashion and consumption. His anthology, *Shoes: A History From Sandals to Sneakers* (with Dr. G. Riello), was published by Berg in 2006. He is Chair of Design History in the Faculty of Design, Architecture, and Building at the University of Technology, Sydney, Australia; and the foundation Chair of Fashion Studies at Stockholm University, Sweden.

Francesca Muscau holds a BA from the University of Milan, Italy, and received her PhD in Comparative Literature from the State University of New York at Buffalo in 2002. Her thesis investigated the interpretation of the Italian Renaissance in Victorian literature and culture, with particular emphasis on the fin de siècle. She has been a lecturer both at the University at Buffalo and at South Bank University, London, United Kingdom. Her research interests include fashion, gender studies, art theory and the literary *fin de siècle*. Her current research includes the cultural history of the figure of the spinster.

Vanessa Osborne received her PhD from the Department of English at the University of California at Irvine. She recently completed a dissertation entitled *Capitalizing Culture: Media, Marketing, and the Commodity Form,* which explores how the character of the commodity changes in the wake of developments in media and marketing in the late nineteenth and early twentieth centuries.

John Potvin is Assistant Professor of Eighteenth- and Nineteenth-Century European Art and Design at the University of Guelph, Canada. He is the author of *Material and Visual Cultures Beyond Male Bonding, 1870–1914: Bodies, Boundaries, and Intimacy* (Ashgate, 2008) and is coeditor of *Material Culture in Britain, 1750–1920: The Visual Meanings and Pleasures of Collecting* (Ashgate, 2009). He is currently working on two book-length projects. The first, *Bachelors of a Different Sort, 1885–1940,* explores queer aesthetics, modernity, and domesticity in Britain, while the second, *Black Label: Giorgio Armani, Modernity, and the Tailored Body,* critically explores the Italian designer's influence on tailoring, the body, and global fashion.

Index